Praise for *Un*

"There is no greater tour guide ... ...n Ng – he offers a vivid and comprehensive account of the pro-democracy movement and a city in transition. *Umbrellas in Bloom* is a definitive compendium of on-the-ground reporting, timelines, maps, photographs, illustrations, a glossary, and a who's-who of Hong Kong's politics."
— Tom Grundy, editor-in-chief, *Hong Kong Free Press*

"*Umbrellas in Bloom* is a necessary and worthy read for those who want to better understand Hong Kong and the events that unfolded in 2014. ... It is also a good reminder that the Umbrella movement had some sizeable accomplishments, even if it did not win the big prize."
— Cameron Dueck, *South China Morning Post*

"Insightful, accessible, and a hugely enjoyable read, *Umbrellas in Bloom* is jam-packed with eureka moments. It is populated with deftly drawn characters and sprinkled with just the right amount of wit. Rather than a dry academic exploration of the causes and consequences of the Umbrella Movement, Ng's story is instead a personal account of those 79 days that rocked the city. The movement in all its vibrancy jumps off every page. It is essential reading for anybody wanting to understand the existential crisis currently engulfing Hong Kong."
— Matthew Torne, filmmaker and director of *Lessons in Dissent*

"The Umbrella Movement was a seminal moment in Hong Kong's history. This skillful blending of personal narrative and analysis represents a vital contribution to understanding what happened and indeed what might happen next."
— Stephen Vines, columnist and author of *Hong Kong: China's New Colony*

"*Umbrellas in Bloom* offers a vivid account of the street protests that paralysed parts of Hong Kong for 79 days. With firsthand observations, timelines, charts and explanations of the semiautonomous Chinese territory's arcane political system — an uneasy blend of the relics of undemocratic British colonial rule and new elements of undemocratic Chinese rule — Ng spells out what many Hong Kong people, particularly younger ones, are chafing against." – Didi Tatlow, *The New York Times*

"The umbrella flowers blossomed and withered. Ng captures the lifecycle of the occupy movement with compassion and wit."
– Benny Tai, co-founder of Occupy Central with Love and Peace

"Ng's authoritative account of the occupy movement is compelling and full of surprises. He combines a journalist's precision with a Hong Konger's passionate heart."
– Zeb Eckert, anchor, Bloomberg Television

Praise for *No City for Slow Men*

"Hong Kong lawyer and blogger Jason Y. Ng is back with a new book of insights after casting his perspective gaze over the good, bad and ugly sides of city life. He offers 36 nicely judged, pithy – often punchy – essays to 'inform and empower' readers. Ng's unpretentious writing reveals a frank, cut-to-the-chase view of life – plus, on occasion, a commendably sympathetic nature."
– Guy Haydon, South China Morning Post

"The most engrossing part of *No City for Slow Men* – and, indeed, Ng's writing in general – is his sincerity, laying bare the best and worst of Hong Kong society, as well as his own struggles and insecurities."
– Meredith McBride, TimeOut HK

"Ng's prose is marked by honesty, clarity and wit, and his book is full of insight and humor about a city and a people still coming to terms with who they are and who they want to be."
– Kent Ewing, Asia Times

"Ng writes with erudition and wit. His new book is a fine-tooth comb running through our contemporary issues and obsessions, an essential read for Hong Kongers and all who are in love with our city!"
– Douglas Young, artist, provocateur and founder of G.O.D.

"*HKID* says it best: Hong Kong is stuck somewhere between the Chinese mainland and the rest of the world, and that causes a bit of an identity crisis. Another major theme is the contrast between the lives of expats and locals – with their gambling by way of cards instead of mahjong, the strange sport of rugby and lack of Cantonese fluency. The plight of the domestic worker is an especially important topic, written about with great heart."

– Ray Hecht, *Shenzhen Daily*

Praise for *HONG KONG State of Mind*

"One of the most successful blog-to-book projects in recent memory. It is honest, insightful and immensely entertaining."

– Joseph Chow, editor-in-chief, *Elle HK*

"Refreshingly frank and wry observations on Hong Kong life."

– Matthew Harrison, author of *Benjamin Button* and *Jessica's Choice*

"One of the most relevant books written in English for today's Hong Kong issues."

– Susan Blumberg-Kason, author of *Good Chinese Wife*

"A thoughtful guy not shy about exposing what happens between his ears, [Ng] is a man of principle and daring."

– *Cairns Media Magazine*

"*HONG KONG State of Mind* is a fascinating study of a truly unique city, highly recommended."

– Midwest Book Review

"*HONG KONG State of Mind* holds up a mirror on our city and offers a refreshing perspective on our culture in the new millennium. I couldn't put the book down."

– *Books4You* magazine

Umbrellas in Bloom

Hong Kong's occupy movement uncovered

Jason Y. Ng

BLACKSMITH BOOKS

Umbrellas in Bloom
Hong Kong's Occupy Movement Uncovered

Print ISBN 978-988-13765-3-4
eBook ISBN 978-988-79638-8-2
Copyright © 2019 Jason Y. Ng
Maps, diagrams, illustrations, photographs
(unless otherwise indicated) © 2019 Jason Y. Ng
www.jasonyng.com

First printing March 2016
Second printing June 2016
Third printing August 2019

Published by Blacksmith Books
Unit 26, 19/F, Block B, Wah Lok Industrial Centre
37-41 Shan Mei Street, Fo Tan, Hong Kong
www.blacksmithbooks.com

Illustrations and maps by Daniel Ng
Cover design by Ada Ng
Cover photograph by Joel Odesser

For the future of Hong Kong,

and our youth who shall inherit it

Contents

Part 4 – Wilting

Appendices

Introduction

Flowers bloom and flowers wilt. They flourish, wither and die, before new buds reappear in the next season. In this endless cycle of birth and rebirth, there are two truths we hold to be self-evident – that change is the only constant, and that beauty is not diminished but magnified by its transience.

That is the context in which we must approach the 2014 mass protests in Hong Kong, the largest anti-government insurgency the city has seen and a referendum on its relationship with China. We must analyze and accept the episode for what it was: a step on our epic journey to full democracy. That's why we prefer the word "movement" to "revolution," because all that happened was more akin to the 15-year social awakening during America's civil rights struggles, than to the one-off regime changes in the recent Arab Spring. To put things in perspective, many African Americans are still fighting their battle half a century later.

If England has its Tudor rose and Japan its chrysanthemum, then Hong Kong has crowned a new national flower: the yellow umbrella. In the fall of 2014, a twist of fate transformed that foul-weather friend – the humble household item that everyone ignores when the sun shines but desperately seeks when the rain pours – into a symbol of courage and defiance. Suffragists used it to keep off not the rain but tear gas and pepper spray. Its defensive, functional nature has made it a powerful symbol for a peaceful uprising. The versatile raingear also opens and shuts like a living thing. For 79 days, yellow umbrellas blossomed, grew and faded. And such is the cycle of life – what we have just said about change and beauty rings true for the political movement that is named after them.

This book is the last of a trilogy. It is a follow-up to *HONG KONG State of Mind*, a candy box of observations about Asia's hyperactive city, and *No City for Slow Men*, a more somber probe into our social and existential issues. It turned out that all the quirks and quandaries expunged in the first two installments were a mere prelude to the third – they were small waves that multiplied and swelled into a tsunami. Taken as a whole, the three volumes track the arc of Hong Kong's post-colonial development, from euphoria to frustration, to rage and rebellion.

The purpose of this book is twofold: first, to record history, and second, to reclaim it.

History is not a chronology – it is more than dates and events. History is a teacher, critic, mirror, weapon, agent of change and arbiter of truth. So much history begged to be written during those 11 weeks in Hong Kong; recording it is a delicate and sacred task. This book documents my firsthand account of the blood, sweat and tears at the three main protest sites as a writer and a freelance journalist. Yet, it is in my capacity as a *citizen* that I feel most duty-bound to preserve the past against not only the test of time but also the trials of state-sponsored revisionism that are furiously underway.

Anyone who has watched Akira Kurosawa's masterpiece *Rashomon* knows that a single event can have vastly different – and often contradictory – interpretations, depending on who is doing the talking and why. Sure enough, competing versions of the truth about the Umbrella Movement have made their way into the public discourse. Local bookstores in Hong Kong are now flooded with a glut of Beijing-backed counter-movement propaganda (so far all in the Chinese language) aimed at doing one thing: controlling the narrative and drowning out dissent.

How sad it would be if 15, 20 years later, our children learned about these events through whitewashed news sources and bowdlerized literature. For posterity's sake, it is incumbent on each of us to seize back the narrative – my second motivation for writing this book. Since the fall of 2014, Hong Kong has entered a new political era in which common sense is turned off, outright lies are delivered deadpan, and a spade is no longer called a spade. To borrow George Orwell's prophetic words: war is peace, freedom is slavery, ignorance is strength. The need to reclaim history has taken on an unprecedented urgency.

But that's not all. The occupy movement is under increasing attack not only by those in power, but also by the young men and women who took part in it. Disillusioned with inexperienced student leaders and embittered by their failure to achieve tangible political results, many protesters are now taking out their anger on the movement and calling it a farce or a waste of time. Proving that history is not without irony, the very people who were awoken and inspired by the occupy movement have now become its harshest critics. Their change of heart has broken mine – but it has motivated me all the more to mount a rebuttal.

This book will not and does not purport to please everyone. Readers of different political stripes may find parts of it too liberal, too sentimental, too critical of some groups and not critical enough of the others, too focused on one protest site and too perfunctory with the other two. As much as I have tried to cover all angles (and fill in the gaps by interviewing key decision-makers and participants), the picture I present is seen through my own viewfinder and therefore unavoidably idiosyncratic. It is but one version of the truth being argued in the Court of Rashomon. My failings will, I can only hope, encourage others to pick up a pen and contribute to the debate. When it comes to recording and reclaiming our history, the bookshelf can never get too crowded.

Not a day has gone by since the last protest site was dismantled that I haven't thought about the protests and the protesters who turned them into so much more. The Umbrella Movement has shown me possibilities in our future that I did not know existed. It has brought out qualities in our citizens that I did not think they possessed. It has reminded me that, no matter how hopeless and helpless we feel, Hong Kong is still a place worth fighting for. I was given a front row seat to behold the human spirit in full bloom. If I did nothing else in my life, if that was all that I ever did, it would have been enough. I have always wanted to do something to show my gratitude for this life-changing experience. And so I try, in the only way a writer knows how: I write.

Jason Y. Ng
Hong Kong, 2016

Foreword by Joshua Wong

It felt like only yesterday when 200,000 citizens took over the streets in Hong Kong in support of the unprecedented Umbrella Movement, when I took questions from over 100 foreign correspondents at a makeshift press conference, when our city of 7 million received the kind of media attention not seen since the Handover in 1997.

As a leader of the Umbrella Movement, I am hopeful that this book – the first in the world to chronicle the protests in the English language – will enable readers everywhere to better understand our political reality, our 30-year pro-democracy struggles that set the stage for the occupy movement, and its evolution from a series of mass protests into a modern day miracle – albeit one that failed to extract concessions from Communist China.

A year on, the media focus on Hong Kong has faded. Even so, the world will see that citizens awoken by the Umbrella Movement will continue their fight against Goliath, and that they will take that fight from the streets to the voting booth and into the legislature. No matter the outcome, our resolve is unshakable.

Readers may disagree on the wisdom of the occupy movement, but they will agree that it has hastened the development of a Hong Kong identity and a local subjectivity. When I heard young people shout "I am a Hong Konger" in the middle of a highway that runs through the heart of our financial district, I knew at that very moment that it is only a matter of time until we find ourselves in another popular uprising, one that will galvanize the city even more than the last.

Joshua Wong
Founder of Scholarism,
One of *Fortune* magazine's Top 10 World Leaders 2015

憶起雨傘運動裡佔領的空前盛況，二十萬人的集結仍是歷歷在目，那時在馬路的記招會面對著過百計外媒記者追訪，這種國際層面的關注實在可以跟九七年的香港主權移交相提並論。

作為整場佔領的學生代表，我只盼各位讀者在閱畢全世界第一本以英文寫成的回顧傘運書籍以後，能夠了解香港政局的來龍去脈，那個從三十年前開始的民主運動是怎樣定下基礎，最終創造了雨傘運動這個奇蹟。可惜奇蹟亦未足以動搖中共威權。

縱然如此，我仍寄望世界各地的公民明白，即使香港今天已不獲國際舞台關注，但在佔領以後覺醒的香港人，仍在公民社會和政壇裡奮力一戰，抱著知其不可為而為之的決心，跟這個如巨人哥利亞的政權抗爭下去。

也許你對佔領街道抱持不同觀點，但不容否認的是這場雨傘運動促成香港主體的建構，正當年輕一代那年在政經中心和交通命脈的大馬路上吶喊：「我是香港人」，我就知道香港人就有一天，會促成一場比雨傘運動更振奮人心的群眾運動。

黃之鋒
學民思潮召集人
2015年《財富》雜誌全球十大領袖

Foreword by Chip Tsao

It is said that post-handover Hong Kong is a sad city that the world has written off, like Cinderella rushing home after the clock has struck midnight. Or is it more like a jigsaw puzzle with all the pieces in place but a picture that remains murky?

Blending knowledge with duty and passion, Jason's "Hong Kong Trilogy" presents our city judiciously to the global reader and the future historian. His meticulously documented account of the city turns an ill-fitted puzzle into a colorful tapestry laid out for all the world to see.

In this final installment, his words emit an piercing light similar to that of Thomas Paine's eyewitness narratives of the American and French Revolutions. It parades our government – the Bastille of the Far East – and explains why it deserves some kind of shaking up, if not a storming. He ties the mass protests of 2014, symbolized by the umbrella, to other popular uprisings in China, Taiwan, Thailand, Egypt, Ukraine, and the United States.

Reading Jason's book reminds me that Hong Kong's story is not yet finished. A few brave young hearts in the territory are still beating with resolve and conviction. They have given our old colonial fairy tale new life, adding more drama and a revolutionary twist. Like Thomas Paine,

Jason is more than a journalistic outsider. He is one of the story's protagonists. Jason gives voice to a great generation that deserves to be heard and preserved.

Chip Tsao
Columnist and broadcaster

About the Illustrator

Daniel Ng is a Hong Kong-born, New York-based architect. He specializes in luxury hotel and commercial space designs, and has worked at such leading international firms as Hellmuth, Obata & Kassabaum (HOK) and Kohn Pedersen Fox (KPF).

Ng's recent works include the Peninsula Hotel in Shanghai, and the St. Regis Yalong Bay Resort in Sanya, Hainan Island. He is also part of the team of architects involved in the US$4 billion rebuilding of LaGuardia Airport in Queens, New York.

Ng spends his spare time writing and drawing. He pens a column titled "Archi/Talk" for *Keypad*, a bilingual lifestyle magazine, and keeps a blog sharing his childhood memories in Hong Kong. Ng takes after his artist father and adorns his blog articles with his own pencil sketches. For *Umbrellas in Bloom*, he has created 24 whimsical illustrations that underscore the surrealism and otherworldliness of the student-led political movement.

Ng currently lives in New York with his family. His professional portfolio and personal pursuits can be found on his website at www.danielng.com. Daniel Ng is the author's brother.

Acknowledgments

The author would like to thank Daniel Ng for the superb drawings and maps featured in this volume; Ada Ng for the cover design and Joel Odesser for the cover photograph; Mark Herz, Matthew Fairclough, Kelvin Ng and Pete Spurrier for their editorial support; the patient staff at the Foreign Correspondents' Club where most of the chapters were written and nearly all of the interviews were conducted; and Blacksmith Books for standing behind this project, which required gumption and grit.

This book would not have been possible without the help and inspiration of Dr. Au Yiu-kai, Ray Chan, Tanya Chan, Jack Chang, Alice Chu, Cheung Tin Tang, Edward Chin, Tom Grundy, Afa Pang, Benny Tai, Matthew Torne, Chip Tsao, Joshua Wong, Alvin Yeung, and of course, members of the Water Blowers' Society.

Above all, the author would like to express his heartfelt thanks to his readers and blog followers for their staunch support over the years.

Map of Hong Kong

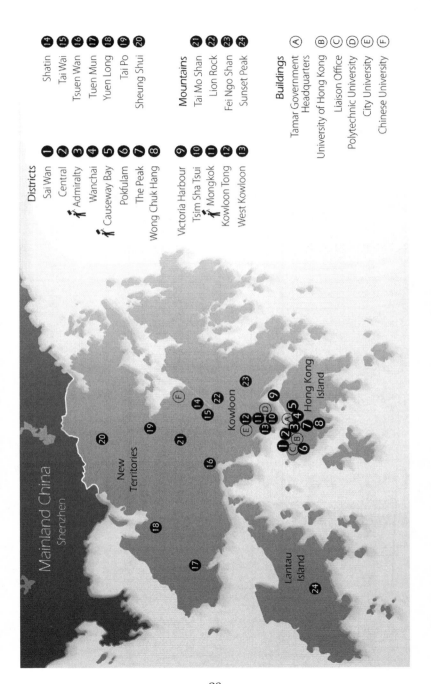

Districts

1 Sai Wan
2 Central
3 Admiralty
4 Wanchai
5 Causeway Bay
6 Pokfulam
7 The Peak
8 Wong Chuk Hang

9 Victoria Harbour
10 Tsim Sha Tsui
11 Mongkok
12 Kowloon Tong
13 West Kowloon

14 Shatin
15 Tai Wai
16 Tsuen Wan
17 Tuen Mun
18 Yuen Long
19 Tai Po
20 Sheung Shui

Mountains

21 Tai Mo Shan
22 Lion Rock
23 Fei Ngo Shan
24 Sunset Peak

Buildings

Ⓐ Tamar Government Headquarters
Ⓑ University of Hong Kong
Ⓒ Liaison Office
Ⓓ Polytechnic University
Ⓔ City University
Ⓕ Chinese University

Part 1

Germination

"Freedom is never voluntarily given by the oppressor;
it must be demanded by the oppressed."

– Martin Luther King, Jr.
Letter from Birmingham Jail

The Day When Everything Changed

September 28th, 2014 – it was a Sunday just like any other.

The mid-autumn breeze whispered, car horns blared from a distance. Arching banyan trees clung to a steely wall of office towers. The noon sky sprawled, ashen by cloud and smog. It was as beautiful a day as a city choked by perennial air pollution could get.

But something seemed amiss this afternoon, as it had every day for the past 17 years.

3:30pm

I had been watching the live coverage on television all morning and decided to answer the call to action. I gathered a few essentials – cell phone, notebook, pen, face towel and swimming goggles – and left my apartment. I WhatsApp'ed my brother Kelvin and asked him to meet me at Lippo Centre in Admiralty.

From there, the two of us walked to the section of Connaught Road that had just been occupied by protesters and regular citizens who had come out to support them. We were about 50 yards from the Tamar Government Headquarters, the epicenter of a massive student protest.

Only 14 hours before, at that very epicenter, professor Benny Tai had taken the stage and the microphone. With leaders from the Hong Kong Federation of Students by his side, the sweaty professor officially launched Occupy Central – an act of civil disobedience to take over the city's financial district to demand universal suffrage. It was a high-profile political campaign two years in the making that finally took hold and merged with the student protest. A perfect storm was gathering speed by the minute.

Outside the Government Headquarters, there were throngs of people all around us, the average age somewhere between 20 and 25. Their growing euphoria was suffused with tension and trepidation. Many among the crowds were wearing lab goggles and raincoats to guard against pepper spray. Some put cling wrap over their eye gear for extra protection.

Tanya Chan, vice chairlady of the Civic Party, was speaking into a bullhorn. She had shaved her head as part of the pan-democrats' pledge to defeat a Beijing-backed electoral reform bill in the legislature. A student wove through the crowd with a loudspeaker repeating her words. Chan urged citizens to hold the line outside the Bank of China Tower to stop police from advancing. She also warned them about undercover officers infiltrating the crowds to collect intelligence. "Strike up a conversation with anyone who looks like a cop and ask him why he is here," she said, "Look for men who are beefier than the average scrawny student!" Her remark drew a few nervous laughs.

4:30pm

From afar, somebody yelled "Saline water! We need saline water NOW!" Other supplies were also needed: face masks, umbrellas and drinking water. Kelvin and I went to see what we could do to help. We joined the human chain passing sundry items from one side of the eight-lane Connaught Road to the other. They were for protesters who had been pepper-sprayed by police on Tim Mei Avenue, one of the several frontlines. The girl next to me, who might have been 15, shoved a carton of fresh milk into my hand. "Pass it on," the teenager yelled. Milk was supposed to sooth the eyes by neutralizing the irritants in the pepper spray. There was order in this chaos: everyone was a commander and everyone was a foot soldier.

We hit a lull in the calls for supplies. I told Kelvin I needed to use the bathroom and we walked to the nearby Queensway Plaza shopping mall. On our way back, I suggested we grab a few things for the frontlines. My brother had overheard that saline water was running low, and so we spent the next 45 minutes scouring Wanchai for pharmacies, because other volunteers had already emptied the shelves within a 300-yard radius of Admiralty.

6:00pm

As Kelvin and I were paying for saline water at a neighborhood drugstore, we saw a text message on our phones. "Police have just fired tear gas into the crowds!" The text was from my sister-in-law who had been monitoring the latest developments on her television at home. We sensed the gravity of the situation and began running with our purchases back to Admiralty. The trip took just 10 minutes, but it felt like an eternity.

As we approached Connaught Road, we began to hear harrowing accounts from students who had retreated from Tim Mei Avenue. A young man, catching his breath and pointing at the government building behind him, said, "The police hoisted a black banner; we had never seen a black banner before. Now we know: black means tear gas." The girl next to him chimed in, "It stung like hell."

Many started cursing at the police officers standing guard in the area. "Have you all gone mad?" shouted one woman. "How could you do this to unarmed students? Don't you have children of your own?" asked another.

6:30pm

Over the next hour, we kept hearing shots being fired. *Boom boom boom*, like fireworks on Chinese New Year's Day. The use of tear gas had caught everyone by surprise. It recalled an episode in the 2012 chief executive election, when the then-candidate C.Y. Leung was accused by his opponent Henry Tang of proposing at a cabinet meeting that riot police and tear gas be unleashed on protesters. Leung vehemently denied it at the time and ended up winning the race anyway. It looked like the man who now held the highest office in the city had just fulfilled his opponent's words.

Tear gas might have been commonplace elsewhere in the world, but it wasn't in Hong Kong. The last time it was used was during the 2005 World Trade Organization Conference to disperse angry South Korean farmers protesting outside the convention center in Wanchai with

The Umbrella Man stands in defiance during the 9/28 Crackdown

placards and Molotov cocktails. Leung's decision to deploy lachrymators against unarmed students this time, despite the political price he would inevitably pay, suggested that he had been given direct orders from Beijing to do whatever it took to clear the streets before citizens returned to work on Monday morning. In so doing, Leung had irreversibly redrawn the relationship between Hong Kong people and their government.

8:00pm

As night fell, the tension rose. Harcourt Road – an eight-lane thoroughfare that connects to Connaught Road – was strewn with broken umbrellas, water bottles and lone shoes, left behind by fleeing protesters. Mobile phones were rendered useless. Someone said the government had ordered service providers to switch off all 3G signals in the area. Kelvin asked me if I had downloaded FireChat, an app that allowed short text message exchanges between smart phones without a Wi-Fi or mobile connection. I said I hadn't, but I would as soon as my connection resumed.

We moved to a footbridge outside the Police Headquarters on the ominously-named Arsenal Street. There, high above ground, we saw a formation of riot police wearing army helmets and gas masks advancing steadily from Wanchai toward Admiralty. They were carrying AR-15 rifles and tear gas launchers; some of them had quivers of rolled-up warning flags strapped to their shoulders. Lit only by the streetlights' amber glow, the scene was eerily reminiscent of the streets of Beijing on that fateful June night in 1989.

Many on the bridge began screaming at the crowd below: "Run! Riot police are approaching! Run!" That's when I saw one of the police officers unfold a black banner. Seconds later, shots of tear gas arced through the dark sky, followed by clouds of white smoke billowing from the ground. The advancing fumes smelled like something between burning rubber and a very pungent mustard.

Pandemonium ensued. A stranger came up to me and Kelvin and said, "You two need these," and handed us two face masks. My eyes started to sting and I put on my swimming goggles. We ran with the retreating crowd and took shelter in the nearby Harcourt Garden.

As I would later learn from the news, 87 canisters of tear gas were fired in Admiralty within the two-hour window, many of them at close range at demonstrators. People I spoke to said that the show of police force – tear gas and rifles – was ordered by C.Y. Leung for one purpose: to provoke a panic. Experience in other cities has shown few weapons to be more effective against protesters than mass hysteria. It is what makes people trample on each other, throw bricks at police or even set vehicles on fire – all the justification that the authorities needed to order an all-out crackdown.

Provocation might also explain the rather curiously designed warning banners used by law enforcement tonight. There were three types of scrolls in the flag-bearer's quiver: the yellow one read "You are in breach of the law. You may be prosecuted"; the red one read "Stop charging or we use force"; and the third one had writing on both sides – the black side read "WARNING: TEAR SMOKE" and the orange side read "DISPERSE OR WE FIRE." Each time before tear gas was fired into the crowd, riot police would hold up the double-sided banner, with the black side facing the protesters. The only plausible explanation for the unusual (and potentially confusing) design – other than that the police department was trying to cut costs by sticking two flags together – was that it would allow field commanders to deploy lachrymators and, expecting protesters to lose control and retaliate with violence, immediately flip the flag around and fire rubber bullets.

If that was indeed Leung's intention, then he had vastly underestimated his opponents. Far from losing control, protesters remained composed and organized. Evacuation from the tear-gassed area was orderly, as was the distribution of face masks and eye goggles. Self-appointed ushers spontaneously took positions at each intersection, reminding fellow protesters to keep calm and keep moving. Those who refused to leave put their hands in the air to signal non-violence. When one excitable citizen arched his back ready to pelt a water bottle at the advancing police, five protesters would rush over to hold him down. "That's exactly what the cops want you to do," one of them would say. "Don't give them an excuse to arrest all of us!"

9:30pm

There were rumors that riot police would start dispersing the crowds with rubber bullets and even live ammunition. Kelvin and I agreed that we should heed the ushers' warning and leave Admiralty for our own safety. My brother lived in Wanchai and I in Pokfulam. We said goodbye to each other and parted ways.

By then almost every road between Wanchai and downtown Central had been blocked, either by police or by makeshift blockades set up by students. Not a car or double-decker bus was in sight. There were people running on the streets but I didn't know why. A man told me that protesters were planning to occupy streets in Wanchai, Causeway Bay, Mongkok and Tsim Sha Tsui. "Crush us in Admiralty and we go everywhere else," he said in defiance. It reminded me of something my mom once told me about our backyard: if we wanted to get rid of dandelions in the lawn, stepping on them would only send the seeds into the wind and they would pollinate everywhere. And pollinate they did tonight. Far from driving away the crowds, the tear gas had brought many more citizens to the streets as the night advanced. One estimate put the number at 150,000. A grassroots rebellion was multiplying at the speed of the Internet.

I walked two miles to Sai Ying Pun, before finding a taxi to take me home. During my 30-minute trek, I downloaded the FireChat app recommended by Kelvin. I joined a few chat groups and saw users with strange names exchanging intelligence on the frontlines. Some said police had started arresting anyone seen wearing a yellow ribbon, while others claimed they spotted a Chinese armored vehicle crossing the Western Tunnel and heading toward Admiralty. It was hard to tell rumor from truth. I felt like a fugitive in a cold war spy movie. A single thought kept running through my head: *what is happening to my city?*

Perhaps years later, citizens would look back and tell themselves that this was a good night. Like bitter Chinese medicine, what went down today would make us stronger and better. But like that bitter Chinese medicine, it was difficult to swallow.

10:30pm

Home had never felt safer and more needed. I took a shower and sat idly in bed. What had transpired in the last few hours suddenly hit me, as images and sounds finally sank in. I started to sob, and my hands shook despite myself. Tonight in Hong Kong, there were prayers, tears and a lot of unanswered questions. I turned on my computer and started writing. My article, titled "Six Hours in Admiralty," would be posted in the online edition of the *South China Morning Post* in a few hours. I wanted the world to know.

3:30am

With 24-hour news looping on television, I began to fall asleep. As I drifted in and out of consciousness, I thought about the significance of the past 12 hours. Tonight, Hong Kong took its place on a long list of cities forever linked to an anti-government revolt, and Admiralty was written into history's hall of fame alongside Cairo's Tahrir Square and Kiev's Maidan Nezalezhnosti. Tonight, September 28th entered the calendar as a date to be feared by the authorities on every anniversary and commemorated by citizens for generations for come.

Chinese people often refer to historical events by the month and day it took place, like "64" for the Tiananmen Square Massacre on June 4th, 1989 and "71" for the handover of Hong Kong to China on July 1st, 1997. We now have a new phrase – "928," the day that would forever divide our post-colonial history.

It was a Sunday unlike any other.

香港政制簡介

Hong Kong Politics 101

Before we begin, a warning.

Hong Kong's electoral system is bizarre, convoluted and, to the uninitiated, remarkably dull. Putting the pieces together is like assembling a jigsaw puzzle without the picture: you don't know where to start. The only thing worse than trying to understand it, is having to explain it. In years past, everyone who has brought up the subject has failed to register a pulse in the hearts of our politically indifferent citizens. Say the words "super majority" or "geographical constituencies" and people roll their eyes and run for cover.

A tall order notwithstanding, it is imperative that we make sense of our one-of-a-kind electoral design, for it holds the key to figuring out the genesis and purpose of the Umbrella Movement. After all, politics is a lot like grammar – we ought to know the rules before we break them. As we will soon see, our system is engineered to entrench vested interests, maximize government control and disable political opposition. Every complaint citizens make, every resentment they harbor, and every social injustice they endure can be traced to a singular source: an absence of government accountability. It is this singularity that puts the call for universal suffrage at the front and center of the largest social uprising in Hong Kong's history.

One country, two systems

The electoral system we have today is spelled out in the **Basic Law**[1], Hong Kong's mini-constitution, which was based on the **Joint Declaration** signed in 1984 by British Prime Minister Margaret Thatcher and Chinese Premier Zhao Ziyang.

The drafting of both the Basic Law and the Joint Declaration makes Homer's *Odyssey* look like a walk in the park. It was the result of a labored negotiation between two world powers in the lead-up to the **Handover**, when the city would cease to be a crown colony and 6.5 million[2] people would return to the same autocratic regime from which their parents and grandparents had escaped. On July 1st, 1997, Hong Kong would become a special administrative region (**SAR**) under Communist rule.

The looming threat of a regime change had sparked an exodus of Hong Kong's elite. During the 1980s and 1990s, hundreds of thousands of business owners and professionals emigrated to English-speaking countries like Britain, the U.S., Canada, Australia and New Zealand. To stem the brain drain, then **Paramount Leader** Deng Xiaoping famously promised that "horses will continue to race, and dancers will continue to dance" after 1997[3].

Deng's pragmatic solution for Hong Kong was memorialized in the Basic law, which guarantees the city a "**high degree of autonomy**" in all aspects other than national defense and foreign affairs. Citizens are granted the kind of civil liberties not enjoyed anywhere else in China, including unrestricted freedom of expression and an independent

---

1 – Terms in boldface are defined in *Appendix V - Glossary*.

2 – During the 17-year period between 1997 and 2014, the population of Hong Kong went from 6.5 million to 7.2 million. The average annual growth rate of 0.64%, one of the lowest in the world, has to do with the city's high cost of living.

3 – Deng paid a high-profile visit to Hong Kong in the 1980s and was so impressed by the British colony that he decided not only to preserve it but also to model pilot cities like Shanghai and Shenzhen after it.

judiciary. This so-called "**one country, two systems**" framework allows Hong Kongers, who are separated from their cousins in mainland China only by the heavily polluted Shenzhen River, to maintain their cherished way of life free from Communist meddling. They can continue to drive on the other side of the road (on the left side instead of the right), use their own currency (the Hong Kong dollar instead of the *renminbi*), speak their own language (**Cantonese** instead of **Mandarin**) and write with their own set of characters (traditional instead of simplified Chinese). They are even allowed to access Facebook and Twitter (which are blocked on the mainland).

According to the Basic Law, however, the "one country, two systems" policy has an expiration date: June 30th, 2047, 50 years after the Handover. Deng was reasonably confident that half a century would be plenty of time for his vision for a New China to win over – and Sinofy – the Westernized Cantonese speakers in the south. Likewise, Hong Kongers were reasonably confident that the Communist regime would not last long enough to see that day come.

While Britain and China agreed on the broad strokes of Hong Kong's post-Handover destiny, the finer points of negotiation – such as how to gradually democratize the electoral system by allowing citizens to choose their leader and lawmakers – were left unresolved. With neither the diplomatic leverage over Beijing nor the motivation to expend its political capital for the sake of its former subjects, the British government capitulated on most of the open issues. And so when the clock struck midnight on July 1st, 1997, a Frankenstein electoral system heaved into grotesque existence.

The Chief Executive

It is the highest office in Hong Kong. Think of it as the CEO of a company, the mayor of a city, or even the president of a country – except that, unlike Singapore, Monaco or the Vatican, Hong Kong is *not* its own country. It is at best a "territory" or a "region." A special administrative region.

The **Chief Executive** is the liaison between Hong Kong and Beijing. Put less diplomatically, he is the buffer between a regime that craves control and a population that resists it. When he performs the role properly, the Chief Executive keeps the economic machine well-oiled and the hoi polloi hunkered down. At the same time, he is expected to advise Communist China on how to assimilate the new subjects without ruffling too many feathers. To achieve both objectives, the snake oil salesman must convey the demands of Hong Kong people to his Communist master, before peddling unpalatable policies back to his people.

Out with the old, in with the red on Handover Day

In reality, the Chief Executive parrots the words of Beijing instead of advising it, and he haggles on behalf of vested interests rather than the people. Still, we can't put all the blame on one individual, when the real culprit is the system itself. Annex I of the Basic Law stipulates that:

"The Chief Executive shall be elected by a broadly representative Election Committee in accordance with this Law and appointed by the Central People's Government."

The **Election Committee** consists of 1,200 members representing various commercial and industry sectors. Because most of them are associated with big businesses or special interest groups, the committee is stacked with Beijing loyalists and pro-establishment elitists. It also leads to anomalies like the fishing and agricultural sector, which carries a block of 60 seats (or 5% of the votes), when there aren't very many fishermen or farmers left in Hong Kong[4]. The setup allows our political leader to be handpicked by a small group of insiders who are hardly representative of the general population. This so-called **small circle**

---

4 – There are roughly 11,000 acres of farmland in Hong Kong. In 1995, locally produced vegetables totaled 100,000 tons (17% of the domestic demand). By 2013, the output dropped to a meager 17,600 tons (less than 2% of the domestic demand).

election ensures the twin goals of "stability" (translation: control) and "prosperity" (translation: crony capitalism) that the authorities use to justify the lack of popular participation. Unless and until every citizen gets a free vote, the Chief Executive will always answer only to those who put him in power.

What's more, not everyone who sits on the Election Committee is selected by actual human beings. A large portion of the 1,200 members are chosen by trade organizations and corporations that carry company votes. This political oddity, known as "**corporate voting**," is yet another way of protecting the interest of the wealthy elite who are beholden to Beijing. It gives a new meaning to the term corporatocracy – rule by business interests.

Beginner's bad luck

Hong Kong has had three Chief Executives since the Handover – all anointed by the unelected Election Committee (see Table 1).

Term	Name	Career	Legacy
1997 – 2005	Tung Chee-hwa	• Scion of a shipping empire. • Elected in 1996 with 320 out of 400 votes (beating retired Chief Justice Yang Ti-liang and property tycoon Peter Woo). • Re-elected in 2002 (unopposed). • Resigned in 2005 for poor governance.	• 1997 Asian Financial Crisis. • 2003 SARS outbreak, burst of property bubble and 2003 Mass Rally. • Creation of Cyberport and Science Park. • Proposal to develop the West Kowloon Cultural District.

2005 - 2012	Donald Tsang	• Son of a policeman. • Career bureaucrat: Financial Secretary and Chief Secretary under Tung Chee-hwa. • Elected in 2005 after Tung stepped down (unopposed). • Re-elected in 2007 with 649 out of 800 votes (beating the Civic Party's Alan Leong).	• Failure to pass the 2005 electoral reform bill. • 2008 financial tsunami. • Express Rail-link controversy in 2010. • Passing of the 2010 electoral reform bill. • Completion of the Tamar Government Complex in 2012. • Bribery scandals in 2012 resulting in imprisonment in 2017.
2012 – present	C.Y. Leung	• Son of a policeman. • Property management company executive. • Adviser to Tung Chee-hwa and head of Donald Tsang's cabinet. • Elected in 2012 with only 689 out of 1,200 votes (beating businessman Henry Tang and the Democratic Party's Albert Ho).	• Patriotic Education saga in 2012. • HKTV controversy in 2013. • Umbrella Movement in 2014.

Table 1. Chief Executives of the SAR

Shipping tycoon **Tung Chee-hwa**[5] and career bureaucrat **Donald Tsang** both won with an overwhelming majority in 1996 and 2007, respectively. Tung received 82% of the votes, while Tsang got 84%. As is the case in North Korea, members on the Election Committee tend to cast their votes in unison before breaking into thunderous applause.

---

5 – Names in boldface are further explained in *Appendix III – Who's Who of Local Politics.*

Unlike his predecessors, **C.Y. Leung**, the main villain in the Umbrella Movement, won the election with only 689 out of the 1,200 votes, just barely a majority (57%). His narrow win in 2012 – and the lack of legitimacy it denoted – earned him the nickname "**689**."

Much to Beijing's displeasure, the first Chief Executive was a disaster of a leader. Tung Chee-hwa's failed policies and a streak of bad luck made him a political piñata. Under his watch, the city was hard hit by the **Asian Financial Crisis** in 1997 and again by the **SARS outbreak** in 2003. The natural disaster was followed by manmade ones – the burst of a property bubble as a result of an ill-advised housing policy and a poorly timed decision to enact an **anti-subversion bill**[6]. All that culminated in the **2003 Mass Rally** that drew 500,000 angry protesters to the streets, the largest demonstration Hong Kong had seen since the rally in support of the **Tiananmen Square Protests** in 1989.

Tung's shocking incompetence forced the Communist leadership to rethink Deng Xiaoping's original hands-off approach for Hong Kong and begin to micromanage the SAR. One of its decisions was to empower the **Liaison Office**, the de facto Chinese embassy in Hong Kong. Located in Sai Wan (west of Central), the outpost is tasked to coordinate Beijing's policies with the SAR government. More importantly, it is to keep a close eye on the affairs in Hong Kong and, if necessary, intervene. Any intervention by the Liaison Office must be done quietly because Article 22 of the Basic Law specifically prohibits any department of the Chinese government from meddling in local matters.

Fahrenheit 689

In 2005, Tung Chee-hwa was fired by Beijing and replaced by Donald Tsang. The second Chief Executive did Hong Kong neither good nor harm – he hardly did anything at all. Nicknamed "Greedy Tsang," the son of a policeman preferred wining and dining on the government's expense account and later got into trouble for renting a penthouse apartment from a wealthy Chinese businessman at below-market rate[7]. Unlike

---

6 – Article 23 of the Basic Law stipulates that the SAR government shall "enact laws on its own to prohibit any act of treason, secession, sedition, subversion against the Central People's Government..." The 2003 attempt to pass an anti-subversion bill sparked widespread concern over the suppression of dissent and speech freedom in Hong Kong.

7 – Tsang failed to declare his rental arrangements and went on to approve a licensing bid by Digital Broadcasting Corporation, a radio station of which his landlord Bill Wong was a major shareholder. Tsang was formally charged in October 2015 and found guilty in February 2017, becoming the highest-ranking official ever to be convicted in Hong Kong.

Tung, Tsang at least managed to keep Hong Kong on an even keel and finish his two terms in office.

Things quickly went south again when C.Y. Leung succeeded Tsang in 2012. Also the son of a policeman, Leung is a self-made millionaire with a good poker face and a honeyed tongue. A classic Machiavellian, his poise and eloquence are matched only by his ambition. Leung has done remarkably well for himself: at age 30, he became the vice chairman of the Hong Kong branch of Jones Lang LaSalle, a multinational property management firm; by age 41, he was president of the Hong Kong Institute of Surveyors. In 1984, Beijing named him Secretary General of the Basic Law Consultative Committee advising on the drafting of the city's constitution. It was during his time serving as a policy adviser to Tung Chee-hwa that Leung set his eyes on the **Government House**. Since then, every step he took and every person he befriended would get him closer to that goal.

Far more disconcerting than his ambition was – and is – the unconfirmed rumor that C.Y. Leung is a member of the Chinese Communist Party (**CCP**), a charge he has repeatedly denied. There are an estimated 3,000 CCP members in Hong Kong, all of them have sworn secrecy and operate underground. Several prominent figures, including founder of the Democratic Party **Martin Lee** and former underground Communist operative Florence Leung, have argued with conviction that only a party member could win Beijing's trust to head the Basic Law Consultative Committee at the age of 34. The day after C.Y. Leung was elected Chief Executive in 2012, the CCP's official news site *Renminwang* issued a congratulatory press release and referred to him as "Comrade Leung," an appellation reserved only for one of their own. If Leung is indeed a closet Communist, then the "one country, two systems" framework would be in serious jeopardy, as all party members are expected to abandon personal judgment in favor of orders from party seniors. As we will see, that is not too far from Leung's track record since he took office in 2012.

C.Y. Leung's election win had much to do with the Liaison Office. Then Deputy Director Li Gang played a pivotal role in lobbying for Leung against his opponent Henry Tang, the candidate favored by the pro-establishment camp in Hong Kong. To bring down Tang, the Liaison Office reportedly dug up dirt about him, including a sordid extramarital affair and illegal home renovations[8]. In the end, Leung won by a narrow margin (689 out of 1,200 votes) and his rise to power further emboldened the Liaison Office. Since 2012, the outpost has become an *éminence*

---

8 – Tang and his wife were caught adding a basement and wine cellar to their Kowloon Tong mansion without prior authorization from the Housing Department. Ironically, illegal structures were also discovered at C.Y. Leung's adjoining houses on the Peak but the discovery came only after his election win.

grise that governs the city behind the scenes, just like the man standing behind the curtain in *The Wizard of Oz*. The local press calls it "rule by Sai Wan."

The Legco

As its name suggests, the Legislative Council is the legislature of Hong Kong. Think of it as our parliament – a forum for lawmakers to propose, debate and vote on bills.

There are 70 seats in the **Legco**, half of which are called **geographical constituencies** and the other half **functional constituencies** (see Figure 1). This bicameral arrangement is not dissimilar to the Senate and the House of Representatives in the United States Congress, or the House of Commons and the House of Lords in the British Parliament. Unlike lawmakers in America, a vast majority of the functional constituencies – all but the five "**super seats**" which I will explain later – are *not* democratically elected. Unlike the British Lords[9], the functional constituencies have the power to reject bills proposed or passed by the elected house.

For ease of reference, I will hereinafter call the functional constituencies the "Upper House" (also because the system gives them the upper hand) and the geographical constituencies the "Lower House."

All 35 seats in the Lower House are voted into the Legco by a general election involving the city's 3.5 million registered voters. The same cannot be said about the Upper House. With the exception of the five super seats, each of the remaining 30 functional seats is handpicked by a small circle of constituents within its own trade or interest group. For instance, the engineering functional seat is nominated and selected by a few thousand registered engineers, just as the legal seat and the IT seat are selected by lawyers and IT professionals, respectively.

Like the Election Committee that chooses our Chief Executive, the Upper House suffers from the same anomaly of corporate voting. Hong Kong holds the dubious distinction as the only jurisdiction in the world where corporations, a legal fiction, are vested with the power to elect legislators who will go on to shape real policies that affect real people. Case in point: the electoral base for the insurance seat is made up of not a single individual but rather 130 insurance companies.

---

9 – The U.K. Parliament Act of 1911 removed the power of the House of Lords to veto or amend bills proposed by the House of Commons.

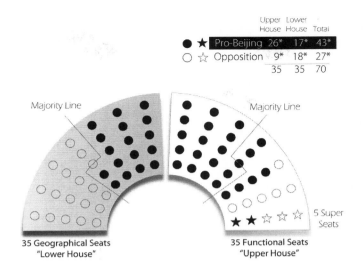

* As of the time of the occupy movement.

Figure 1. Make-up of the Legco

A tale of two camps

In Hong Kong, the opposition comprises the pan-democrats (or **pan-dems** for short), an informal coalition of pro-democracy political parties. They include the **Democratic Party**[10], the **Civic Party**, the Association for Democracy and People's Livelihood (**ADPL**), **People Power**, the League of Social Democrats (**LSD**), and other small parties. The pan-dems typically carry between 25 and 27 of the 70 Legco seats, not enough to have a majority to block most government-proposed bills, but sufficient to prevent a super majority needed to approve constitutional matters (more on that later).

The remaining 45 or so seats in both houses are taken up by the **pro-Beijing camp**. The red coalition is subdivided into two wings. The business-friendly wing, such as the **Liberal Party** and the Business and Professionals Alliance (**BPA**), consists of wealthy business owners and special interest lobbyists. They favor conservative fiscal policies and benefit from the government's pro-business agenda.

---

10 – Political parties in boldface are further explained in *Appendix IV – Major Political Parties in Hong Kong*.

The loyalist wing, on the other hand, is motivated not by business interests but handouts from the CCP and sometimes genuine patriotism for the motherland. Many of them are mercenaries hired by the Liaison Office and other Communist operatives to say and do whatever they are told. When **Chris Patten**, the last colonial Governor of Hong Kong, famously prophesied that the city's autonomy would not be taken away by Beijing but instead given away bit by bit by citizens in exchange for personal gains, he might have had these people in mind.

The largest political parties representing the loyalists are the Democratic Alliance for the Betterment and Progress of Hong Kong (**DAB**) and the Federation of Trade Unions (**FTU**). They carry the highest number of Legco seats and are known for buying votes with anything from paid meals and kitchen appliances to bus tours and concert tickets. Their tactic has spawned the Cantonese catch phrase "*se zai beng zung*," which literally means snake soup banquet, vegetarian meal, mooncake and glutinous rice – the four freebies that have proved especially popular among senior and low-income voters.

The pro-Beijing camp has a natural advantage over the pan-dems: the full backing of the Communist machine. The DAB and the FTU are much better funded than any of the opposition parties, which rely on the proverbial 20-dollar checks from regular citizens. The pro-Beijing coalition also runs better coordinated election campaigns by comparison. Whereas the pro-democracy votes are often split between the moderates (like the Democratic Party) and the radicals (such as People Power and the LSD), the Liaison Office will see to it that their teams do not siphon off votes from each other by going head-to-head within the same district.

Electile Dysfunction

The functional constituencies predate the Handover. Ironically, they were conceived in the mid-1980s by the colonial government with the hope of increasing local participation in the legislative process by recruiting representatives from a cross-section of the economy. What began as an innocuous – some say well-intended – concept, however, ended up as a political nightmare that would haunt the city long after it reverted to Chinese rule. Its small and uneven electoral base, combined with a few tricks slipped into the Basic Law during the Sino-British negotiation, has made the Upper House the government's most effective weapon against political opposition and social progress.

So how do 30 unelected functional seats manage to control the 70-member Legco? The answer lies in a number of constitutionally protected oddities designed to give the Upper House virtually complete control over the legislature.

Trick No.1 – Under the Basic Law, any bill introduced by the government requires a simple majority vote by all 70 Legco seats voting together. Because almost the entire Upper House is stacked with Beijing loyalists, the government has no difficulty securing the 36 votes it needs to pass its own bills. That means government-led initiatives, no matter how wasteful and unpopular, almost always sail through the Legco without a hitch.

The only exception to this simple majority requirement is government-proposed bills relating to constitutional issues such as electoral reform or any amendment to the Basic Law. These politically sensitive matters require a super-majority vote, or at least 47 out of the 70 votes. Two-thirds is a high threshold: the pan-dems need only 23 seats in the Legco to block any such bill. For instance, an unpopular electoral reform bill was defeated by pan-dem lawmakers in 2005.

Trick No.2 – If that isn't confusing enough, the legislative process then takes a schizophrenic turn. While government-proposed bills require either a simple or super majority vote of both houses voting *together*, any bill proposed by an individual Legco member must go through two rounds of voting. It must first be passed by the Lower House before being *separately* voted on by the Upper House. This two-step mechanic is called the **separate vote count**, and it applies *only* to legislator-proposed bills (and not government-proposed ones). As a result, bills drafted by the opposition that the government or big businesses do not care for, such as a proposal to raise the minimum wage or form a subcommittee to look into the Chief Executive's dubious business dealings, will invariably get voted down by the Upper House, even if the bills manage to get through the Lower House.

Trick No.3 – Things get more bizarre still. The Basic Law prohibits Legco members from proposing any bill that concerns constitutional matters (e.g. electoral reform) or involves the use of government funds (e.g. raising unemployment benefits or introducing a comprehensive pension plan). Because almost every social policy requires public funding, this limitation has all but stripped individual Legco members of their ability to discharge their role as policymakers. They are left with limited power to amend or defeat government-proposed bills – like a boxer who is only allowed to block but not to throw punches.

These convoluted rules are summarized in Table 2.

Legco rules	Bills proposed by government	Bills proposed by Legco member
Limitations on scope	None.	Must not involve constitutional matters or use of government funds.
Voting mechanics	Upper and Lower Houses voting *together*.	Separate vote count: Upper and Lower Houses voting *separately*.
Approval requirement	Simple majority (36 or more votes) for most matters. Super majority (47 or more votes) for constitutional matters.	Simple majority vote by <u>each</u> of the Upper House and the Lower House.

Table 2. Legco, an uneven playing field

If all of that sounds like gibberish to you, that's because it is. All you need to remember is this: *functional constituencies are very bad for us and we should get rid of them.*

Designed to rubber stamp government policies and stonewall the opposition, the Upper House was why taxpayers forked out HK$70 billion (US$9 billion) to fund the wasteful **Express Rail-link** infrastructure project[11], why the investigation into C.Y. Leung's alleged conflicts of interest in the **West Kowloon Development**[12] was dropped, and why the government is sitting on trillions of dollars in foreign reserves and still refuses to set up a social security plan.

---

11 – The megaproject involved the construction of a local railroad system to connect Hong Kong to mainland China's massive high-speed rail network. It fitted the dictionary definition of a white elephant not just because the link-up was overpriced and unnecessary (there was an existing track that could have been used), but also because it raised serious constitutional issues by setting up Chinese border controls in the SAR. It was Hong Kong's version of Boston's "Big Dig" disaster in the 1980s.

12 – Leung was one of 10 panel judges in the 2001 concept planning competition for the construction of the West Kowloon Cultural District, but he failed to declare that his company DTZ Holdings had acted as a consultant to one of the contestants.

The Upper House is also why we can't blame some of the more outspoken pan-dems, like members of People Power and the LSD, for resorting to over-the-top antics in the Legco. Lawmakers like **Long Hair** and **Albert Chan** are known to hurl effigies and placards at the Chief Executive, and filibuster almost every government bill. Reasoned debate and thoughtful dialogue – methods preferred by the more moderate pan-dems – may work in a normal democracy in the West. But Hong Kong is *not* a normal democracy.

So long as the functional constituencies continue to take up half the Legco seats, none of the moderates' high school debate team tactics will do ordinary citizens any good. Instead, firebrands like Long Hair subscribe to the political adage that "if it ain't fixed, just break it." They use their theatrics on the Legco floor to draw public attention to the gross injustice of our legislative process. Even though their righteous indignation is often mistaken for thuggery, any self-respecting legislator would have done the same. If you found yourself in a poker game with a four-card hand or on a soccer team with no goalie, would you keep playing or would you kick and scream?

The reasons Long Hair keeps throwing objects at C.Y. Leung are summarized in Table 3 overleaf.

Electoral reform

Hong Kong is faced with two problems. First, we have an unaccountable leader selected by a small group of insiders. Second, we have an equally unaccountable legislature dominated by the same small group of insiders.

The one-two punch of our dysfunctional electoral system has bruised the city with bad policies and unjust laws. Over time, the bruises have turned into festering wounds. Short of genuine reform to overhaul the system, the lack of accountability will remain the biggest stumbling block that prevents Hong Kong from reaching its full potential and becoming the world city that it desperately aspires to be.

Fact	*Implications*	*Examples*
Pro-Beijing camp carries a majority in Legco (both houses together)	Government-proposed bills are uniformly approved by the pro-Beijing majority.	Funding approvals for wasteful infrastructure projects such as the Express Rail-link in 2010 and the third airport runway in 2015.
Pro-Beijing camp does *not* carry a super majority in Legco (both houses together)	Government-proposed bills relating to electoral reform and other constitutional matters cannot be passed without the cooperation of the opposition.	The 2005 electoral reform bill failed to pass without pan-dem support. The 2010 electoral reform bill was passed after Democratic Party and ADPL lawmakers switched sides at the 11th hour.
Pan-dems carry a majority in the democratically elected Lower House (geographical constituencies)	The opposition can propose its own bills and have them passed in the Lower House, but as a result of the "separate vote count" requirement for legislator-proposed bills, those bills are invariably defeated in the Upper House.	Long Hair's proposal to investigate C.Y. Leung's alleged conflicts of interest in the West Kowloon Development was passed in the Lower House but defeated in the Upper House.
Pro-Beijing camp carries a majority in the unelected Upper House (functional constituencies)	The Upper House will veto every bill proposed by the opposition even if it passes the Lower House.	Ditto.

Table 3. Legco facts and implications

Of the two problems, the second one is considered more damaging because real political power resides with the legislative branch. While the Chief Executive sets the policy agenda, it is the Legco that approves or rejects each item on it. Anything that C.Y. Leung proposes, from social programs to infrastructure projects, likely requires government funding and he needs the Legco to play ball. As we have seen, the functional constituencies remove these checks and balances by marching in lockstep with the Chief Executive and acting as a gatekeeper to veto unwanted bills initiated by the opposition. That is why the pan-dem coalition has made abolishing the Upper House – or at least curtailing it – the cornerstone of its political platform.

Donald Tsang's government tried twice, once in 2005 and a second time in 2010, to quell public outcry by initiating snail-paced electoral reform. The challenge was to come up with a solution progressive enough to satisfy the pan-dems without pushing Beijing's limits. The first attempt to reach that elusive goal was dead on arrival, when the conservative **2005 Reform Bill** fell far short of the pan-dems' expectations and failed to get a super-majority vote in the Legco to pass it.

In 2010, it was *déjà vu* all over again. To make sure Tsang came up with something more constructive this time (including the abolition of the Upper House), the hawkish LSD had an idea. Five pan-dem legislators – three from the LSD and two from the Civic Party, each representing one of the five electoral districts – resigned from the Legco at the same time to trigger a citywide by-election to fill their vacancies. The by-election was viewed as a **De Facto Referendum** that would give the general public a chance to take a stand on the **2010 Reform Bill**. The idea was that if citizens voted the resigned lawmakers back into the Legco, it would be construed as a "yes" vote supporting a more progressive electoral reform package. The plan worked brilliantly: it got the bureaucrats so nervous that Tsang begrudgingly agreed to take part in an unprecedented – and rather embarrassing – televised debate against the much more eloquent **Audrey Eu** (seasoned litigator and chairlady of the Civic Party) to defend his feeble reform proposal. Hong Kong was as close as it had ever been to finally ridding itself of the functional constituencies.

Sadly, the hopes to take down the Upper House were dashed after the Democratic Party and the ADPL met with representatives from the Liaison Office at the 11th hour without conferring with their pan-dem allies. The closed door meeting resulted in the two parties making a sudden U-turn and voting to pass the 2010 Reform Bill – even though it was widely considered to be even more conservative than the proposal that they vetoed in 2005.

One of the features in the 2010 package was an increase in the number of members on the Election Committee from 800 to 1,200 – which really wasn't much of an improvement at all. What's more, instead of curtailing the functional constituencies, the 2010 package added five new seats to each of the Upper House and the Lower House, raising the total number of Legco seats from 60 at the time of the reform proposal to the current number of 70.

The five new seats in the Upper House were dubbed the "**super seats**," so called because, unlike the existing 30 functional constituencies that are selected from industry sectors, the new ones would be chosen from a pool of existing district council members and have a broad electoral base comprising 3.5 million registered voters. These super seats would also have a high nomination threshold, which favors large political parties (like the Democratic Party) and precludes smaller ones (like the LSD) from ever winning them. Many believed that the new feature was a bone thrown by the Liaison Office to get the Democratic Party to switch sides. Indeed, in the 2012 general election that followed the passing of the reform bill, three of the five super seats went to the Democratic Party and the ADPL.

The Democratic Party came under heavy fire for its change of heart. Once the beacon of democracy, party members were accused of betraying their allies by accepting a bad reform package in exchange for a handful of new Legco seats – like Judas and his 30 pieces of silver. Because of them, critics argued, Hong Kongers had lost a golden opportunity to abolish the Upper House once and for all. Long after the reform was passed, the Democratic Party continues to pay a hefty political price in elections and fundraising campaigns. In the 2012 Legco election, its share of the popular votes plunged to an all-time low of 14%, down from 43% in the first post-Handover election in 1998[13] (see Figure 2). Party seniors such as **Albert Ho** and **Emily Lau** have become more despised than even some of the pro-Beijing loyalists. So much for being a beacon of democracy.

Political indifference

If you have managed to get this far without skipping ahead or falling asleep, then you deserve a gold star. You have a longer attention span than 95% of the people in Hong Kong. And if you have been paying attention to what you have read, then you deserve another gold star. While giving yourself a pat on the back, you should be wondering how a

---

13 – The Democratic Party's popularity has been slowly declining since the Handover due to the emergence of new pan-dem players such as the Civic Party and the LSD, which was considered one of the key motivations for it to forge a "dangerous liaison" with the Liaison Office in 2010.

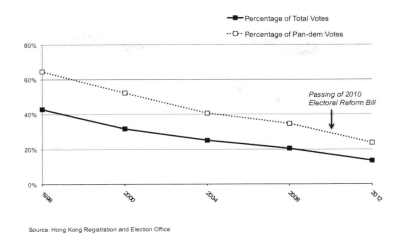

Figure 2. Declining popularity of the Democratic Party since the Handover

political system so blatantly unfair and patently wrong has managed to fly below our radar for so long.

Grotesque as it is, the topic of electoral systems rarely comes up in everyday conversation. Citizens do not feel the sting on a personal or, crucially, economic level. Even if they do, few care enough to invest the time to figure out the minutia of voting procedures. Most people would rather get a rectal exam than listen to a three-hour lecture on separate vote count and corporate voting.

Every now and then, a *cause célèbre* like the Express Rail-link controversy will bring to light some of the systemic injustices. As soon as the news cycle runs out, however, the headlines shift back to celebrity gossip and stock market performance. Citizens shake their heads in mild annoyance and return to their daily grind. After all, young graduates need to find jobs, families need to pay mortgages, and retirees need to make ends meet. People rarely pause to think that those 30 unelected functional seats are the very reason why the job market is stale, property prices continue to skyrocket, and the elderly and the poor have no social safety net to fall back on.

Contrary to popular belief, Hong Kong people are not politically apathetic. Every July 1st, tens of thousands brave the punishing summer heat to take to the streets to vent their frustrations toward the government. Half a million citizens joined the 2003 Mass Rally to oppose the anti-subversion bill and defend freedom of expression.

If it isn't apathy, then what is it that makes so many dive for cover when we talk about electoral reform?

Professor Michael DeGolyer, founder of the HK Transition Project, observed that in Hong Kong, topics such as employment, housing and welfare are uniformly pigeonholed as "social issues" rather than "political issues." As such, ordinary citizens rarely connect the dots between their everyday problems and what happens on the Legco floor or at the ballot box. Furthermore, there is a strong sense among the masses that wealth is trapped at the top, power is entrenched among the ruling elite, and the unwritten rules of a corporatocracy are immutable and irrefutable. Politics, like golf and polo, is an exclusive sport played by the upper crust of society. In other words, Hong Kongers are not politically *indifferent*; they are politically *jaded*. So while people are vocal about what they don't like *socially*, not many are willing to participate *politically*. Because of that, the turnout at street demonstrations is much higher than the turnout at the voting booth.

There is an elephant in the room, but no one says anything. Some see a 5-ton animal but can't make out what it is. Others pretend it isn't there because they don't think it has anything to do with them. So the elephant continues to roam free and trample on everything in its path. But all that is about to change.

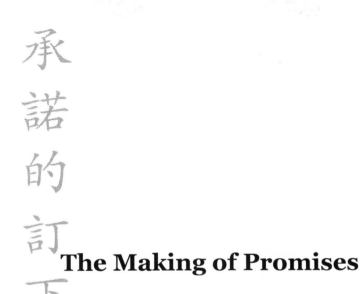

The Making of Promises

Universal suffrage – the extension of the right to vote to every adult citizen – is the axis around which the entire Umbrella Movement turned. The need to bring Hong Kong's electoral system in line with that of the rest of the civilized world is not only a collective wish for pro-democracy activists, it is also written in our law.

To show that the British weren't completely asleep at the switch during the Handover negotiations, they did make sure that the Basic Law provides for the gradual democratization of Hong Kong. To our dismay, however, they left open the question of how and when.

A basic right

Article 45 of the Basic Law has this to say about the Chief Executive selection:

"The method for selecting the Chief Executive shall be specified in the light of the actual situation in the Hong Kong Special Administrative Region and in accordance with the principle of gradual and orderly progress. The ultimate aim is the selection of the Chief Executive by universal suffrage upon nomination by a broadly representative nominating committee in accordance with democratic procedures."

Article 68 uses almost identical wording with respect to the Legco election:

"The method for forming the Legislative Council shall be specified in the light of the actual situation in the Hong Kong Special Administrative Region and in accordance with the principle of gradual and orderly progress. The ultimate aim is the election of all the members of the Legislative Council by universal suffrage."

In the local vernacular, the twin goals to give citizens a free vote to elect their leader and lawmakers is dubbed "**dual universal suffrage**." Ever since the Handover, the pan-dems have been pressuring the SAR government at every Legco session and street rally for a timetable and a roadmap to implement Articles 45 and 68.

2003 was a watershed year for post-Handover Hong Kong. The SARS outbreak that started around Chinese New Year and went on for five terrifying months killed hundreds and decimated the local economy. Tourism plunged and unemployment shot to a historical high. The mystery virus turned a normally jam-packed city into a virtual ghost town. At the same time, property prices hit rock bottom as a result of the critically wounded economy and Tung Chee-hwa's "85,000 Housing Plan" – an aggressive proposal to flood the property market with 85,000 new residential units every year – that led to the largest man-made property crash in our history. Tens of thousands of citizens lost their homes to foreclosure, and homeowner's suicide by jumping off buildings and burning charcoal at home (to self-induce carbon monoxide poisoning) became a trend.

The series of unfortunate events culminated in the 2003 Mass Rally, where 500,000 citizens – over 7% of the entire population – took to the streets to vent their anger over ineffective disease control, bad policies, and the poorly timed attempt to enact an anti-subversion bill. Days after the massive protest, the government withdrew that bill from the Legco and then Security Secretary **Regina Ip** was forced to step down. 20 months later, Tung Chee-hwa resigned from office citing an arthritic leg and Donald Tsang was hastily sworn in.

Hu Jintao, Chinese President and Paramount Leader at the time, was starting to lose faith in the SAR government and its ability to govern the city. Meanwhile, the calls for dual universal suffrage by as early as 2007 were getting louder by the day. As the political climate became more toxic and public frustration boiled over, the Chinese government knew that ignoring those demands would further destabilize Hong Kong and threaten Tsang's administration. The 2005 Reform Bill, designed to cool the temperature, was vetoed by the pan-dems. Beijing needed to come up with something else.

The two promises

In 2007, the **Standing Committee** of the National People's Congress, the central legislative body of the Chinese government, issued a decision agreeing to implement Article 45 by 2017 and Article 68 by 2020. The edict, known as the **2007 Decision**, crushed the pan-dems' hopes for dual universal suffrage by the next general election in 2012. Instead, Beijing handed Hong Kongers a rain check and told them to wait 10 and 13 years before they could freely select their leader and lawmakers.

There is no consensus as to why President Hu bothered making these concessions at all. Some observers believed the Chinese government needed to keep Hong Kong open and free to attract foreign investment to fund the country's breakneck economic growth. Others believed the city's stability was important for self-preservation. With growing factional infighting within the Communist leadership, a mishandling of the delicate situation down south might be just the opportunity that rival factions up north needed to undermine, even upend, Hu's hold on power. Hong Kong might have been only a square on the Paramount Leader's chess board, but any skilled player knows that one wrong move is all it takes to lose a game. For the sake of his own credibility and supremacy, Hu had to throw Hong Kongers a bone.

There was also the **Taiwan** angle. Even though the sole objective of the Communist regime has always been self-perpetuation – to cling to power for eternity – there have been pet projects like outer space exploration and territorial expansion. Reunification with Taiwan is another one of them. To end the 65-year standoff with the renegade island, China wanted to hold up Hong Kong as the poster boy and demonstrate to the Taiwanese people that the "one country, two systems" model could work for them too. Botching the democratization of Hong Kong would not only sour the already tenuous cross-strait relations, it would also confirm a longstanding fear shared by 23 million self-ruled islanders: "Hong Kong today will be Taiwan tomorrow."

Given both domestic and diplomatic considerations, even the normally uncompromising Beijing had to bite the bullet and find a way forward for Hong Kong, if only to keep up appearances. Without better alternatives, kicking the can down the road seemed an expedient solution. The top priority at the time was to defuse a political time bomb and the 2007 Decision did just that. It bought Hu some valuable time – all 10 years of it. After all, 2017 and 2020 were political light years away and the hot potato would be handed down to the next generation of Communist leadership set to assume power in 2012.

Promise-maker's remorse

The pan-dems knew full well that achieving dual universal suffrage would be an uphill battle. Doing so by 2007 or even 2012 was more a rallying cry than a bottom line. In other words, getting Beijing to agree on a timetable – any timetable – was already a huge political victory. At the time, most citizens agreed that democracy was worth the wait. Better in 2017 and 2020 than never.

The waiting period following the 2007 Decision has been a bumpy ride. In 2008, the city was mired in another financial downturn, triggered by the subprime mortgage crisis in the U.S. followed by the second property market crash in five years. The political temperature was rising once again. To the ire of its pan-dem allies, the Democratic Party handed Donald Tsang's government the votes it needed to pass the disappointing 2010 Reform Bill, adding more seats to the functional constituencies instead of abolishing them altogether.

There were enough distractions in the city for citizens to take their eyes off the 2017 deadline. We blissfully – and naively in hindsight – assumed that things would sort themselves out in advance of 2017 and 2020. Dual universal suffrage was a bridge to be crossed when we got to it, despite the many operational details still to be worked out. The vague wording in Article 45 such as "broadly representative" and "in accordance with democratic procedures" needed to be debated and defined. Composition of the **Nominating Committee**, central to the election's procedural fairness, had not even been discussed.

More worrying still, there were misgivings that Beijing might find a way to renege on its promises. While a smooth democratization of Hong Kong would let off steam in the SAR and impress a watching Taiwan, it also entailed great political risk for China.

The big question facing Beijing was: *what if Hong Kongers chose their leader unwisely and put someone like Long Hair in the Government*

House? That worry was ill-placed, because citizens of the SAR are pragmatic enough to avoid anyone who would openly defy China or lacked the experience to operate the bureaucratic machine. Nevertheless, even a moderate like **Anson Chan** (Chief Secretary under Governor Chris Patten) or the Civic Party's Audrey Eu could spell trouble. One candid interview with the *Washington Post* or the BBC about the Chief Executive's stance on the **Tiananmen Square Massacre** or the imprisonment of Nobel Peace Prize laureate Liu Xiaobo would undo years of brand building for the Communists. The world's second largest economy – a superpower that had sent astronauts to the moon and put more new billionaires on the *Forbes List* than any other country – would not be dressed down on the world stage, least of all by one of their own.

There were also the wealthy elite in Hong Kong to worry about. A free and fair election in 2017 would favor candidates who answered to the average voter. That meant more social spending and fewer business-friendly policies. Local tycoons and powerful trade groups feared that the new sheriff in town could put an end to the quid pro quo between government and big businesses, and turn Hong Kong into a Scandinavian welfare state. During the Umbrella Movement, C.Y. Leung went so far as to tell a *New York Times* reporter that a freely elected Chief Executive would "skew government policies toward the poor." Leung's gaffe was less a Freudian slip than a real concern expressed by the super rich. There is an age-old assumption that Beijing needs the help of local property tycoons such as Asia's second richest man **Li Ka-shing**[14], Henderson Land's **Lee Shau-kee** and Wharf's **Peter Woo** to effectively govern Hong Kong. And the tycoons were telling Beijing to rethink its promises.

All that, however, pales in comparison to the biggest worry facing the Chinese government. What was there to prevent citizens on the mainland from looking at their proud Hong Kong cousins and demanding the same basic rights? China had been putting out fires daily with local insurgencies and regional uprisings across the country, particularly in Tibet and Xinjiang. State control over the press and the Internet was barely keeping pace with the rapid sharing of information on social media and the free exchange of ideas among the middle class who were able to travel overseas and read English news online. The last thing Beijing needed was a spark of inspiration from Hong Kong that could trigger a chain reaction and threaten the nation's one-party rule.

All things considered, the CCP concluded that perhaps it was best to keep Hong Kong just the way it is: in a state of perpetual adolescence and

---

14 – In 2015, Li lost his title as Asia's richest man to Jack Ma, founder and executive chairman of China's e-commerce juggernaut Alibaba.

The Occupy Trio: from left, Chu Yiu-ming, Benny Tai and Chan Kin-man

never reaching political maturity. No one wants to know what happens when Peter Pan grows up.

Occupy Central

With 2017 fast approaching, there was growing skepticism among the pan-dems over how the Communist leadership would reconcile its governance concerns with the commitment it made years ago. Among the skeptics was a soft-spoken academic who refused to be a sitting duck.

Benny Tai was a 50-something associate law professor at the University of Hong Kong (HKU). When he was not teaching constitutional law, Tai kept himself busy with human rights campaigns. In his younger days, he served as legal counsel to the Democratic Party working alongside founder Martin Lee. Years of toiling in the pro-democracy trenches had taught the professor one thing: people make promises they can't always keep.

In January 2013, Tai published an article in the *Hong Kong Economic Journal* proposing a pre-emptive move to pressure Beijing to make good on the 2007 Decision. The official campaign was called "Occupy Central with Love and Peace" (**OCLP**), modeled loosely after the 2011 Occupy Wall Street movement at Zuccotti Park in New York City. To do that, Tai recruited two like-minded friends: **Chan Kin-man** and **Chu Yiu-ming**. Chan did his doctorate at Yale and was an associate professor of sociology at the Chinese University of Hong Kong (CUHK). Reverend Chu was a Baptist Church minister and a human rights veteran. He was also one of the key organizers of Operation Yellowbird to smuggle hundreds of wanted protesters out of China after the Tiananmen Square Massacre.

In March 2013, two months after Tai published his initial OCLP article, the **Occupy Trio** held a press conference at a church to announce the campaign. The written manifesto they held up in front of reporters was long on ideology and lofty goals, but somewhat short on where, when and how it would happen. Like Occupy Wall Street, OCLP involved protesters bringing their own tents and camping out in the city's financial district (fortunately, Hong Kong's winter is much more tolerable than New York's). But OCLP went one step further. Occupiers would paralyze the downtown Central area and create so much disruption to business activities and daily life that Beijing would be cowed into letting Hong Kong people freely choose their leader in 2017 without any strings attached or clever tricks with semantics.

Holding the city hostage was expected to involve confrontations with law enforcement, and that's where the "love and peace" came in. As soon as OCLP began, the government would mobilize the police to clear the streets. Tai stressed to both supporters and critics that there would be no resistance of arrest or violent clashes. Demonstrators would be rounded up, taken away and charged with unlawful assembly[15]. They would be detained for questioning and released on bail. After that, depending on the public reception of the first sit-in, demonstrators might or might not return to occupy Central again. Regardless of that decision, anyone arrested would be tried, convicted and sentenced. They would become prisoners of conscience and the faces of a new and improved pro-democracy movement celebrated by the local and international press.

Behind the scenes, the Occupy Trio began putting together various support functions: medical doctors to treat injuries, defense lawyers to handle arrests, and site marshals to keep the sit-in orderly. Their first battleground was to be Chater Garden, a small public park in the heart of Central opposite the iconic Bank of China Tower designed by Chinese-American architect I.M. Pei. Occupiers were prepared to camp out in the park for two to three days starting on October 1st, 2014. The organizers did not share any explicit details with the press for fear of ruining the surprise. They believed that keeping the authorities in suspense was one of the campaign's greatest strengths.

---

15 – Under Hong Kong's Public Order Ordinance, "unlawful assembly" is defined as the congregation of three or more individuals conducting themselves in a manner in breach of the peace. The crime is punishable by up to five years in prison.

Civil disobedience for dummies

OCLP was intended as a threat. No one wanted to see the financial district shut down, not even Benny Tai. The campaign could be likened to the tactics of a frill-necked lizard: the reptile will gape its mouth and spread its frill until it scares predators away. It doesn't actually want to fight. To generate as much noise and media frenzy as possible, the co-founders repeatedly prolonged the deliberation period[16], during which they held numerous workshops, debates, training sessions and rehearsals without divulging any plan of attack.

OCLP was a tough sell in an economic city like Hong Kong. Before Tai introduced the concept of civil disobedience to the public in 2013, few people had even heard of the phrase, let alone understood what it meant. The Cantonese translation *gung man kong meng* sounds pedantic and dull. Martin Luther King, Jr. and John Lewis may be household names in the West, but they are virtually unheard of in Asia. In the months leading up to OCLP, Tai and his fellow co-founders found themselves telling and retelling the story of Rosa Parks, the African American woman who was arrested for refusing to give up her seat on a bus to a white passenger, and the story of the peaceful suffragists in Selma, Alabama crossing the Edmund Pettus Bridge in protest and being brutally attacked by state troopers on what historians called "Bloody Sunday." In most cases, it was the first time the audience had heard about the American Civil Rights Movement, or how the efforts of unarmed citizens eventually led to the passing of the landmark Voting Rights Act of 1965 which guaranteed every American, irrespective of race, the right to vote without intimidation or encumbrance.

In addition to unfamiliarity, illegality was another aspect of OCLP that alienated the average law-abiding citizen. Benny Tai spoke passionately about how marchers in Selma violated a court injunction banning illegal assemblies to oppose race-based voter registration legislation, and how Mahatma Gandhi breached the Salt Act by walking 24 days to a coastal town in India to make salt from seawater. Even OCLP sympathizers were shocked to hear a law professor talk so openly about breaking the law and going to prison. All their lives, pragmatic Hong Kongers are taught to follow instructions in school and then take the well-trodden path of desk jobs and mortgage payments in the real world. A criminal record was far too high a price to pay for political ideals, considering that it would almost certainly bar them from applying for student visas to study abroad or landing a government job at home.

---

16 – In the 19 months between the announcement of OCLP in March 2013 and the originally scheduled launch on October 1st, 2014, there were three rounds of deliberations, in June 2013, March 2014 and May 2014.

OCLP was a long shot from the get-go. To the organizers, it was a gun they wanted to carry but did not wish to fire. To its supporters, the looming threat of arrest or even prison gave them second thoughts. On many public and private occasions, Benny Tai expressed his lack of confidence in the eventual turnout. He admitted that the campaign had less than a 50% chance of success and that he would be lucky to attract a few thousand participants. Like everyone else, Benny was in for a big surprise.

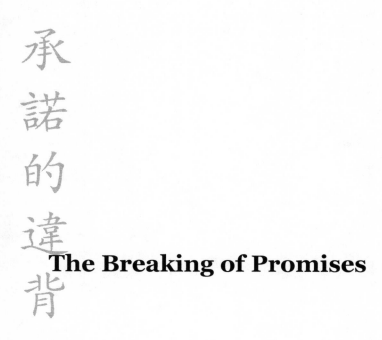

The Breaking of Promises

A broken promise feels like a kick in the groin no matter how much we prepare ourselves for it. It isn't so much about the disappointing outcome, but rather the embarrassment of naïvely believing in the sanctity of the written or spoken word. Call a Hong Konger a selfish bastard or a social climber and he will shrug it off – because he probably is. But call him a gullible fool? Now that really hurts.

OCLP was meant to be a pre-emptive move on the off-chance that Beijing went back on its word. There were times when the Occupy Trio were criticized for not having enough faith in their motherland that it would do the right thing. On August 31st, 2014, however, all the bickering ground to a sudden halt and pro-democracy groups were left in stunned silence. That day, the Standing Committee announced the first and the last word on the implementation of universal suffrage for the 2017 Chief Executive election. If the 2007 Decision gave the city a flame of hope, then the so-called **8/31 Framework** snuffed it out completely and conclusively.

The warning shots

Back in March 2013, the same month that the co-founders held a press conference to announce OCLP, Beijing dropped the first hint that things weren't going to be simple. Qiao Xiaoyang, Chairman of the Standing Committee's Legal Subcommittee, told the pro-Beijing camp at a meeting that any Chief Executive candidate must be someone who "loves China and loves Hong Kong." Never mind what that meant and who would get to decide if the requirement was met. Qiao's comment fueled already widespread speculation that Beijing had every intention of sabotaging our free vote by pre-screening candidates with highly subjective criteria.

On October 17th, 2013, C.Y. Leung announced the creation of an **Electoral Reform Taskforce** to be headed by Chief Secretary **Carrie Lam**. Two months later, the taskforce issued a consultation document titled "Methods for Selecting the Chief Executive in 2017" to kick start the first round of public consultation for the **2015 Reform Bill**. It was meant to be an open invitation for anyone to submit proposals on the implementation of Articles 45 and 68 of the Basic Law, including the central question of the size and composition of the Nominating Committee for the 2017 Chief Executive election.

The consultation process, under the banner "Let's Talk and Achieve Universal Suffrage," ended in May 2014. During the five-month period, the government received thousands of proposals from political parties, academics, advocacy organizations and special interest groups. A few weeks later, on July 15th, C.Y. Leung submitted a report to the Standing Committee summarizing the range of opinions expressed by members of the public. Everything appeared to be going by the book, even though it all seemed too good to be true.

And it was. On June 10th, 2014, while OCLP was still in the deliberation stage and a month before C.Y. Leung submitted his report to the Standing Committee, the **State Council of China** issued a 54-page document to clarify a few things on the "one country, two systems" framework in Hong Kong. The **6/10 White Paper** asserted China's total and complete jurisdiction over Hong Kong, stating that the high degree of autonomy enjoyed by the city came from the Chinese government and was therefore subject to its unquestioned authority. It was a not-so-subtle reminder to Hong Kongers that their way of life lay at the mercy of the CCP. More importantly, it was a stern warning to OCLP organizers not to test the party's patience. Far from achieving its intended goals, however, the 6/10 White Paper only added to the growing cross-border distrust and handed Benny Tai another talking point about Beijing's inclination to curtail, as opposed to expand, Hong Kong's political freedom.

Bubble burst

On August 31st, the Standing Committee issued its edict on electoral reform under Article 45 of the Basic Law. The 8/31 Framework stated, among other things, that:

> "*When the selection of the Chief Executive of the Hong Kong Special Administrative Region is implemented by the method of universal suffrage:*
>
> *1. A broadly representative Nominating Committee shall be formed. The provisions for the number of members, composition and formation method of the Nominating Committee shall be made in accordance with the number of members, composition and formation method of the* **Election Committee**...;
>
> *2. The Nominating Committee shall nominate* **two to three candidates** *for the office of Chief Executive in accordance with democratic procedures. Each candidate must have the endorsement of* **more than half** *of all the members of the Nominating Committee...*" (emphasis added)

Under these new guidelines, citizens would have the right to choose their leader in 2017 by popular vote as promised. But the devil was in the details. The framework required that the Nominating Committee be modeled after the existing 1,200-member Election Committee. End of discussion. The intention was to allow the Communists to stuff the Nominating Committee with Beijing loyalists, just as they did with the Election Committee. The nomination process would function as a sieve to screen out any candidate that Beijing did not approve, thereby giving it effective control over the outcome of the election despite the one-person-one-vote concession. In other words, universal suffrage would exist in form but not in substance. It calls to mind the famous line by Henry Ford when he introduced the Model T in 1909: "Our customers can have any color they want as long as it is black."

The 8/31 Framework – and subsequent clarifications by party officials – also imposed or invented other limitations that had no legal basis under the Basic Law. For instance, there were new requirements that the total number of candidates on the ballot be capped at "two to three," that each candidacy be backed by majority support (or 600 votes)[17] of the

---

17 – In past chief executive elections, candidates only needed one-eighth of the total votes of the Election Committee to secure a nomination. The majority vote requirement in the 8/31 Framework was therefore considered a major step back. To produce more than one nominee, each Nominating Committee member would have to be given more than one vote.

Nominating Committee, and that the Chief Executive be someone who "loves China and loves Hong Kong." These additional barriers to entry were as arbitrary as they were amateurish – classic Communist nonsense that would make a law student laugh and his professor cringe.

C.Y. Leung had to share a big part of the blame. Like a bad salesman who falsifies invoices to boost his month-end figures, Leung completely sanitized the findings of the public consultation. In former Governor Chris Patten's words, Leung and the Electoral Reform Taskforce "told the emperor what they thought he wanted to hear, not what the situation really was." The report they submitted to the Standing Committee on July 15th significantly downplayed the city's profound concerns over the nomination process. Instead, it characterized the recycling of the much-hated Election Committee as part of the "mainstream consensus." The looming threat of OCLP – the biggest political story in 2014 – received no mention at all. Although the airbrushed report was hardly the sole basis for the 8/31 Framework (CCP leaders are known to peruse Hong Kong newspapers every day), it did give Beijing the right to tell us that we got what we asked for.

Another glaring omission in Leung's report was the so-called **civil nomination** option. It was a progressive interpretation of Article 45 that would allow individual citizens to nominate Chief Executive candidates, thereby circumventing the pre-screening Nominating Committee. Not surprisingly, the proposal received enormous public support and was incorporated into all the three proposals in an electronic poll jointly organized by OCLP and HKU on June 22nd, 2014. An estimated 800,000 citizens (or over 20% of the city's 3.5 million registered voters) participated in the **6/22 Referendum** via the "PopVote" smart phone app[18], which was intended to offer Beijing a true picture of public opinion in Hong Kong.

Don't spit on my face and call it rain

The 8/31 Framework was a non-appealable ruling on the 2017 Chief Executive election. Carrie Lam even called it the "rap of a gavel" to signal its finality – so much for her "Let's talk" slogan. The six-month public consultation turned out to be a sham, and the political monkey show was nothing short of fraud.

---

18 – The smart phone app was hit by multiple cyber-attacks and was down for a number of days. In the interim, thousands of citizens lined up outside makeshift polling booths set up at HKU and Polytechnic University to cast their vote. The main reason for the large turnout was believed to be the 6/10 White Paper, which suffragists considered to be Beijing's pre-emptive strike against OCLP and an indication that the CCP would renege on the 2007 Decision.

Outraged, all 27 pan-dem legislators signed a pledge on the same day to veto any electoral reform bill modeled after the 8/31 Framework. To those who had criticized the Occupy Trio for not having enough faith in their motherland, it was an "I told you so" moment. At a joint press conference with the pan-dems, Benny Tai called August 31st "the darkest day of Hong Kong's democratic development." His worst fear now confirmed, the law professor heaved a heavy sigh and said, "our dialogue [with Beijing] has reached the end of the road."

You can't blame Tai for being dramatic. In one broad stroke, the Standing Committee thwarted hopes for real democracy in Hong Kong. We couldn't tell which was more frustrating: that Beijing had backed out of its promise, or that it didn't think or know it had. Despite the uproar, mainland and SAR officials continued to defend the election framework, insisting that China had kept its side of the bargain by granting one-person-one-vote to the citizens of Hong Kong. They maintained that democracy comes in all shapes and forms, and that even though Beijing's brand might look different from what the pan-dems had expected, it was nonetheless the real thing. Think of it as "Chinese-style democracy," like a Shenzhen-made "Hi-Phone" knock-off or the all-knowing "Goojje" search engine.

To drive home the point, Zhang Rongshun, Vice-chairman of the Standing Committee's Legislative Affairs Commission, called the Nominating Committee a "brilliant invention" and a "contribution to democracy." He told reporters that "the more I look at it, the lovelier it gets." Liaison Office Director **Zhang Xiaoming** compared it to a "beautiful maiden yet to be discovered."

Following that logic, Hong Kongers should have stopped complaining and shown a little gratitude toward their biggest benefactor. That was why the words "greed" and "ingratitude" came up frequently in state rhetoric when referring to the city's reaction to the 8/31 Framework. The cheaters turned the table around and accused the cheated of taking a mile when given an inch. They said it with so much conviction that less informed citizens began to wonder if they should just "pocket it first" – to use Carrie Lam's own catch phrase. It bore out that old adage: if the Communists can't convince you, they will try to confuse you.

Most educated Hong Kongers saw right through the smoke and mirrors. The twisted logic put forward by the Standing Committee – that free choice meant choosing from two to three pre-selected candidates who must embrace the CCP – defied common sense and fell far short of the "international standard" of universal suffrage demanded by the pan-dems. As one of the five permanent members of the United Nations Security Council, China would be well-served to consult the UN Human Rights

Committee on the International Covenant on Civil and Political Rights, to which China is a signatory. The human rights committee would gladly explain to Beijing that "universal suffrage" includes the right to vote as well as the right to stand for office – one cannot go without the other[19].

It would almost have been better if Beijing had just called the spade a spade. In other words, if the Chinese government were to renege on the 2007 Decision, then it should at least have the decency to say: "Sorry, folks, we thought better of what we said before and we changed our minds." The restrictive election guidelines in the 8/31 Framework were as much an insult to Hong Kongers' intelligence as they were an embarrassment for this so-called *qiang guo* (the Mandarin phrase for superpower). For all its economic achievements and outer space breakthroughs, China couldn't seem to fulfill its commitment to a small island.

In the end, the city waited seven years for nothing. In our long and arduous struggle for democracy, every disappointment we begrudgingly swallowed and every concession we reluctantly made was all for naught. We began to think about what would happen to the *other* promise – universal suffrage for the 2020 Legco election – and wonder when the other shoe would drop. The likelihood that we would finally get rid of the functional constituencies and freely elect all 70 Legco members by 2020 appeared more remote than ever. If there was one thing we learned from all this, it was that the next time the Communists ask us to trust them, we should do what anyone would when they see a lunatic: smile and slowly walk away.

The young and the fearless

The first citizens to act on their outrage over the 8/31 Framework were, apropos, our students. They were the ones who fired the first shot in an anti-government protest that would change the course of our history.

On September 13th, 2014, two weeks after the Standing Committee bombshell, **Scholarism** organized a mass demonstration outside the **Tamar Government Headquarters**. Participants at this **9/13 Tamar Demonstration**, most of them secondary school students in their mid-teens, heeded the organizers' call to wear a yellow ribbon as a show of solidarity. Although no one knew why they had picked that particular color, yellow would forever be associated with the massive uprising that would soon follow.

---

19 – After the Umbrella Movement erupted, UN Human Rights Committee rapporteur Konstantine Vardzelashvili weighed in on the controversy and reiterated the importance of the right to nominate. He flatly called Beijing's election guidelines in the 8/31 Framework "unreasonable."

Scholarism was a student activist group founded in 2011 by **Joshua Wong** when he was just 14. Sporting a bowl haircut and signature black-framed spectacles, Wong was a pint-sized force of nature to reckon with – he had a 12th grade education and a doctorate in charisma. While his teenage friends were still playing video games and reading comic books, Wong was already debunking political myths on radio talk shows and challenging the establishment on televised debates. The self-described "middle class kid" was a prodigy, a savant and a Hollywood child star wrapped into one.

Nicknamed G-phone[20], Joshua Wong rose to political stardom in summer of 2012, when he mobilized scores of teenagers – none of them even old enough to vote – for a nine-day hunger strike outside the Government Headquarters to protest against a **Patriotic Education Plan**. The curriculum, officially called "Moral and National Education," was to be introduced in every primary and secondary school in Hong Kong to inculcate a stronger Chinese identity and a sense of belonging to the motherland. Most citizens saw it as part of the Communists' social engineering program to brainwash and indoctrinate young minds.

Wong seized on the growing anti-Communist sentiment, captured the imagination of his peers with his eloquence, and called on tens of thousands to join his mass rally. His campaign eventually forced C.Y. Leung to withdraw the curriculum. The watershed moment not only catapulted Wong to international fame, but it also jolted citizens out of their political jadedness. It taught them that grassroots campaigns, if properly run, could bring about real policy changes. Since the David-versus-Goliath story in 2012, Wong had been using his new celebrity status to fight an even bigger cause: dual universal suffrage.

Scholarism was a club for high school activists. Its university counterpart was the Hong Kong Federation of Students (**HKFS**), an organization formed by the student unions of the city's eight accredited universities. At the time of the occupy movement, the federation was led by secretary general **Alex Chow** of HKU and his deputy **Lester Shum** of CUHK. The HKFS and Scholarism were so-called "non-incorporated" political forces – neither of them was an official political party or held any Legco seats. When it came to making or breaking government policies, these groups chose the streets over the Legco floor or the ballot box. Why vote for someone else to do what you can do yourself?

On September 22nd, 2014, the HKFS organized a five-day citywide **9/22 Class Boycott**. They staged a student protest at CUHK, long

---

20 – Wong's Cantonese name, Chi-fung, sounds like "G-phone." In addition, the hyperactive teenager is always seen texting on his iPhone, which gives the nickname a double meaning.

The incomparable Joshua Wong

considered the most politically progressive university in the city. Instead of attending classes, 13,000 students assembled on University Mall, the main pedestrian thoroughfare on the CUHK campus in Shatin, to listen to Alex Chow address a cheering crowd. The HKFS also invited professors and well-known commentators to take turns giving speeches to the assembly. The campaign, and the impassioned response it received from both teachers and students, bore the hallmarks of the class boycott organized by Beijing University students in 1989.

The following day, the HKFS moved their protest to Tamar, where they joined supporters of Scholarism who had been demonstrating against the 8/31 Framework for over a week. The merger of the two operations – the 9/13 Tamar Demonstration and the 9/22 Class Boycott – gave the student leaders a big shot in the arm. The Scholarism-HKFS coalition would continue over the course of the occupy movement, and would propel the three musketeers – Alex Chow, Lester Shum and Joshua Wong – to pop-star status.

On September 26th, Scholarism extended the 9/22 Class Boycott from universities to secondary schools across the city. That evening, Joshua Wong announced that he would escalate the Tamar sit-in and called on his followers to climb over a 10-foot-high fence to reclaim a public space – the courtyard outside the east wing of the Government Headquarters that protesters dubbed "Civic Square" – that had been walled off by the authorities and turned into a fortress. Law enforcement responded with pepper spray and arrested Chow, Shum and Wong the following afternoon, which drew even more students to the demonstration calling for their release. Within 24 hours, the number of protesters at Tamar grew from mere hundreds to 80,000.

When Benny met nerdy

By then, a full 21 months had passed since Benny Tai penned his lofty newspaper article about civil disobedience. The Occupy Trio had been dragging their feet, not for a lack of conviction but a result of their risk aversion and the interminable wait for the "right moment" to arrive. Their constant assessment and reassessment of the situation was a textbook case of Hamletism – paralysis by analysis. It came to a point when the HKFS and Scholarism felt they could no longer depend on the adults and had to take matters into their own hands.

The arrest of the student leaders on September 26th, and the subsequent surge in student turnout at Tamar gave the Occupy Trio a "YOLO" (you only live once) moment. It was the jolt they needed to finally initiate the launch sequence to fire up their civil disobedience campaign. Shortly after midnight on September 28th, Benny Tai took to the stage set up outside the Legco Building and announced the "activation" of OCLP[21], three days ahead of its original October 1st start date.

After dawn, citizens began showing up in Admiralty in droves. By noon, the crowds had overwhelmed the Admiralty subway station and spilled onto Harcourt Road. Like the Occupy Trio, concerned citizens couldn't sit at home in front of their television sets and watch unarmed teenagers get pepper sprayed by police like an intrusion of cockroaches and hauled away like captured animals.

---

21 – The Occupy Trio were not welcome by everyone at Tamar. Many student protesters feared that OCLP would "pollute" the purity of the 9/22 Class Boycott and "hijack" the campaign. Nearly half of the protesters at Tamar threatened to quit the protest that night, which promoted Long Hair to get on his knees in public and beg the outgoing students to stay, saying "Win or lose, we are all in it together!"

The convergence of Benny Tai's OCLP, Scholarism's 9/13 Tamar Demonstration and the HKFS's 9/22 Class Boycott turned out to be much more than the sum of its parts. The three worlds collided at the intersection of idealism and courage, and created a perfect political firestorm that would catch both the SAR government and Beijing off guard. Nearly two years in the planning, OCLP technically lasted only 16.5 hours[22] – from 1:40am on September 28th, when Benny Tai launched OCLP, to 6:00pm that same day when riot police fired the first shot of tear gas and turned it into the 79-day Umbrella Movement.

---

22 – Some may disagree with this statement and argue that OCLP lasted 67 days, from September 28th through December 3rd when the Occupy Trio turned themselves in to police, thereby completing the final stage of their civil disobedience campaign.

A Season of Discontent

People in Hong Kong are miserable.

At least that's what a United Nations survey said. The city ranked 72nd in the *2015 World Happiness Report* published by the UN Sustainable Development Solutions Network. Even people in war-torn Kosovo and Libya are more satisfied with life than we. None of the Rolex watches and Chanel handbags[23] we own seem to do much to cheer us up.

But it hasn't always been that way.

---

23 – More Rolex watches are sold in Hong Kong than anywhere else in the world. They are the ultimate status symbol for middle class men, more so than expensive cars (not everyone drives in Hong Kong) or big houses (most people live in small apartments). For women, it is the Chanel 2.55 handbag, the accessory *de rigueur* among female office workers.

The bygone era

Hong Kong came of age in the 1960s and 1970s, when the economy experienced double-digit growth by supplying the world with toys, clothing and consumer electronics. Mainland Chinese escaping from poverty and political turmoil provided the talent and labor to fuel the city's economic ascent. We used to make things, and we traded what we made for access to better housing, education and opportunities. We called it the "**Lion Rock Spirit**," the belief that we reap what we sow, that hard work and a quick mind are the rungs of the social ladder, and that our children will make it even if we didn't. It is our answer to the American Dream and our only discernible cultural identity.

That trademark can-do spirit carried the city through the 1980s and much of the 1990s. Those two decades were the Fragrant Harbor's golden age, the Pearl of the Orient's heyday. With affluence came influence. During that period, Hong Kong was selling much more than just manufactured goods – we were a purveyor of culture and all things cool. Our films and popular music delighted audiences across Asia, and super stars like Leslie Cheung and Anita Mui were household names in the Chinese-speaking world and beyond. The city's economic and cultural prowess in the region was second only to Japan, the world's No. 2 economy at the time.

Then came the Handover in 1997 and it has been all downhill since. The city seemed to have peaked, plateaued and begun a slow decline. We were battered by one crisis after another: the Asian Financial Crisis in 1997, the SARS outbreak in 2003, the burst of a housing bubble in the same year, and another round of financial market meltdowns in 2007.

While neighboring economies like South Korea and Singapore managed to ride out the economic cycles, Hong Kong lost its balance and never quite regained it. It wasn't about the numbers – the **Hang Seng Index** and employment rate rebounded after each downturn – it was something else. Somewhere and somehow, the belief that we were in control of our destiny, that we could do anything and be anybody if we put our minds to it, started to drain away. The Lion Rock Spirit began to look more like a web of lies fabricated and perpetuated by the wealthy elite. The Hong Kong Dream was turning into a living nightmare, and the city was becoming ordinary and replaceable.

So what is it that made us lose our way?

The property market

In our city of 7 million, every story begins and ends with the property market. Anyone who has spent any time in Hong Kong, or knows anything about Hong Kong, is aware of the city's housing crisis. With only 127 square miles of usable land – half the size of San Francisco – citizens are constantly clamoring for space. Limited supply is exacerbated by both domestic and foreign demand. "Hot money" from the mainland – resulting from China's growing affluence and the use of Hong Kong as a safety deposit box to park hidden fortunes – continues to push property prices through the stratosphere.

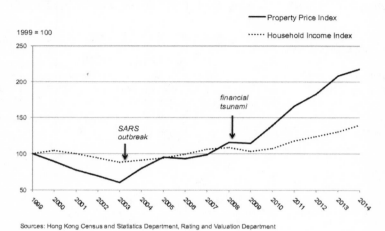

Sources: Hong Kong Census and Statistics Department, Rating and Valuation Department

Figure 3. Property prices and median household income between 1999 and 2014

In the 15-year period leading up to the Umbrella Movement, property prices grew by over 220% (see Figure 3). Year after year, Hong Kong maintains a top three ranking in the world's costliest cities to buy property. The title may make for good cocktail conversation, but for the people who have to live with that grim reality, it is a punch to the stomach. It's not that the city does not have enough apartments, but that many of them are left empty by non-residents who buy them for investment, while others are hoarded up by property developers to create an artificial shortage[24].

---

24 – According to a study by HKU's Department of Real Estate and Construction, out of 146 residential property projects that commenced between 1990 and 2014, only 65 (or 45%) were completed and occupied. The remaining 81, which would have provided an estimated 100,000 homes, were "frozen" by property developers instead of being brought to market. Developers sat on these units and delayed sale by filing repeated applications for minor construction modifications.

Some of the newly built residential complexes have such low occupancy rates that entire buildings look pitch dark from the outside at night.

As property prices continue to skyrocket, competition for smaller, more affordable housing intensifies, resulting in a market anomaly: shoebox apartments in more remote areas are outpacing luxury homes in terms of rent increases. In the meantime, the number of applicants on the waiting list for public housing has nearly tripled from 90,000 in 2003 to 260,000 in 2014. Escalating property prices mean that dignified living conditions are out of reach for even the middle-class. There is something to be said about a city where people can afford luxurious European vacations and six-figure Swiss timepieces, but still don't have a decent home to return to at day's end.

The law of supply and demand has put a handful of property developers on the list of the world's richest. Powerful oligarchs benefit from skewed land sale practices under which government land is auctioned off in such large plots that effectively bar smaller competitors from submitting a bid. They also benefit from business-friendly building regulations that allow them to inflate sellable gross floor area (GFA), so that homebuyers end up paying 30% to 40% more for needless space such as oversized bay windows and ornate lobbies. Each time we look at stunning postcard-perfect pictures of residential towers rising out of Victoria Peak, we marvel not at the beauty of a vertical city, but the twisted manifestation of crony capitalism[25].

Since wealth begets wealth, the super-rich continue to gobble up businesses and turn their property empires into colossal conglomerates. Their tentacles have reached into every corner of the economy, owning not just real estate but also supermarket and drugstore chains, utilities companies, public transport operators and mobile phone service providers (see Figure 4 overleaf). Hong Kong is often compared to the Monopoly game board. While the super-rich carve up the city and stake out their turf, the rest of society keep going around the board and paying rent wherever they land.

In Hong Kong, property tycoons like Li Ka-shing and Lee Shau-kee are more famous and talked about than movie stars. To the hoi polloi, they are the gods and they are the devils. Getting a 30-year mortgage means putting on the shackles and becoming indentured servants. Their

---

25 – In 2014, Hong Kong was ranked number one by *The Economist* on the "crony capitalism index," as it was in 2007 when the survey was first conducted. The ranking was based on the total wealth of a country's billionaires relative to its gross domestic product (GDP). The British newsmagazine observed that Hong Kong is "packed with billionaires in crony industries" and that the city has also long been "lax on antitrust."

Conglomerate (chairman)	Residential property	Commercial property	Hotel chains	Retail chains	Food & beverage	Public transport	Telecom & utilities
Cheung Kong / Hutchison / PCCW *(Li Ka-shing & Sons)*	✓	✓	✓	✓	✓		✓
Henderson Land *(Lee Shau-kee)*	✓	✓	✓	✓	✓		✓
Sun Hung Kai Properties *(Kwok Brothers)*	✓	✓				✓	✓
Wheelock Properties *(Peter Woo)*	✓	✓	✓	✓	✓	✓	✓
New World Development *(Cheng Yu-tung)*	✓	✓	✓	✓		✓	✓
Jardine Matheson / Hongkong Land *(Sir Henry Keswick)*	✓	✓	✓	✓	✓		
Swire Pacific *(J.R. Slosar)*	✓	✓	✓			✓	
MTR Corp. *(Raymond Chien)*	✓	✓				✓	

Source: Hong Kong Stock Exchange filings

Figure 4. Reach of the property conglomerates

monthly paychecks go straight into the masters' deep pockets in the form of mortgage payments, grocery bills, bus fares and utilities charges. At times, the Monopoly game board feels more like a Ouija board – the next move is determined not by the throw of a die but by a paranormal force that pushes the players around.

The more citizens resist, the tighter the grip becomes. Powerful property developers have both the government and pro-establishment legislators wrapped around their fingers. The pan-dems have made numerous attempts to break up the cartels and sever the quid pro quo relationship by, for instance, passing a comprehensive competition law to prohibit price fixing, bid rigging, exclusive dealing and market monopolization. Thanks to the functional constituencies, these bills have either been defeated or watered down on the Legco floor[26].

Whereas the grown-ups are slaves to the property tycoons, many of the youth have given up on home ownership altogether. There is a general sense of hopelessness among university graduates from the realization that they can never keep pace with property prices no matter how hard they work and how much money they save. The down payment alone has priced most of them out of the market and made them put off their life plans indefinitely. Young couples who dream of living in a three-bedroom with one child end up squeezing three people into one bedroom.

Our runaway property market does more than deprive us of comfort and space, it is also threatening to snuff out the city's entrepreneurship and creativity. At over HK$20,000 (US$2,500) per square foot in monthly rent, Russell Street in Causeway Bay is the most expensive luxury street in the world, surpassing even Fifth Avenue in Manhattan and Champs-Élysées in Paris. Heart-stopping retail rent is scaring small business owners, artists, bakers, musicians and athletes into giving up their dreams and settling for a safe desk job. The bold and the beautiful all opt for the dull and the mundane.

Over time, the city is left with bankers, insurance agents and real estate brokers. The once-revered Hong Kong cinema and Cantopop are both facing extinction, in part because of piracy and content sharing on the Internet, but in larger part because of the lack of oxygen for local talent to

---

26 – After over a decade of delays and bickering, the Competition Ordinance was finally passed in the Legco in June 2012 and went into effect in December 2015. The bill had been significantly diluted by pro-business lawmakers. Among other things, individuals would not have the right to file lawsuits against anti-competitive behavior and would have to lodge complaints through a newly established Competition Commission. In addition, the law contains numerous exemptions that would effectively exclude 95% of small and medium-sized enterprises and nearly all statutory bodies.

thrive. In 2013, the number of locally produced films hit a record low of 42, down from a high of 238 in the golden years of the 1990s. Nowadays, even an A-list pop singer would be lucky to sell a few hundred copies of a new music album. Citizens can only cling to the past, remembering bygone superstars as if they were deceased family members. We watch with abandon as Hong Kong goes from a net exporter of pop culture to a net importer of music, movies and drama series.

Affluence, but for whom?

Property prices are not the only thing that puts Hong Kong on a top 10 list. Among the world's wealthiest economies, Hong Kong has one of the highest Gini coefficients, a widely used measure of income inequality. According to the government's own figures, over 1.3 million people – or close to one-fifth of the population – live below the poverty line. The post-Handover financial bonanza that came with forging closer ties with the mainland has eluded a large segment of society.

The yawning gap between the rich and the poor is more than just a statistic or superlative. We see real life manifestations of it every day. Across the city, senior citizens well into their 70s and 80s can be seen picking through garbage bins looking for soda cans or pushing heavy carts of scrap metal or cardboard boxes up hilly streets. An estimated 400,000 people (one out of 18) live in so-called "subdivided flats" or "coffin houses," a common feature in urban slums like Sham Shui Po and Yau Ma Tei. Families of four or five cram into apartment units the size of a parking space without proper plumbing or air-conditioning. But just as well, because they can't afford to run the A/C anyway.

Decades ago, the haves and the have-nots signed an unwritten pact that upward mobility is achievable, no matter how long it takes to get there. The masses were willing to embrace trickle-down economics as long as there was light at the end of the tunnel and ways to climb the ladder. The carrot was dangled close enough to keep their mouths shut, but far away enough to keep them hunkered down.

Since the Handover, collusion between government and big businesses, made possible by a legislature that rubber stamps pro-business policies, has become more severe and in-your-face. Political battles are no longer won and lost, but bought and sold. Corporate elites are recruited to take up powerful ministerial positions in the government, while retired bureaucrats are hired by the private sector as advisers and consultants. The blatant display of political nepotism is fueling a growing sentiment that the "unwritten pact" is just a rich man's lie. It is one thing to be poor, but it is quite another to know that our children and our grandchildren will stay poor no matter how hard they try.

The sense of social injustice is made worse by a demographic shift. Hong Kong has one of the fastest aging populations in the world. By 2040, a mere generation away, people aged 65 or above are expected to account for 30% of the city's population. Old-age poverty is a ticking time bomb that can be defused only by thoughtful, long-term population policy. Nevertheless, demands made by activists and the pan-dems for a comprehensive pension plan have fallen on deaf ears, despite the government sitting on HK$800 billion (US$100 billion) in foreign reserves. Each time these issues are raised with officials, they show little compassion and even less interest. Why should they? Public funding should be invested in the future rather than wasted on the old. There is a strongly held belief among bureaucrats that those who can't look after themselves when they are old must have been lazy when they were young.

Development, but for what?

For as long as we can remember, the city has operated on the notion that progress can only be achieved through more development. To the disenfranchised masses, the word "development" is a euphemism for the destruction of cherished traditions to make room for wasteful government-funded infrastructure projects. Put another way, "urban development" is simply code for a big money-laundering scheme designed to plow taxpayers' hard-earned money back to the wealthy elite through a never-ending series of multi-billion-dollar construction contracts.

Opposition from environmental groups and the pan-dems notwithstanding, historical structures deemed part of the city's collective memory are falling under the wrecking ball of property developers. Heritage conservation is a joke in Hong Kong – it is spearheaded by an antiquities advisory board stacked with businessmen. The demolition of the beloved Star Ferry Pier and Queen's Pier in 2007 and Ho Tung Gardens in 2013 sparked public outrage and led to weeks-long protests. All three sites were leveled for redevelopment shortly thereafter.

In the meantime, the functional constituencies continue to ensure the safe passage of government-proposed funding bills through the legislature no matter the price tag. Examples abound: the HK$70 billion (US$9 billion) Express Rail-link to Shenzhen was approved by the Legco in 2010; the HK$30 billion (US$4 billion) Hong Kong-Zhuhai-Macau Bridge in 2011; and the HK$142 billion (US$18 billion) third airport runway, which did not require Legco approval because it will be funded by a surcharge on every plane ticket – an income tax in sheep's clothing.

Attempts to turn Hong Kong into Asia's technology hub have fallen flat. The Science Park in Tai Po and Cyberport in Pokfulam – both brainchildren of Tung Chee-hwa – turned out to be glorified property developments without any real focus on technology. C.Y. Leung's proposal to set up an Innovation and Technology Bureau was delayed for years by pan-dem filibusterers, who accused it of being yet another pork barrel project to benefit political friends. As a result, Hong Kong continues to behave like a one-trick pony prancing in its own La-la Land of banking and finance, while neighboring economies like South Korea and Singapore are branching out into clean energy, life sciences and nanotechnology.

Perhaps our being stuck in this rut is more by design than by circumstance. Cynics believe that Beijing has made a conscious effort to keep Hong Kong a "single industry city," in order to make its economy more fragile and the population more tractable. Just as pet birds are easier to tame if their wings are clipped.

Erosion of civil liberties

Hong Kongers may be miserable, but at least they can complain about it.

In 2002, a France-based monitoring group called Reporters Without Borders published its first World Press Freedom Index. Hong Kong ranked 18th among the 150 countries and territories surveyed, the highest in all of Asia.

The SAR is a paradox: nowhere else in the world are citizens so deprived of the right to a free vote and yet are given such unfettered freedom of expression. No, we can't choose our leader or half of our lawmakers; but yes, we can phone in to radio talk shows, go on a social media tirade, or kick and scream outside government offices.

Martin Luther King, Jr. once said that "a riot is the language of the unheard." Here in Hong Kong, placards and mass rallies are our mother tongue. Sunday afternoon marches on Hennessy Road have become a way of life – parents and small children will finish their dim sum brunch and head to the streets shouting angry anti-government slogans. The ability to speak our minds is one of our cherished core values and the very thing that distinguishes this "City of Protests" from the rest of China.

The bizarre combination of control and freedom presents a unique set of challenges from a governance perspective. When Hong Kong shouts, Beijing listens – even if it doesn't like to admit it. To the bosses up north, the turnout at the annual **July 1st rally** is a barometer of public sentiment and the demonstrators' battle cries are a referendum on social issues. The 2003 Mass Rally that drew half a million citizens to the streets put enough pressure on China that Tung Chee-hwa had to withdraw the controversial anti-subversion bill. The same thing happened with the Patriotic Education Plan in 2012. Because of its political importance, the turnout of any given political protest has become the subject of great contention. The organizers will tout one number, and the police will report a much lower one.

Nevertheless, Beijing's tolerance for dissent has its limits. There is a popular metaphor Hong Kong people use to describe the gradual erosion of their freedom of expression: a slow-boiled frog. To cook a frog, it is said, one must turn the heat low enough so that the critter doesn't notice the rise in temperature and jump out of the pot. Ignorance is bliss, and for the frog swimming merrily in the pot, deadly.

In much the same way, the authorities chip away at our freedom of speech little by little while we go about our daily lives. With each street rally, the police impose more unreasonable restrictions and the Liaison Office hires more counter-protesters to drown out the message. With each official speech, Beijing toughens its rhetoric more to pressure big business – banks, property developers and luxury brands – to cut their advertisements from newspapers and magazines critical of the Chinese government.

But slow-boiling is so 2012. Since C.Y. Leung took office, Beijing has turned the heat way up, whether the frog will notice it or not. These days, the authorities blatantly target uncooperative publications and engineer staff reshufflings at news organizations. **Jimmy Lai**, owner of the anti-Beijing *Apple Daily* tabloid, had his home firebombed and his office stormed by thugs. Lai joined a long line of journalists who have been physically assaulted by or received death threats from their adversaries. Others include Chen Ping of *iSun Affairs*, Shih Wing-ching of *AM730* and radio talk show host Fast Beat.

In February 2014, Kevin Lau, former editor-in-chief of **Ming Pao** – one of the city's major Chinese language newspapers – was stabbed six times by two knifemen in broad daylight outside a restaurant. The assault reeked of a Mexican drug hit or a turf war between rival Russian gangs. While the assailants' motive remained a mystery (some argued it had to do with Lau's reporting of former Chinese Premier Wen Jiabao's hidden fortune), what was clear was Beijing's change of attitude toward dissent from grudging acceptance to violent suppression.

All that prompted Pen America, a New York-based watchdog, to publish a scathing report in January 2015 about the rapid deterioration of press freedom in Hong Kong. The report cited targeted economic pressures on pro-democracy newspapers, cyber-attacks against online media, and unresolved cases of violence against journalists. Hong Kong's ranking on the World Press Freedom Index has declined every year since C.Y. Leung took office (see Figure 5). In 2015, it fell to an all-time low of 70th, below Bosnia and Papua New Guinea. According to Reporters Without Borders (which publishes the index), the trend is attributed to Beijing's interference of the local media through the Liaison Office.

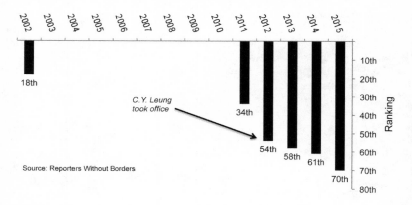

Figure 5. Free-falling press freedom since C.Y. Leung took office in 2012

No discussion of our dwindling freedom of expression is complete without mentioning the **HKTV saga**. At the time of the occupy movement, there were only two broadcasters operating in the free-to-air television market in Hong Kong: **TVB** and **ATV**. To watch these channels, viewers required neither a monthly subscription nor a cable box, just a good old antenna. That explains their popularity in the 1970s and 1980s when alternative forms of entertainment were out of reach for most citizens. Ever since ATV, the perennial underdog, was acquired by mainland Chinese businessman Wang Zheng in 2010, the No.2 in the free television industry had gone from bad to worse, and was eventually taken off the air in April 2016. TVB ended up with a near-monopoly, which has allowed it to churn out banal soap operas and cringe-worthy awards shows without losing its viewership or advertising dollars.

In 2013, in an attempt to open up the languishing free-to-air market, C.Y. Leung's government granted new broadcasting licenses to iCable and PCCW (owned respectively by property tycoons Peter Woo and

Richard Li, son of Li Ka-shing), but rejected the application by Ricky Wong's HKTV, the bid most favored by the public. The decision drew public outrage and spawned wild speculation regarding the underlying political motives. Many believed that Wong was too much of a maverick for Beijing's taste and that, when in doubt, the authorities would rather stick to people they knew they could trust – the Woos and the Lis.

Controlling Hong Kong's media is said to be at the top of Beijing's political agenda for the city – one of the so-called "**Four Great Tasks**" handed to each Chief Executive when they take office (see Table 4).

Task	Goal	Status
Media control	To tighten control on television, radio and the press by installing pro-Beijing management and putting economic pressure on businesses to cut advertisements from media groups critical of the authorities.	• Acquisition of ATV by mainland Chinese businessman Wang Zheng in 2010. • Donald Tsang's appointment of bureaucrat Roy Tang to head the RTHK, a public radio broadcaster, in 2011. • C.Y. Leung's denial of a free-to-air TV broadcasting license to HKTV in 2013. • Acquisition of the *South China Morning Post* by mainland Chinese businessman Jack Ma in 2015. • Growing self-censorship among the press, resulting in the *Apple Daily* and *Ming Pao* being the last two independent newspapers in Hong Kong.
Anti-subversion	To pass national security legislation to suppress anti-Beijing and anti-government speech and activities.	• Tung Chee-hwa's attempt to pass an anti-subversion bill in 2003 sent half a million citizens to the streets in the 2003 Mass Rally, resulting in the withdrawal of the bill and the resignation of then Security Secretary Regina Ip. • Promise made by Donald Tsang and C.Y. Leung that they would not renew discussion of an anti-subversion law during their terms in office.

Patriotic education	To instill patriotism by introducing a pro-Communist curriculum in all primary and secondary schools.	• The Patriotic Education Plan was made a marquee item in Donald Tsang's 2010 policy address. • C.Y. Leung's attempt to introduce the curriculum in 2012 sent 120,000 parents and students to the streets, resulting in the withdrawal of the plan and the meteoric rise of Joshua Wong.
Electoral reform	To create a Beijing-friendly version of universal suffrage.	• The Standing Committee announced the 2007 Decision to implement Article 45 by 2017 and Article 68 by 2020. • The Standing Committee issued the 8/31 Framework in 2014 to significantly restrict the Chief Executive election, which became a key catalyst for the Umbrella Movement.

Table 4. The Four Great Tasks and progress to date

The other three tasks are: passing an anti-subversion law, instituting patriotic education and reining in electoral reform. That explains why the three Chief Executives – Tung Chee-hwa, Donald Tsang and C.Y. Leung – take turns bringing up these unpopular political topics even in the worst of times (such as 2003), rather than focusing on more pressing issues like housing and social security.

Second colonization of Hong Kong

When Jackie Chan famously said that "we Chinese people need to be controlled," the international *kung fu* comedian became an instant social pariah in the Chinese-speaking world. As far as his native Hong Kong is concerned, however, he might have hit the nail right on the head.

Hong Kongers seem destined to be controlled. The city survived 156 years of British rule, only to be colonized again by Communist China in 1997. During the difficult Handover negotiation, Beijing promised the British colony 50 years of semi-autonomy under the "one country, two systems" policy. Now that Hong Kong is finally under Chinese sovereignty, it

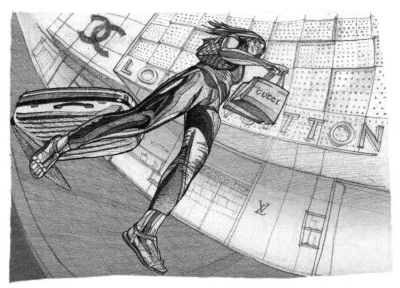

A mainland Chinese shopper walks down Canton Road with a rolling suitcase

doesn't feel like we have much autonomy at all. Day by day, the city is losing its strategic significance to China[27] and is slowly turning into just another mainland city.

To govern its new subjects, the CCP borrowed the Singapore model of economic anesthesia: numbing citizens with middle class affluence while sapping their civil liberties. Efforts to "Sinofy" Hong Kong and to assimilate it with the motherland are happening right under our noses. Under Beijing's orders, the SAR government has spent billions on infrastructure projects like the Hong Kong-Zhuhai-Macau Bridge and the Express Rail-link to Shenzhen, all to speed up the geographical integration of empire and colony. Aggressive plans to urbanize the city's border area in the northeastern New Territories, despite having to displace thousands of local residents, are rolled out in the name of "cross-border economic cooperation." The proposal to introduce the Patriotic Education Plan in 2012 is yet another example of the CCP's attempt to paint the town red.

---

27 – In the 1980s and early 1990s, Hong Kong was the single largest source of capital and foreign investment to fuel China's rapid economic growth. Today, the world's second largest economy no longer relies on Hong Kong – at least not nearly as much – for investment, while the SAR is growing increasingly dependent on economic handouts from China.

In 2003, in the wake of the devastating SARS outbreak, China launched the **Individual Visit Scheme** to revive Hong Kong's economy with tourism dollars, by relaxing travel restrictions on mainlanders visiting Hong Kong. The scheme achieved its stated purpose, but it also had a few unintended consequences. The number of Chinese visitors quadrupled within a decade from 12.5 million in 2005 to a record high of 47.2 million in 2014 – seven times the city's population. In 2005, mainlanders accounted for 54% of the total number of tourists coming to Hong Kong. By 2014, the percentage had jumped to 78% (see Figure 6). Chinese tourists became the culprits for everything from rising consumer prices to bumper-to-bumper traffic.

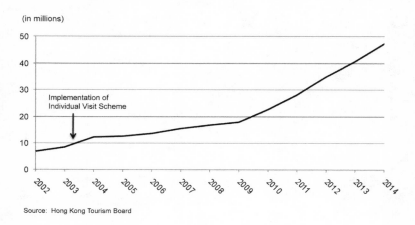

Figure 6. Number of mainland tourists visiting Hong Kong

The scheme also spawned a crop of **parallel traders** – day trippers from Shenzhen and other neighboring Chinese cities who cross the border using multiple-entry permits to stock up on daily necessities – baby formula, shampoo and skincare products – in Hong Kong. The goods are then resold at a higher price on the mainland, where there is great demand for safe, reliable consumer goods[28]. These arbitrageurs are a nuisance to local residents, especially those in border towns like Sheung Shui, Yuen

---

28 – Consumer safety, especially for food products, is a pressing social problem on the mainland. Unscrupulous businessmen are known to sell anything to turn a quick profit. The long list of food scandals in China includes rice contaminated with cadmium, rat meat sold as mutton, fake eggs made from gelatin and paraffin, and "gutter oil" collected from the sewers for cooking. In 2008, tainted baby formula sickened nearly 300,000 infants and killed at least six. The scandal touched off a nationwide firestorm and led to the jailing of both the perpetrators and the activists who demanded justice for the victims.

Long and Tuen Mun who have seen their neighborhoods turned into a ubiquity of pharmacies, jewelers and cosmetics stores.

The unplanned, uncontrolled influx of mainland tourists is driving up prices and drying up supply in Hong Kong, the same way the Russians and the Arabs are in London. In recent years, a growing public outcry has prompted the SAR government to come up with a hodgepodge of stopgap measures to prevent a run on everything from baby formula and diapers to real estate, hospital beds[29] and kindergarten seats. In 2012, a 15% stamp duty was imposed on property purchases by non-permanent residents. Starting in 2013, mainland mothers have been prohibited from giving birth at public hospitals in Hong Kong and no visitor has been allowed to leave the city with more than two cans of baby formula.

The deluge of mainland shoppers, whether genuine vacationers or parallel traders, has transformed some neighborhoods beyond recognition. Before the Individual Visit Scheme, our streets were crowded but not impenetrable. Today, pedestrians are lucky not to be run over by rolling suitcases in popular shopping areas like Causeway Bay and Tsim Sha Tsui. Big city malls used to be upscale but full of variety. They are now dominated by a homogeneity of luxury retailers, making them virtually indistinguishable from an airport duty-free arcade. Out of the 63 retail spaces on Nathan Road between Argyle and Dundas Streets, 39 of them are goldsmiths and jewelers. Shopping, the national pastime for millions of Hong Kongers, has all but lost its appeal – at least domestically. Citizens prefer spending their hard-earned cash in Taipei or Tokyo, where retail means more than Rolex and Cartier.

The Individual Visit Scheme has enriched landlords of prime retail space and the luxury business, while its social costs are being borne by the entire population. Over time, cross-border tensions have intensified. Racial slurs such as locust and *zhinaren* (a derogatory term for Chinese people coined by Japanese invaders more than a century ago) are used liberally on social media in Hong Kong to refer to the stereotypical mainlander who squats, spits, litters, urinates and even defecates in public. To the social conservative, their presence – whether they are tourists, students or immigrants – raises the specter of social engineering by Communist China to dilute our "Hong Kongness."

---

29 – In the landmark 2001 decision, *Director of Immigration v. Chong Fung Yuen*, the Court of Final Appeal – the highest court in Hong Kong – granted permanent residency to any mainland baby born in Hong Kong, even if neither parent is a permanent resident. The ruling encourages an influx of pregnant women from mainland China to give birth south of the border so that their children can enjoy better education and career opportunities. The number of these births surged from 620 in 2001 to over 35,000 in 2011.

On the issue of immigration, the quota for newcomers from the mainland is currently set at 150 per day, or nearly 55,000 a year. Local right-wing groups accuse them of siphoning off resources like welfare, education, housing and healthcare. Worse, some see it as the same demographic invasion that has been happening slowly in minority-dominated Tibet and Inner Mongolia since 1949. Even though Hong Kong has not yet degenerated into the kind of "one country, one system" scenario feared by cynics, a "one country, one people" cultural integration seems to be well in progress.

Some believe that the Sinofication of Hong Kong is more than paranoia or a conspiracy theory. It is a cancer that, if left untreated, will spell the death of Hong Kong within one to two generations. Our resistance to all things mainland Chinese is rooted in our innate distrust of the Communists, as many Hong Kongers from a generation ago were refugees who swam across the Shenzhen River to escape from the Cultural Revolution. By the fickle finger of history, the children and grandchildren of those refugees now find themselves running away from the same oppressors 40 years later.

Our anti-Communist sentiment is often mistaken for jealousy. There is a common misconception among mainlanders that Hong Kong is threatened by China's rapid economic ascent, and that the city's injured pride is standing in the way of a full integration with the motherland. They think that the crybabies down south are throwing a tantrum because the *renminbi* is now worth more than the Hong Kong dollar[30] and the city is losing its competitive edge to Shanghai and Shenzhen. The truth is, many of us would gladly choose an economically weaker but socially stronger society over the one we presently have. If Shanghai or Shenzhen is to take our place as Asia's financial capital or the world's most competitive city, we would be the first to congratulate them. For what's the use of rankings and superlatives if our identity is under threat, if we must play by rules that we have no part in setting up, and if we feel miserable all the time?

A spark

Income inequality, wealth entrenchment, government-business collusion, diminishing freedoms and growing mainland political interference are but some of the burning problems facing Hong Kong. There are a slew of other issues we haven't even touched upon: pollution, food safety, racism, marginalization of the Cantonese language, and a broken education system that drives both students and parents to the

---

30 – In the 10 years between 2005 and 2014, the *renminbi* appreciated against the Hong Kong dollar by more than 30%.

point of exhaustion. Commentators like to point out that it took the British 156 years to transform Hong Kong from a sleepy fishing village to a world class metropolis, but it took the Communists less than two decades to undo the good work and turn it into a tinderbox of frustration and misery.

It is said that people with post-traumatic stress disorder react differently to stimuli. Trauma, stress and disorder are what Hong Kongers wrestle with on a daily basis. Put in that context, the Umbrella Movement was neither a coincidence nor a freak accident. It was a collective reaction to a stimulus – in this case the disproportionate use of police force on unarmed students during the **9/28 Crackdown** – that triggered an all-out rebellion. The broken promises of electoral reform and subsequent protests and police clashes only *catalyzed* the revolt, but they did not *cause* it. They merely provided the spark that set the smoldering city ablaze.

The Day After Everything Changed

Starting a revolution is easy; the real question is what happens the day after.

7:30am

I woke up to flickering lights.

I had put the television on mute and left it on all night. The morning news was on split screen reporting live from all three protest sites: Harcourt Road in Admiralty, Nathan Road in Mongkok and Yee Wo Street in Causeway Bay. The news ticker on the bottom of the screen read "50 bus lines cancelled and 200 more re-routed." "Subway system operational but certain exits remain closed."

So it wasn't a dream after all. The occupy movement really did happen and the city remained as on edge as it was yesterday.

I had slept for about three hours – or three more hours than the protesters got. I changed into my work clothes and left my apartment for the office. I waited for a Central-bound minibus like any other morning. Traffic was light and passengers were muted. Nothing around me offered the slightest hint that a revolution was hotly underway in the heart of the city.

9:15am

I went about my usual routine at my desk: checking email, answering email, filing email. I had both the CNN and the *Apple Daily* web pages up in the background, toggling and refreshing regularly. The stock market opened sharply down – the Hang Seng Index had lost more than 550 points by mid-morning. September 29th might not have been another Black Monday, but an anti-government uprising of this magnitude had spooked fund managers and retail investors. Someone on the trading floor had predicted a nosedive. Two or even three thousand points by market close, an equity trader said.

My boss phoned me and asked me to pop by his office down the hall. "Did you see this?" he said, pointing at his computer screen. My *South China Morning Post* article "Six Hours in Admiralty" had been picked up by various foreign news sites, including BBC News. I braced myself for a lecture on separating my day job from my freelance work, but the lecture never came. "Off the record," he said, "keep it up!" That bit of understanding felt better than a raise.

12:30pm

During lunch, I took the 10-minute walk from my office to Admiralty. On the Pedder Street footbridge, pedestrians could see the on-ramp of the Harcourt Road expressway in the distance. Everyone pulled out their cell phones to take pictures of a sight none of them had seen before: there was not a single vehicle on the highway. Eastbound and westbound traffic had both been blocked by a rampart of trash cans and steel barriers held together by household cable ties. An eerie silence swaddled us like a blanket – the usual cacophony of car horns and bus engines had given way to whispers and camera clicks. One of the busiest streets in the city at one of the busiest hours of the day had become indistinguishable from a post-apocalyptic ghost town.

Connaught Road is a gallery of 20ᵗʰ century monuments. It is home to the world's first Mandarin Oriental hotel, a World War II memorial, a city hall built in the 1960s and the colonial Hong Kong Club. Normally teeming with cars and buses, this magnificent stretch of asphalt had become a public park. Students sat along the curb, some checking the latest news on their phones, others chatting softly with each other. Still others busied themselves with chalk and markers. They were making signs in both Chinese and English: "Free Hong Kong," "Power to the People," "Universal Suffrage Now." Some of the signs targeted the suffragists themselves: "This is not a carnival," "Don't forget why you are here."

There were large piles of donated supplies: bottled water, crackers, face masks, saline water and umbrellas. Lots and lots of umbrellas. Items were carefully sorted by category but unguarded. No one grabbed more than what they needed, and there were more items being dropped into the piles than there were being taken out. I made a mental note of what was needed most and made plans to stop by the supermarket the following day.

12:45pm

I arrived in Admiralty outside the Far East Finance Centre. Standing at the highest point of the arched Harcourt Road – roughly 20 feet above ground – I began to survey the area. On my right, Cotton Road Drive had been barricaded, meaning all traffic to and from Midlevels (the mountainous residential enclave) had to be diverted. On my left, the Tamar Government Headquarters and the Chief Executive's Office next to it looked lifeless and deserted. Down below, shops and banks were temporarily shuttered to keep out looters – except that there were no looters to be found.

Then there were the people – thousands of people – as far as the eye could see. Harcourt Road was part bazaar and part college campus. There were students talking in small groups, passers-by engaging strangers, and volunteers handing out drinks and snacks. There were retirees and office workers who had taken the day off or called in sick. All of them had answered calls on social media to come out to boost the turnout. Crowds were thin in the early morning and they feared that the police might swoop in to clear the area; but by the lunch hour, numbers were back in the thousands.

Protesters move water-filled barriers down Connaught Road

Police presence was scant compared to just 24 hours earlier. Law enforcement had pulled back significantly, a sign that Beijing was re-strategizing and that the SAR government was awaiting new instructions. Given the public relations disaster last night, the police had been ordered to stand down to avoid making a bad situation worse. Besides, there were no vandals or arsonists to arrest, no brawlers or rioters to disperse. There were just peaceful, polite protesters. A few feet away from where I was standing, a chorus of school girls appealed to the uniformed officers. "Please take a day off or go on strike," they urged. "Democracy is for your children too."

1:45pm

I returned to the office after lunch. The afternoon droned on uneventfully. Email, conference calls, and more email. The Hang Seng Index closed with a 449-point drop – not nearly as bad as many had predicted. Retail stocks suffered the most, as investors worried about the impact on tourism during the October Golden Week, one of the two week-long national holidays in mainland China that typically sends millions of visitors to Hong Kong.

Carrie Lam, Chief Secretary and second-in-command in the SAR government, had made an announcement earlier in the day that the National Day firework show on October 1st would be cancelled. The last thing the government needed was more citizens congregating in public. Lam had also announced that the next phase of electoral reform – the second round of public consultation – had been suspended due to an "unfavorable political climate." Soon after these announcements, the pan-dems held their own press conference calling for both Lam and her boss C.Y. Leung to step down. The HKFS and Scholarism announced they would indefinitely extend the citywide class boycott.

By then, images of unarmed citizens engulfed by swaths of tear gas had been beaming across the Internet and received wall-to-wall coverage by every major newspaper and news channel around the world. They gave the protests a catchy new name: the "Umbrella Revolution."

6:30pm

I left the office and took the same 10-minute walk back to Admiralty. I felt a gravitational pull back to the protest site. The sun began to set on the horizon, casting long shadows of people streaming toward Harcourt Road. Office workers in their dark suits wove through teenagers in school uniform. No one knew how many more had come out tonight – nor did anyone really care. Public turnout normally mattered a great deal to protest organizers because it was a measure of public support. Tonight we didn't need a number to tell us that.

The evening heat was oppressive and the humidity stifling. I sat down on the ground and wiped my neck with a face towel handed to me by a teenager. The crowd was listening to a speaker I didn't recognize. You didn't need to be a famous politician to take the microphone. In fact, there were no leaders to give orders or take charge. This wasn't Occupy Central any more – the place where I was sitting wasn't even part of Central. Benny Tai's campaign had ended with the tear gas crackdown 12 hours ago and evolved into something bigger and better.

A few minutes into our sit-in, volunteers carrying plastic bags stopped by and offered us water, cookies, paper fans and wet naps. Others were cooling down the crowds with mist sprayers and distributing cooling patches to be placed on the forehead. I felt parched and asked for water. Five people must have heard my request and came charging toward me with water bottles. I took one from the student nearest me, who then thanked me for accepting his offer. He also reminded me to recycle the plastic bottle at the drop-off tent near the KFC restaurant.

8:30pm

At the urging of student patrols, I left jam-packed Admiralty and walked back toward Central where there was more space. All the cloud-hugging skyscrapers, those modern cathedrals of glass and steel, looked strangely out of place tonight, as were the shiny sports cars trapped in the nearby City Hall parking garage. I wondered if any of these 80-story buildings had made us better people, people who were half as generous and benevolent as the student protesters. Or half as happy? I jotted down a few thoughts in my notebook as I inched westward with the migrating crowd.

At the Pedder Street and Chater Road intersection, a crowd gathered to listen to a crash course on treating pepper spray burns. Standing on a soapbox, the speaker was a young girl who looked about 18. "Don't douse water on your face or else the chemicals will drip down your body and irritate your skin," the teenager warned. "Do this instead." She expertly demonstrated how to tilt the head to one side and rinse one eye after the other using water poured into the tiny bottle cap. "And one more thing," she continued, "you are now at the westernmost frontier of the Central occupation. It is my duty to warn you about your liability should you get arrested for illegal assembly."

After the young girl finished, the audience clapped and broke up into small groups. I approached her before she disappeared into the crowd. The teenager gave me a once over and demurred when I asked her for her name and the name of the university she attended. She must have been warned about undercover cops and Chinese spies infiltrating the protest zone. I told her I was a freelance reporter and just wanted to ask a few simple questions. "I'm a nobody," she replied, "I'm not newsworthy. I just want to share with others what I know."

9:15pm

From Central I began making my way to Causeway Bay. It would have been a 10-minute bus ride, only that public transport had been re-routed like twisted metal. So I walked instead – it would take me 45 minutes.

Causeway Bay was the smallest of the three encampments: just a single city block of Yee Wo Street and a short stretch of Hennessy Road. But it was still a sight to behold. The normally bustling shopping enclave was now an outdoor town hall filled with speakers and listeners. A few curious mainland tourists took pictures with their new iPhone 6's but did not stay to talk to the suffragists.

Sitting on the tram tracks beneath the circular Yee Wo Street footbridge, I realized I hadn't had dinner. Compared to Admiralty, Causeway Bay had only basic resources and supplies – just bottled water and umbrellas. There were no free sandwiches being passed around or all-you-can-eat snack buffets. I decided to grab a burger from the nearby McDonald's. Suddenly I felt an urge to walk around the site and collect takeout orders from perfect strangers. I figured I was going to the restaurant anyway, and it would be silly to come back with just one burger. On any other day, my action would elicit suspicious looks from people – in Hong Kong, nobody offers anything without wanting something in return. But tonight was different. Tonight, everybody gave more than they took.

Munching my Sausage McMuffin, I overheard a young man ask his friend, "How long do you think Beijing will allow this to continue? A week? 10 days?" We all knew that the sit-ins couldn't and wouldn't go on forever. What we didn't know was that we would be asking the same question the young man had just asked for 79 days. As I washed down my burger and French fries with the free water I took from one of the piles, I told myself how wonderful it would be if this new way of life could last forever.

*   *   *

The mid-autumn breeze whispered, cicadas sang. Arching banyan trees swayed willfully against a brooding wall of office towers. The night sky sprawled, like a black cloak dotted with silver stars. It was the most beautiful night I had seen in Hong Kong.

Umbrellas and raincoats, the humblest of household objects, had been thrust onto the world stage, as had tens of thousands of students who had used them to fend off tear gas and pepper spray. Tonight, their trusty raingear would be needed once again – the Hong Kong Observatory had issued a rain and landslide alert for a coming thunderstorm. But protesters had more than a downpour to worry about. In the days and weeks that followed, they would be hit with the urban equivalent of the Ten Plagues of Egypt, and their endurance would be tested by alternating thug attacks and police crackdowns. Many would be harassed, assaulted and arrested, as the authorities scrambled to fight the raging fire by any means possible.

Part 2

Growth

"Birds born in a cage think flying is an illness."

– Alejandro Jodorowsky

Cops and Mobs

The natural reaction to a fire is to throw things at it: water, sand or any dirty old rag.

In the case of a mass protest that threatens a government's credibility and legitimacy, the authorities naturally turn to the men in uniforms. Law enforcement is the first line of attack and the last line of defense. Police officers are trained to follow orders and are, from the ruling regime's point of view, expendable. When in doubt, send in the guards to do the dirty work. Let them deal with a political problem that no one knows how to solve.

That was C.Y. Leung's thinking behind the 9/28 Crackdown before he learned the hard way that the occupy movement was a war that foot soldiers could not win. In the age of cell phone journalism and keyboard activism, battles are fought with pictures and videos instead of batons and rubber bullets. With Beijing breathing down his neck, Leung needed to formulate new strategies to put out the fire before it burned him alive.

The spin doctors

When it comes to swaying public opinion, two can play the game. Almost immediately, spin doctors working for the government came up with a new set of vocabulary to perform damage control. At press conferences and in television interviews, officials substituted the Cantonese words for tear gas, pepper spray and water cannon with the more benign sounding "tear smoke," "pepper agent" and "watering hose." Pro-Beijing newspapers sang the praises of heroic policemen taking long shifts and canceling family vacations to keep the peace in the protest zones.

On September 30th, Day 3 of the Umbrella Movement, the Hong Kong Police began hosting a daily televised news conference to brief the media on the latest developments. The real motivation was to seize the narrative and spoon feed viewers at home a daily dose of government propaganda to discredit the occupy movement. The briefings played up the violent clashes in Mongkok, made a spectacle of disgruntled business owners inconvenienced by the roadblocks, and exaggerated or even fabricated incidents of delayed medical care due to snarled traffic[31]. To deliver these pointed messages, Hong Kong's Finest needed a new face – someone more media savvy than the unpopular Police Commissioner Andy Tsang (better known by his nickname the "Bald Eagle").

Enter Steve Hui, head of the police force's Public Relations Bureau. With a likeable face and a head of slicked-back hair, Hui took the helm as announcer-in-chief. Addressing reporters every afternoon at precisely 4:00pm, he was promptly dubbed "**Four O'clock Hui Sir**[32]." Like a newscaster, Hui read from his script behind a desk, in both Cantonese and English, before taking questions from journalists. His famous lines "Thank you kindly for the question" and "I will now recap in English" became instant catchphrases on social media. A Facebook page created in his honor received tens of thousands of likes in the first week. When a different officer took his place one afternoon, netizens booed and demanded their idol be brought back the next day. The idolatry was all in jest, of course – Hui's popularity was like being rich in Monopoly: it wasn't real. Just the same, his TV show went some way to soften the hard edges of the police's image.

In the meantime, uniformed officers had all but disappeared from the perimeters of the protest zones. Police presence had dwindled to a lone patrolman walking a lazy beat. To some, the absence of law enforcement was a sign of its restraint and a chance for protesters to catch their breath.

---

31 – Dubious stories of medical tragedies abounded. In one incident, an old woman phoned in to a radio show and alleged that her taxi was stuck inside the Cross Harbour Tunnel for five hours, which caused her to miss the chance to see her beloved cancer-stricken daughter-in-law on her deathbed. Public records showed that there was no such congestion reported at the tunnel on that day. In another incident, a man wrote on his Facebook wall about his friend's wife giving birth to a baby girl at Ruttonjee Hospital in Wanchai, with traffic delays causing the newborn to suffer brain damage. The Facebook post went viral, before one user pointed out that there was no maternity ward at Ruttonjee.

32 – "Sir" is a colloquial honorific for teachers, police officers and other men in positions of authority.

To others, it was a deliberate attempt by the authorities to create a power vacuum for a different kind of crackdown.

Send in the thugs

If water doesn't work, try that dirty old rag.

On October 3rd, Day 6, masked thugs fanned out at all three encampments, starting with Mongkok and quickly spreading to Causeway Bay. By nightfall, angry mobs had moved into the movement's nerve center in Admiralty. They called themselves "pro-Hong Kong citizens" – vigilantes who had self-organized to clear the streets and restore public order. They had taken matters into their own hands because they believed the cops had been too lenient toward the students.

Throughout the day, social media was ablaze with graphic cell phone videos of physical and sexual assaults: students with their school uniforms ripped to shreds, volunteers with blood streaming down their faces, and girls screaming "Help me!" while being groped on their chests and legs. These assailants – who should be called domestic terrorists – were systematic in targeting protesters and journalists, among them a TVB reporter and a NOW TV photographer. The Hong Kong Journalists Association and the Foreign Correspondents' Club issued stern statements condemning the **10/3 Mob Attacks**.

Both government officials and the pan-dems (including the Occupy Trio) urged students, especially young girls, to leave the occupied areas and remove any yellow ribbons. The **yellow ribbon** was a symbol of the occupy movement, as was the umbrella that gave the movement its name. Pro-Beijing groups had taken notice and come up with a symbol of their own: a **blue ribbon** in support of police officers. Many of the thugs in Mongkok were seen wearing the blue ribbon.

Later that evening, Joshua Wong took to the podium on Harcourt Road to confirm reports that throngs of blue ribbons had overrun Mongkok and Causeway Bay. Wong's speech was followed by a series of emotional accounts from students who had been kicked and punched by mobsters earlier that day. One girl, still sobbing, recounted her experience of being molested in broad daylight. Another girl said a man tried to grab her and said, "You should expect some hanky-panky in a street protest!"

Whoever was behind the 10/3 Mob Attacks might have leaked the plan or somehow tipped off the universities. The night before, on October 2nd, professors Peter Mathieson and Joseph Sung – respective presidents of HKU and CUHK – made a sudden visit to Admiralty. Looking deeply troubled and speaking with a great sense of urgency, the two went up on stage to urge protesters to "put safety first, take care of yourselves and avoid conflicts." Nobody at the time thought it was anything more than trite advice from their gray-haired school principals. Hindsight suggested that perhaps the two knew something that the students didn't, and were trying their best to warn the protesters against dangers they weren't at liberty to disclose.

The thug attacks began on October 3rd and continued in fits and starts in the weeks that followed. They appeared coordinated, well-timed and even choreographed. The self-proclaimed "disgruntled citizens" came and went in waves. They wore construction masks and black T-shirts that looked like an underground army uniform. They taunted protesters, shouting "What are you waiting for? Hit me back!" as a way to incite a street brawl that would get the students arrested for assault. When asked by reporters why they had shown up at the protest, they stuck to the same scripted, defensive answer, "Nobody sent me. I came here of my own accord."

Rent-a-mobs

There was plenty of circumstantial evidence for reasonable people to conclude that the thug attacks were the handiwork of the Chinese government and its apparatchiks. Since the 10/3 Mob Attacks, unauthenticated price lists began to circulate on social media: a few hundred dollars for showing up, double the amount for punching someone in the face. BBC News showed hidden camera footage of a blue ribbon being handed cash by a middleman. The *South China Morning Post* (**SCMP**) reported WhatsApp messages from an anonymous mafia boss offering the unemployed HK$800 (US$100) for a day's work.

In one incident, police found a six-inch knife in the backpack of a blue ribbon. When confronted, the middle-aged man, clearly not very bright, replied, "It was for... for my durian... et cetera, et cetera, et cetera." Durian is a tropical fruit with a hard spiky shell and is in season during late June to August. The man's bumbling response – *"lau lin mut mut mut"* in Cantonese – went viral on YouTube and became one of the most repeated expressions in 2014, used whenever a person was caught telling a poorly constructed lie.

In another incident, a man threatened to jump off a footbridge in Admiralty if protesters did not leave the streets so that his three children could go back to school. The man expertly climbed to the roof of the bridge and walked confidently along the narrow span. For theatrics, he dropped his old mobile phone to the ground three stories below. When onlookers started to lose interest, he held a box cutter against his neck. After he was finally subdued by the police, the man was found to be a member of the Hong Kong Stuntman Association, believed to be hired by counter-protester groups to stage a mock suicide to sway public opinion.

In Hong Kong, resorting to the underworld to handle tricky situations is an open secret and a time-honored tradition. Local mafias such as Wo Sing Wo and 14K are collectively called the "**Triads**," a term coined by the British in the colonial days in reference to the triangular crest of one of the prominent gangs. Triad members are typically hired by moneylenders to collect unpaid debts or by property brokers to intimidate stubborn residents who hold up lucrative redevelopment projects.

Likewise, fighting crowds with crowds is nothing new in Asia. Rent-a-mobs are routinely deployed during political unrest in Thailand and the Philippines. They are a weapon of choice not only because links to a mastermind are hard to prove, but also because they give the authorities a convenient excuse to use force. A scuffle between yellow and blue ribbons in Mongkok, for instance, would give police the legal and moral authority to clear the area.

Public condemnation of the 10/3 Mob Attacks was immediate. The finger pointed directly at the Liaison Office for mobilizing the Triads to rough up protesters. The use of hired thugs has too been part of the Communist playbook, the same way Mao Zedong mobilized the Red Guards during the Cultural Revolution to purge dissenters. Citizens with a long memory may recall an episode in 1984 when Deng Xiaoping, China's Paramount Leader a generation ago, openly endorsed the Triads in Hong Kong by declaring that "there are many good guys among them." During C.Y. Leung's bid for the Government House in 2012, there were allegations (supported by eye-witnesses) that the Liaison Office had summoned a well-known mafia boss nicknamed "Shanghai Kid" to attend a pre-arranged dinner to coerce a group of Election Committee members to vote for Leung.

Much to the authorities' chagrin, the plan failed miserably. Instead of being scared into staying home or heeding the government's call to withdraw for their own safety, citizens came out in droves to protect their young. Just like the use of tear gas had backfired the week before, the thug attacks drew a bigger, more determined crowd. If the 9/28 Crackdown had sparked the Umbrella Movement, then the 10/3 Mob Attacks had given the campaign another boost. Turnout at all three protest sites had been dropping since the October 1st National Day public holiday, but the gruesome accounts of physical and sexual assaults had thrust the movement back to the forefront of the public consciousness.

A student protester holds up an umbrella for a police officer

Bad Samaritans

"**Peanut eater**," which means a passive bystander in colloquial Cantonese, was used by hardy protesters to shame fellow citizens who stood and watched while others braved pepper spray and police batons to defend the frontlines. Their inaction was likened to that of an audience enjoying a show while eating peanuts[33].

The expression was also used to describe the men in uniform. The sudden appearance of gang members in the protest sites threatened to turn the city into a mob rule, and law enforcement did little or nothing to stop them. Amnesty International condemned the police for abdicating their duty to protect civilians. They pointed to uniformed officers seen standing idly by with their arms folded, and those who took advantage

---

33 – In the old days, movie-goers ate peanuts instead of popcorn at theaters.

of the mayhem to remove steel barriers commandeered by students. One blue ribbon summed up the rationale well: "The students can't break the law [by occupying the city] and expect police to keep them safe."

Law enforcement was accused of not only condoning Triad members, but also aiding and abetting them – by guiding them into the occupied areas, or faking an arrest only to secretly release the suspect on a quiet street corner. In response to mounting allegations, Security Secretary Lai Tung-kwok held a press conference during which he vehemently denied claims of collaboration between police and organized crime syndicates. On a radio show, cabinet member Lam Woon-kwong dismissed the allegations as "fairy tales."

From bad to black

The word "excessive," when applied to the use of police force often means pepper spray aimed at the eyeball or a baton landing right at the rib cage. In the case of one Ken Tsang, the word took on a kick-in-the-groin and sick-to-the-stomach meaning.

In the small hours of October 15th, Day 18, a group of protesters breached police barricades on the four-lane Lung Wo Road near the Tamar Government Headquarters. They began blocking traffic with trash cans and other objects. It was around that time when a group of seven plainclothes officers handcuffed Civic Party member and registered social worker Ken Tsang and carried him to a dark corner where they punched and kicked him for close to five minutes. The cops could have done it in the back of a police truck or in the privacy of an investigation room – but they simply couldn't wait. Unbeknownst to the assailants, the entire incident was caught on video by a TVB cameraman.

TVB broadcast the footage in its morning news program and the clip went viral on the Internet. The so-called **Dark Corner Beating** recalled the brutal assault of African-American taxi driver Rodney King by Los Angeles Police Department (LAPD) officers that sparked a series of deadly riots in 1992. Security Secretary Lai scrambled to do damage control – his second time in less than two weeks – and promised a fair and independent investigation into the incident. But what was done was done and for the whole world to see. If it weren't for the cameraman's good work[34], no one would have believed that members of one of the most respected police forces in Asia were capable of such savagery. Without the video, the truth about Tsang's beating would have been lost

---

34 – The video went on to win the Best TV News Item Award at the 55th Monte Carlo TV Festival and the Edward E. Murrow Award for exemplary news reporting.

in a never-ending he-said-she-said squabble, for who would believe one arrestee over seven trusted officers?

From unconfirmed allegations of cop-and-mob collusion to a caught-in-the-act display of police brutality, event after damning event had decimated the image of the Hong Kong Police Force. Unflattering nicknames like "black cops," "police canine" and *"gong'an"* (the Mandarin word for policemen) began to pop up on social media and enter the mainstream lexicon. In the end, the expendables were discarded, and the police's reputation and morale became the first casualty in the battle for democracy. No amount of charm offensives by Four O'clock Hui Sir could undo the damage done.

軟
硬
兼
施

Carrots and Sticks

In the fall of 2014, preparations were busily underway in Beijing for the celebration of the 65th birthday of the People's Republic. The calendar was peppered with red-letter days and state functions, starting with the National Day festivities on October 1st and followed by Premier **Li Keqiang**'s official visit to Germany on October 10th. The party season culminated in the Asia-Pacific Economic Cooperation (APEC) Summit in mid-November. Under the theme "shaping the future through Asia-Pacific partnership," the three-day gathering of heads of state would be proudly hosted by the city of Beijing[35]. Barack Obama and Vladimir Putin had already RSVP'ed.

You can imagine Beijing's reaction when it heard what happened in Admiralty on September 28th. Overnight, citizens became warriors and outlaws became international rock stars. An anti-government uprising in Hong Kong was both an embarrassment for the CCP and a *lèse-majesté* that threatened its absolute authority. And the timing couldn't have been worse. The last thing that China needed was a diplomatic black eye at the APEC Summit that would give the Americans an excuse to dress down the host in front of other world leaders, or to use its human rights record

---

35 – The APEC Summit was originally set to take place in Hong Kong. In February 2014, the Chinese government announced that the venue would be moved to Beijing, presumably to avoid the event being derailed by OCLP.

as a bargaining chip in trade negotiations. This *qiang guo* was not about to let a bunch of pesky teenagers ruin its party.

If Beijing had learned one thing about running the world's largest nation, it would be that they should never send an idiot to do a Communist's job. The time for heads to roll in the SAR government would come, but right now the CCP needed those paper-pushing fools in C.Y. Leung's camp to do whatever it took to make the nuisance go away. In the meantime, the Communist leadership put together a response team to closely monitor the unfolding crisis. They set up a command center at Bauhinia Villa, a high-end resort in Shenzhen owned by the Liaison Office, where senior party officials met regularly – and secretly – with Leung and members of his cabinet.

Beijing's quandary

If the Umbrella Movement – or any kind of pro-democracy uprising – had taken place in mainland China, the People's Liberation Army (**PLA**) would have been mobilized within hours to nip it in the bud. Demonstrators would have been arrested en masse and the Internet would have been temporarily shut down for "maintenance."

Fortunately, Hong Kong is not (yet) the mainland. A heavy-handed suppression would almost certainly backfire because of the glare of social media and the presence of the international press, as was the case on September 28th. From the start, Beijing had ruled out the nuclear option: a Tiananmen-style crackdown[36]. The Communists knew that if they mobilized so much as a single armored vehicle across the Shenzhen border or fired a single bullet into the crowd, it would destroy any remaining pretense that modern China is capable of handling political discord without a military response. Worse, it would spell the end of Hong Kong as we know it: anyone with any means would get on the first plane and flee the city.

The absence of a clear leader in the occupy movement also caught the Chinese authorities flat-footed. There was not one person to target or take down. None of the old tricks in the Communist playbook – bribery, frame-up, character assassination – would work on the protesters. Even

---

36 – There were unconfirmed reports in the media that C.Y. Leung and Liaison Office Director Zhang Xiaoming originally supported a bloody crackdown on September 28th and that the SAR government had gone so far as to issue a notice to major public hospitals telling their emergency rooms to prepare for a large number of causalities that night. It was said that the operation was vetoed by President Xi Jinping who did not want any fatalities weeks ahead of the APEC Summit.

if Benny Tai were to accept their hush money or Joshua Wong were to be locked up for fabricated charges, another one just like them would step up and take their place.

What's more, senior leadership in Beijing had enough problems on their hands. The country had just gone through a once-in-a-decade leadership change in 2012 when **Xi Jinping**, scion of a well-known party elder, succeeded Hu Jintao as the Paramount Leader (see Table 5). Soon thereafter, Xi began a high stakes operation to purge political enemies under the guise of an anti-graft campaign. He went after both elite cadre members (the "tigers") and minor officials (the "flies") with equal tenacity. By September 2014, factional infighting within the senior leadership had reached a fever pitch.

China is an autocracy. What the country lacks in multi-party dissent, it makes up for in factional politics. Exactly how many factions there are and who plays on whose team is unclear[37]. Most observers believe there are two main coalitions: the **Princeling Faction** and the **Youth League Faction**. The Princeling Faction, represented by Bo Xilai[38] and Xi Jinping, consists of descendants of Communist China's founding fathers who fought the Kuomintang (**KMT**) during the Chinese Civil War. Born with a red spoon in their mouths, they hold high-level political positions by virtue of their family names and powerful connections. By contrast, the Youth League Faction is made up of career bureaucrats who come from ordinary backgrounds but make up for their lack of pedigree with hard work and loyalty. Leaguers like former Paramount Leader Hu Jintao and current Premier Li Keqiang joined the CCP or its little league version – the Communist Youth League – at a tender age and worked their way up the food chain.

To give an idea of President Xi's epic power consolidation and the dangerous games he was playing, in late 2013, he placed former security czar and military top brass Zhou Yongkang (a member of the Shanghai Clique) under investigation for corruption. On December 5th, Day 69 of the Umbrella Movement, Zhou was arrested and stripped of his party membership. Seven months later, he was sentenced to life in prison after a secret trial. The disgraced general was the first ever **Central Politburo Standing Committee** member in the CCP's 65-year history to be taken down, breaking the unwritten rule that the Central Politburo

---

37 – Factions include, among others, the Shanghai Clique (headed by former Paramount Leader Jiang Zemin), the Qinghua Clique, the Populists, the Elitists, the Princelings and the Youth Leaguers.

38 – A flamboyant princeling, Bo Xilai served as the party secretary of the national central city of Chongqing and a member of the Central Politburo. While in office, Bo initiated a high profile anti-graft campaign and a revival of Maoism, both aimed at purging political opponents.

Standing Committee is politically off limits. In doing so, Xi might have overextended himself: one misstep and the new emperor could find himself in a coup d'état that would cost him everything[39].

Reign	Paramount Leader	Faction	Legacy
1978 - 1989	Deng Xiaoping	N/A	• "Reform and Openness" initiative beginning in 1978 that opened up the Chinese economy. • Negotiation with Britain in the 1980s regarding the handover of Hong Kong. • Tiananmen Square Massacre in 1989.
1989 - 2002	Jiang Zemin	Shanghai Clique	• China's accession to the World Trade Organization in 2001. • Major infrastructure projects including the Qinghai–Tibet Railway and the Three Gorges Dam. • Widespread corruption, nepotism and a growing income gap. • Aggressive stance on Taiwan.
2002 - 2012	Hu Jintao	Youth League	• Sustained economic growth. • International events including the 2008 Beijing Olympics and the 2010 Shanghai World Expo. • Outer space program and infrastructure projects including the world's largest high-speed rail network. • Softened stance on Taiwan.

---

39 – In 2012, for instance, Bo Xilai attempted a coup d'état against fellow princeling Xi Jinping. Xi emerged from the political struggle unharmed, while the failed coup cost Bo his political career and almost his life. Months later, Bo was found guilty of corruption and sentenced to life imprisonment. His wife also received a life sentence for the murder of British businessman Neil Heywood.

2012 – present	Xi Jinping	Princeling	• Champion of the "Chinese Dream." • Anti-graft campaign to consolidate power and stem the hemorrhage of state funds. • "One Belt, One Road" economic connection with Central Asia and North Africa. • Umbrella Movement in 2014.

Table 5. Leadership of the New China

The ripples of factional tensions in Beijing could be felt a thousand miles away in Hong Kong. On October 8th, Day 11, C.Y. Leung was embroiled in a political scandal for failing to declare a HK$50 million (US$6.4 million) payment by an Australian engineering company called UGL. Details of the arrangement were leaked to the Australian press, and the curious timing – less than two weeks after the start of the Umbrella Movement – stirred up speculation that the leak was orchestrated by a rival faction wanting to topple Leung to weaken Xi Jinping's credibility.

If any other government official in the SAR were caught doing what Leung did, the person would likely have been investigated by the **ICAC** (Hong Kong's FBI) and handed a stiff prison sentence. That is unless the person had the backing of the Liaison Office and Beijing. In the end, the **UGL Scandal** failed to gain traction and the issue flamed out after a few days. C.Y. Leung came out of the controversy unscathed, proving himself to be a certifiable Teflon politician. The saga was evidence that Xi Jinping – who favored stability by supporting Leung – still had the upper hand over his political rivals. At the same time, the news leak underscored the depth and the breadth of the power struggles within the Communist leadership, and how the occupy movement presented both opportunities and threats depending on one's agenda and affiliation.

The olive branch

Beijing was not interested in military intervention. Meanwhile, the alternating recipe of cops and mobs failed to make a dent in the protesters' determination to stay on the streets. It was time the authorities tried something else: negotiation.

A life-size cardboard cut-out of Chinese President Xi Jinping holding up a yellow umbrella in Causeway Bay

After repeated delays and multiple cancellations (see Table 6), Beijing finally gave the nod for the SAR government to sit down and talk to the suffragists. On October 16th, Day 19, C.Y. Leung announced that the Electoral Reform Taskforce would meet face-to-face with student leaders at a mutually agreed location on October 21st. The sudden U-turn had much to do with the Dark Corner Beating that happened the day before, which had re-galvanized the city and reenergized the occupy movement.

The October 16th agreement to talk was a significant step for the movement. It was the first time the authorities acknowledged that the protests were more than an illegal act. Student activists were finally taken seriously and treated like equals, to be seated at the table across from senior government officials. Observers compared the **10/21 Talks** to the famous scene in May 1989, when student leaders from Beijing University wearing headbands and pajamas were received by the Communist leadership at the Great Hall of the People.

Date	Talk	Cause	Action
Sep 28th (Day 1)	ON	9/28 Crackdown.	• The HKFS issues an ultimatum to C.Y. Leung demanding talks within 48 hours. • Two days later, Carrie Lam agrees to hold a dialogue with protesters.
Oct 3rd (Day 6)	OFF	10/3 Mob Attacks.	• The HKFS suspends plans to hold talks with Carrie Lam.
Oct 7th (Day 10)	ON	The occupy movement enters its second week; the HKFS faces increasing pressure to try something new.	• Government officials and the HKFS agree to hold talks on Oct 10th.
Oct 9th (Day 12)	OFF	The HKFS announces a "non-cooperation campaign" against the SAR government.	• Carrie Lam puts the Oct 10th talks on hold.
Oct 16th (Day 19)	ON	Dark Corner Beating.	• C.Y. Leung announces that government officials will hold talks with student leaders.

Table 6. The on-again-off-again relationship between the government and student leaders

The talks took place at the Hong Kong Academy of Medicine in Wong Chuk Hang and were moderated by Lingnan University president Leonard Cheng. The event was broadcast live by every television station in the city. The protesters were represented by core members of the HKFS, and the government delegation included Carrie Lam and the rest of the Electoral Reform Taskforce. C.Y. Leung recused himself from the talks and for good reason. After narrowly escaping the UGL Scandal,

Leung decided to keep a low profile and step away from the glare of the media for the time being.

Because the negotiation was televised, both sides stuck to their rhetoric. The students reiterated their demands for a free election without any restrictions, and the government insisted that the voting methods could not deviate from the 8/31 Framework. At times, the talks sounded more like a high school debate than a serious dialogue. While the live event made for great prime time entertainment – it was one of the most watched broadcasts in the city's television history – it did little to end the impasse on the issue of electoral reform.

The only pleasant surprise on that evening was the poise and eloquence of the HKFS delegates. The talks were good publicity for the student leadership, and a chance for them to make a compelling case for universal suffrage in front of millions of viewers. The students were assertive without being disrespectful, conscious of the mistakes made by their predecessors in the Tiananmen Square Protests. During the talks at the Great Hall of the People, overly confident student leaders like Wu'er Kaixi[40] lectured senior party leaders about the need for political reform, and their perceived arrogance was considered one of the causes for the heavy-handed crackdown a few weeks later.

Toward the end of the evening, Carrie Lam promised to draft a document to supplement the (whitewashed) report C.Y. Leung submitted to the Standing Committee back in June. The new document would summarize the protester's demands and be hand-delivered to the Beijing-based **Hong Kong and Macau Affairs Office**. It was another empty promise, of course. Lam refused to commit to a submission date for the supplement or what it would contain[41]. Just the same, the event helped to raise the public profile of Alex Chow and Lester Shum, and made new political stars out of student union presidents **Yvonne Leung**, **Nathan Law** and **Eason Chung**.

---

40 – A Beijing-born ethnic Uighur, Wu'er Kaixi was one of the most prominent student leaders of the Tiananmen Square Protests. He was best known for interrupting and dressing down Premier Li Peng in a televised meeting during the pro-democracy movement. After the June 4th crackdown, he became the second most wanted person in China and fled the country with the help of Hong Kong activists through a coordinated rescue effort known as "Operation Yellowbird."

41 – A supplemental document, titled *Report on the Recent Community and Political Situation in Hong Kong*, was eventually submitted to the Hong Kong and Macau Affairs Office in March 2015, three months after the Umbrella Movement had ended.

An old man's appeal

If the first carrot from Beijing was an offer to sit down and talk, then the second one would be a plea from an old man.

On October 25th, Day 28, Beijing summoned former Chief Executive Tung Chee-hwa out of retirement to entreat the students. At a hastily organized press conference, the 77-year-old urged protesters to go home to their parents, before the unrest inflicted any more harm to the city's economy and social harmony. Although the Chinese government wouldn't intervene militarily, said Tung, it also would not change its mind about the 2017 election. He went on to defend the 8/31 Framework as "real universal suffrage" and call C.Y. Leung's multi-million-dollar payment by UGL "normal business activities." With teary eyes and a trembling voice, Tung sounded like a heartbroken grandfather trying to talk some sense into his wayward grandchildren.

Tung took office in 1997 as an energetic Chief Executive but left in 2005 without finishing his second term. Hong Kongers remember him as a disgraced bureaucrat – incompetent, confused and out of touch with mainstream society. For Beijing to ask a washed-up politician to waste his breath pleading with protesters, and to do so at a press conference instead of a sympathetic visit to the encampments, spoke volumes about how little the Communist leadership actually understood the people of Hong Kong. The move indicated China's increasing desperation or a complete misjudgment of the situation, or both.

Economic sanctions

Where there is a carrot, there must also be a stick – it's the first law of Chinese politics. Hong Kong is an economic city after all, and citizens go where the money goes. To squeeze where it hurt the most, Beijing did what the United Nations does to Iran and North Korea: trade embargoes and economic sanctions.

On October 1st, Day 4, the Chinese government temporarily suspended the issuance of travel visas to mainland tour groups coming to Hong Kong. The Individual Visit Scheme was not affected because of the large number of cross-border families and business owners who commute between the two places every day. The moratorium, which lasted for seven days, served a dual purpose: to limit the number of mainlanders exposed to the poison of anti-government protests and to stem the flow of tourism dollars as a reminder that social unrest can be costly. To Beijing's annoyance, the travel ban was greeted with enthusiasm by

Hong Kongers who for years had been complaining about being overrun by Chinese tourists.

The travel ban had a second prong that worked in the opposite direction. On November 15th, Day 49, Alex Chow, Nathan Law and Eason Chung were stopped from boarding a Beijing-bound flight at the Hong Kong International Airport. Their travel documents – the home return permits[42] – were confiscated and destroyed by the airport authorities. The trio had planned to meet with party leaders in Beijing or stage a demonstration in the capital city if they were not granted an audience.

In the weeks that followed, other members and associates of the HKFS and Scholarism were also refused entry into mainland China and **Macau**, even for holiday or family visits. The target audience of the embargo was not only the activists themselves, but also anyone doing business on the mainland or needing to travel there for work – that is most professionals in the finance and service industries. The second prong of the travel ban had bite: pragmatic citizens would rather not risk their career prospects by having their photos taken by undercover police at the protest sites and becoming *persona non grata* in the eyes of the mainland authorities.

In fact, all it took to be added to the border control blacklist was to be stopped by a police officer near one of the protest zones and have your HKID card checked. In Hong Kong, every citizen is required by law to carry an identity card at all times. Police can demand anyone stopped on the street to produce the document with or without probable cause. It was believed that law enforcement was systematically compiling a roster of troublemakers and relaying the information to mainland customs so that they could be red-flagged and prevented from crossing the border. Local media estimated that the blacklist had around 1,500 names and was growing.

To turn up the heat even more, Beijing threatened to take back or at least delay some of the economic handouts to the city. The **Shanghai-Hong Kong Stock Connect** is a platform that allows mainland investors to purchase stocks listed on the Hong Kong Stock Exchange, and Hong Kong investors to do the same with Shanghai-listed stocks. The scheme was first announced by Premier Li Keqiang in April 2014 as a "gift to Hong Kong people" and was scheduled to go live in October that year. After the Umbrella Movement erupted, the Chinese authorities postponed the launch date for unspecified reasons, even though all technical aspects of the platform were said to be ready.

---

42 – Hong Kong-born citizens may travel to China without a passport or visa. They may apply for a "home return permit" to get in and out of mainland China as often as they wish. Many members of the pan-dem camp had their permits revoked and have not been able to set foot on the mainland since.

On November 10th, Day 44, Chinese securities regulators suddenly announced that the Stock Connect platform would go live within a week. Observers found the timing of the announcement highly suspect – it came the day after a face-to-face meeting between President Xi Jinping and C.Y. Leung ahead of the APEC Summit. The theory was that during their closed door meeting, Xi finally authorized the clearance of the protest sites and Leung gave his personal assurance that the operation would be completed without a hitch. That meant the economic sanctions could also be lifted.

Trading activities on the platform, however, were disappointing. Daily trading volumes fell far short of expectations and even the head of the Hong Kong Stock Exchange admitted that the scheme was overhyped. The lackluster performance drew jeers and boos from suffragists. They used it as an example to remind fellow citizens that these so-called "gifts" from China were never as good as promised. Many of them, like the Individual Visit Scheme, were more a curse than a blessing.

No means no

Halfway through the occupy movement, political commentators and insiders began to observe a pattern in Beijing's stance toward the protests. The CCP was willing to entertain any ideas to put an end to the insurgency – hence the combination of carrots and sticks – so long as they followed three basic ground rules: no compromise, no negotiation and no bloodshed (see Table 7).

The outright refusal by Beijing to either compromise or negotiate was a clear indication that the hawks within the Communist leadership had the last word. The hardliners pointed to four threats:

- a loss of credibility and a sign of weakness;

- the spread of anti-government insurgencies on the mainland, especially in troubled territories like Tibet and Xinjiang;

- a budding separatist movement in Hong Kong[43]; and

- Western operatives providing financial and other assistance to the occupy movement.

---

43 – The separatist movement in Hong Kong was led by **Chin Wan**, assistant professor at Lingnan University, who advocated the establishment of a Hong Kong city-state independent from the mainland. Chin commanded a cult following on social media before and during the occupy movement.

Ground Rule	Evidence	Rationale
No compromise	• Both Chinese and SAR officials repeatedly told protesters that the 8/31 Framework was immutable, like "the rap of a gavel." • Beijing showed zero interest in any of the alternative proposals regarding the make-up of the Nominating Committee floated by academics, the pandems or even moderate Beijing loyalists.	• Any concessions from the 8/31 Framework would make the CCP look weak. It would also set a bad precedent that could encourage similar uprisings in China. • 17 years into the Handover, the SAR government had failed to instill a "one country" mindset in its people. Beijing was concerned that separatist groups were gaining momentum in Hong Kong. • Beijing was equally concerned that foreign governments might be backing the anti-government uprising and meddling in local affairs.
No negotiation	• Since the 10/21 Talks, the SAR government had refused to hold any follow-up meetings or new rounds of private or public discussion. • The HKFS's requests to have Tung Chee-hwa broker a dialogue with Chinese officials were ignored. • Members of the HKFS were denied entry to the mainland where they hoped to meet directly with senior officials. Their travel documents were revoked.	

No bloodshed	• Police pulled back from all protest sites following the 9/28 Crackdown. • Police attempted to clear Mongkok only to stop halfway, allowing protesters to reoccupy the area. • Hired thugs were used to intimidate and harass students but did not inflict serious injuries. • The PLA was not mobilized to conduct an all-out clearance.	• The APEC Summit in mid-November put China in the global spotlight. • A bloody crackdown would exponentially increase the stakes, and give rival factions within the CCP ammunition to challenge President Xi's authority. • China paid a high price for the Tiananmen Square Massacre and repeating history would jeopardize the country's standing on the world stage and spell the end of Hong Kong.

Table 7. The so-called "Three No's" Policy

The first two threats were a real cause for concern, which was why the CCP had cranked up the state propaganda machine to discredit the protesters and mobilized an army of Internet police to take down sensitive posts on Chinese social media. The other two, however, were figments of imagination drummed up by either ill-informed advisers or fear mongers motivated by their own political agenda.

Everyone knows that separatism has no traction in Hong Kong – past, present or future. We are not Scotland, Catalonia, not even Quebec. The idea of turning a tiny southern Chinese city into an independent state is as far-fetched as Miami trying to secede from the United States – it's never going to happen. With a 2.3 million-strong PLA, China would crush the secessionists like bugs.

As for the unease toward foreign intervention, there is indeed a history of external forces stirring the pot in Hong Kong. In the mid-19th century, it was a European power (the British Empire) that snatched the territory away from China after the Qing court suffered a humiliating defeat in the First Opium War. In the 1960s, it was another foreign power (this time

Mao's China) that orchestrated a violent uprising to subvert the British Hong Kong government that led to the **1967 Leftists Riots**[44].

Fast forward to 2014, there were persistent rumors that the CIA or MI6 had a hand in fomenting the student-led protests. Neither Beijing nor the SAR government was able to produce any evidence to bear out the conspiracy theory. Some observers believed that the "blame the West" campaign was a red herring to divert attention away from the electoral reform debate and deflect accusations of broken promises. Others argued that it was a pre-emptive strike to warn the Americans and the Britons to back off.

Whether they were based on real or imagined threats, the three ground rules left hardly any wriggle room for the SAR government to do anything at all. In the absence of better alternatives, the only strategy was to wait out the storm and hope that the suffragists would tire themselves out or that their disruptions would turn public opinion against them. That said, prolonging the standoff meant that the public relations black eye would keep throbbing, a costly proposition for both C.Y. Leung and Beijing. Time was not on anyone's side.

---

44 – In 1967, during the height of the Cultural Revolution on the mainland, Hong Kong was ravaged by a series of left-wing riots that killed at least 50 people. The extremists were backed by the CCP with the intention to topple the British-appointed colonial government.

The Court of Public Opinion

For two and a half months, the same conversations had been playing out all over the city, from the office pantry to the dinner table, from the radio talk show to the backseat of a taxi. *When will the students go home? What's the point of all this if Beijing won't back down? How will it all end?*

From the first shot of tear gas in Admiralty to the removal of the last tent in Causeway Bay, the Umbrella Movement had been a war of public opinion. Any political campaign predicated on the idea of occupying city streets, whose very premise is to obstruct traffic and paralyze business activities, requires buy-in from those who are most affected by it: the general population.

Public support is a tricky thing. It takes more to maintain than it does to obtain it. In the early days of the occupy movement, the authorities tried to fight 21st century warfare with last century weapons. If this were a soccer game, the government would have lost 0-1 on Day One. Subsequent turns of events such as the 10/3 Mob Attacks and the Dark

Corner Beating continued to widen the suffragists' lead on the scoreboard. As the protests dragged on, however, the novelty of the one-of-a-kind political movement started to wane, as complaints about cancelled bus services and lost sales continued to fester. The students' lead in the game began to narrow, and the tides eventually turned against them.

A city divided

September 28th, 2014 is as much a dividing line in Hong Kong's history as it is in its society. The Umbrella Movement, and the daily disruptions that came with it, had polarized the city along political and ideological lines. The middle class blamed the suffragists for rocking the economic boat and putting the lofty ideals of *some* people above the livelihood of *all* people. In turn, protesters accused non-supporters of selling out the city's future for a paycheck and protecting the very system that enslaved them. Weeks of bickering and name-calling had driven a wedge between parents and children, husbands and wives, teachers and students, the yellow ribbons and the blue ribbons.

There was a misconception, in particular among the foreign media, that all of Hong Kong had rallied behind the protesters, when in fact their sympathizers had always been in the minority. From the start, public reaction toward taking the city hostage was at best ambivalent. Over the 79-day period, support for the protests hovered below 40%. The percentage was much lower among respondents aged between 26 and 39, and lower still among those aged 40 or above. By mid-November, the movement had lost nearly all of the middle-of-the-road "swing votes" and a large portion its core base. Over 65% of the population felt the students should pack up and go home (see Figure 7).

To get a sense of the fierce opposition to the occupy movement, look no further than the comments section on local news sites. Every voice of support for the students was counter-balanced by at least a dozen attacks, and those who opposed the movement did it with far greater intensity than those who supported it. To be sure, some of the responses came from the so-called "**50 Cent Party**" – hired trolls who were paid 50 cents for each insult they hurled at a news article or op-ed column, in part to skew the public debate and in part to intimidate journalists critical of Beijing. Still, the majority of the anti-protest responses were written by readers who wholeheartedly and fundamentally disagreed with the movement. Typical comments included:

> *"The students are lawless thugs and self-righteous agitators for their minority view."*

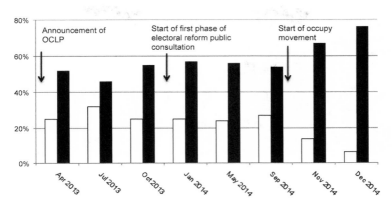

Data from April 2013 to September 2014 come from surveys conducted by HKU's Public Opinion Programme, based on the question "Do you support Occupy Central as a means to demand universal suffrage in 2017?" Data from November to December 2014 come from surveys conducted by CUHK's Centre for Communication and Public Opinion Survey, based on the question "Should protesters evacuate all their occupied areas?"

Figure 7. Changing public support for the occupy movement

> *"They are spoiled brats manipulated by the West to destroy a city that their parents have worked so hard to build."*

> *"Police should go out and start arresting everyone. I do not believe anyone in HK would complain if these hooligans are locked up."*

Much of the negativity was fanned by the Communists' propaganda machine. Under Beijing's order, the DAB, the Liberal Party and other loyalists stepped up their doomsday rhetoric. They made up exaggerated, unsubstantiated predictions about economic contraction, unemployment and market crashes. Even though none of those terrible things materialized, the mere thought of another recession – after what the city endured in 1997, 2003 and 2008 – was enough to make citizens shake their heads and wag their fingers at the outlaws.

The fear-mongering trickled down to corporate management and small business owners. Employers and line managers were known to openly pressure staff to sign anti-OCLP petitions and forbid employees from wearing yellow ribbons in the office or going to the protest sites after hours. HSBC director Laura Cha sent a not-so-subtle message to the tens of thousands of bank employees by downplaying the urgency of electoral reform. At a media event in Paris, Cha said that universal suffrage could wait because "American slaves were liberated in 1861 but were not granted voting rights until 107 years later." Meanwhile, the Philippine Consulate issued a stern warning to the 180,000 foreign domestic workers based in Hong Kong against going near Admiralty, Mongkok or Causeway Bay "to avoid being inadvertently perceived as being part of the protest actions." Offenders faced up to a HK$5,000 (US$640) fine, a 12-month sentence or instant deportation.

The mass media

To find out whether someone is a yellow ribbon or blue ribbon, you rarely have to ask. You simply look at the newspaper he has under his arm.

A headline comparison (see Table 8) will reveal the great divide between pro-democracy media outlets – namely, the *Apple Daily* and *Ming Pao* – and the Beijing mouthpieces and self-censoring publications – namely, everything else. During the occupy movement, each side appealed to its own base and tried to sway the fence-sitters.

Expectedly, pro-Beijing newspapers such as *Wen Wei Po* and *Ta Kung Pao* were the most aggressive against the suffragists. More interestingly, however, the movement exposed the true colors of many self-proclaimed "middle-of-the-road" publications operated by local tycoons with significant business ties in China. Under pressure from Beijing to declare their loyalty, so-called "independent" *Sing Tao* and *Oriental Daily* were forced to come out of the closet and reveal their political orientation. Once they crossed that red line, there was no turning back. They joined *Wen Wei Po* and *Ta Kung Pao* in the graveyard of propaganda papers that get printed every day but read by no one.

Likewise, television broadcasters were pressured to self-censor and whitewash details unfavorable to the government. The most egregious incident happened at TVB. After the Dark Corner Beating video was first aired in the morning on October 17th, senior management at TVB intervened. They attempted to downplay the incident by deleting sensitive wording such as "kicking" and "punching" from the newscaster's script for the more popular 6:30 evening news program. That night, 27 TVB reporters signed a joint petition condemning management's self-censorship and heavy-handed interference with the newsroom. At the peril of their own careers, a few of them went to Admiralty and shared their frustrations on stage. That, followed by several cases of biased reporting of skirmishes between protesters and police, earned TVB the nickname "CCTVB" (after China's state-owned broadcaster **CCTV**).

Media	Pro-Beijing/Pro-establishment	Liberal/Pro-democracy
Newspapers	• Sing Tao • Oriental Daily • Wen Wei Po • Ta Kung Pao • Sing Pao • The Sun • Sky Post • Hong Kong Daily News* • Hong Kong Commercial Daily • Hong Kong Economic Journal	• Apple Daily • Ming Pao * Publication ceased on July 11th, 2015
Headline comparison: Sep 29th (day after the 9/28 Crackdown)	"Occupy Central sparks violence, police clear protest site" – Wen Wei Po "Occupy Central is lawlessness" – Ta Kung Pao "Occupy Central gets out of control" – The Sun "Admiralty is a warzone" – Sing Tao "Chaos! Protesters overrun city, tear gas fired" – Oriental Daily	"Protesters undaunted by police crackdown" – Apple Daily "Police fire tear gas, Occupy Central spreads across the city" – Ming Pao
Headline comparison: Oct 4th (day after the 10/3 Mob Attacks)	"Citizens fed up with occupation fight back" – Sing Tao "Citizens affected by occupiers self-organize to clear protest sites" – Oriental Daily "Citizens angered by illegal occupiers self-organize to clear Mongkok and Causeway Bay" – Wen Wei Po "Citizens have had enough! 10,000 people face off with protesters in Mongkok" – Ta Kung Pao "Stock index goes south, Occupy Central overhang continues" – Hong Kong Economic Journal	"Police and triads conspire to clear occupied areas" – Apple Daily "Counter-protesters attack from dawn to dusk; demonstrators accuse police of inaction" – Ming Pao

Table 8. A survey of Chinese-language newspapers in Hong Kong

The businesses

Understandably, those who were financially impacted by the occupy movement were its most vocal critics. The hardest hit were perhaps the car dealerships along Connaught Road in Admiralty and Wanchai, which saw a near total loss in sales from October through mid-December due to blocked roads. Tour bus operators and retail chains that cater primarily to mainland tourists, such as luxury watch sellers and beauty boutiques, also bore the brunt of traffic jams and a week-long travel ban on mainland tour groups. Dozens of jewelry shops along Nathan Road and Hennessy Road were temporarily shuttered. Chow Tai Fook, a goldsmith chain owned by property tycoon Cheng Yu-tung, claimed that they were forced to temporarily close a third of their 90 stores across the city, 10 of them in Mongkok alone.

Industry lobbyists came out swinging against the protesters, but failed to get much sympathy from the public. Over the years, high-end retailers and tour bus companies had made a fortune from the deluge of mainland tourists, rolling out the red carpet for them but neglecting local consumers. They had displaced small businesses, destroyed old neighborhoods, and clogged highways and main roads. Many citizens viewed *them* as the real occupiers.

Taxi and minibus drivers were affected to various degrees depending on the route. Some of them saw as much as a 30% increase in daily income as a result of improved traffic in certain areas, as many commuters and leisure drivers decided to leave their cars at home, and numerous public bus lines were cancelled or rerouted. Nevertheless, opposition from commercial drivers was fierce and coordinated. Taxi driver unions organized several "slow drive" protests and sent representatives to negotiate with student leaders. Many believed the motivation was political rather than financial. There were allegations that those angry cabbies were paid to stage counter-protests just to sway public opinion. Several large taxi companies reportedly sent out text messages offering HK$1,500 (US$200) for half a day's work.

Some businesses actually benefitted from the occupy movement, including the MTR Corporation – operator of the city's subway system – which saw a 15% increase in ridership. There were also fast food chains, newsstands and convenience stores near the occupied areas that experienced an uptick in sales. The lines inside the McDonald's and KFC at Admiralty Centre were long and constant, as were the ones at the 7-Eleven on the second floor of nearby Queensway Plaza. They were the main sources of food and drinks (and bathrooms) for protesters and their supporters. Some of the staff knew the students by name and were used to preparing large orders that fed a small village.

The real victims – the businesses with the most legitimate complaints – were the mom-and-pop shops in Mongkok and Causeway Bay (Admiralty being a financial district did not have the same issue). They included clothing boutiques, souvenir shops and other retailers that relied on pedestrian traffic but did not sell things needed by the protesters. Students asked for their understanding and held up placards that read "Democracy in progress; sorry for the inconvenience!" In hindsight, protesters should have done much more than offer apologies, for example, by using the power of social media to raise compensation funds or call on friends and supporters to patronize the affected retailers. Left unaddressed, stories of financial hardship added to a growing sentiment among ordinary citizens that the students were as tone-deaf to the outcries of small business owners as the government was to the protesters' political demands.

As for the business tycoons, the Lis, the Lees and the Woos largely kept a low-profile. Their relative silence could be interpreted in one of two ways. Cynics gawked at the way the super-rich built their empires on the backs of the masses, only to turn a blind eye when the city was in trouble. Optimists argued that their reticence under the harsh glare of Beijing's watchful eye equated to tacit support. In fact, a week before the occupy movement began, President Xi Jinping summoned a large delegation of Hong Kong property oligarchs to Beijing for a lecture on why they needed to do more to sell the 8/31 Framework to the public. There was probably some truth in both interpretations.

The blue ribbons

The blue ribbons were divided into two main groups. The first comprised Beijing loyalists who either self-organized or were funded by the Liaison Office to help manufacture dissent. Outspoken leaders included a rogue's gallery of longtime social pariahs such as **Robert Chow**, a washed-up radio host; **Patrick Ko**, a pan-dem reject; and **Leticia Lee**, a housewife who came out of the woodwork and whose frequent gaffes were a reliable source of comic relief. Lee had a long rap sheet and an unfortunate Chinese name (a homophone with "bootleg cigarettes" in Cantonese).

The trio of political streakers – Chow, Ko and Lee – led a number of loosely organized pressure groups with poorly chosen names like Caring Hong Kong Power and Voice of Loving Hong Kong. They functioned as modern Red Guards who showed up at pro-democracy rallies with banners and megaphones to heckle participants and drown out their message. A month before the movement erupted, the trio organized a massive anti-OCLP demonstration consisting mainly of hired participants (who couldn't tell reporters who Benny Tai was or what Occupy Central meant) and senior citizens (who reportedly kept asking each other "when can we

Blue ribbons Patrick Ko (second from left) and Leticia Lee (to his right)

go home?"). Once the day's work was over, the rent-a-crowd would litter the streets with the placards they did not understand and the Chinese flags that they had eagerly waved moments ago. They would then hurry back onto the tour bus to claim their free snake soup banquet meal.

The second group was made up of diehard supporters of the Hong Kong Police Force, most likely friends and family of law enforcement or other government arms. At social gatherings, they openly praised the police for their bravery. On social media, they changed their profile pictures to a blue ribbon and defended allegations of excessive force. They shrugged off the police's inaction during the 10/3 Mob Attacks and dismissed incidents like the Dark Corner Beating as "liberal propaganda." Some of their pro-government Facebook posts were so odious to the center-to-left mainstream that they triggered a wave of "unfollowing" or outright "blocking."

From time to time, the more aggressive blue ribbons penetrated deep into the protest zones, either alone or as a group. They tried to engage protesters for a debate, which often turned into a screaming match or even a physical altercation. Over time, students learned that there was no point in trying to reason with the intruders – neither side could be persuaded. Instead, protesters would either ignore the challengers or start singing "Happy Birthday to You" in English as a way of saying "we agree to disagree." Whenever one person started to sing, others would join in and the growing chorus would usually do the trick and drive the intruders away.

Blue ribbons were motivated either by promises of financial rewards or a personal allegiance to law enforcement, neither of which could be called an ideology. As such, these people were not, and could never be, as strong as the yellow ribbons who were anchored in solid ideological conviction. As history has shown us time and again, personal interests are no match for collective faiths.

The silent majority

Between the blue ribbons and the yellow ribbons were the 50 shades of green[45] – those who fell somewhere between the two. There were the "light blue ribbons" who sided with the government, but found the use of lachrymators and hired thugs a step too far. There were also the "light yellow ribbons" who were sympathetic toward the students but didn't care for the bad traffic and extra commute time.

By far the majority of the population were people who, like Switzerland in the two world wars, declared neutrality toward all things political. To them, a free election would be nice, but they wouldn't bend over backwards to get it. An unofficial poll conducted in early September 2014 showed that over 50% of citizens felt they could live with Beijing's pre-screening electoral design. After all, Hong Kongers went through 156 years of British rule without the right to choose their leaders and the city turned out all right. Neutrality is a time-tested survival skill. Hong Kong is a place to make money and not enemies. Pragmatic citizens know always to stay out of the fight, keep their mouths shut and upset no one.

Refusing to take a position, however, is a position in and of itself. In the minds of the suffragists, the fence-sitters willingly chose indentured servitude over a once-in-a-lifetime opportunity for change. They picked comfortable lies over unpleasant truths. Remember our metaphors about a poker game with a four-card hand and a soccer team with no goalie? The silent majority would rather stay in the game – even though it is unfair, humiliating and impossible to win – than to speak up and risk not being able to play – if you can call that "playing" at all. Netizens

---

45 – Indeed, a group of anti-occupy activists who called themselves "Green Peace" emerged shortly after the start of the movement. They billed themselves as the voice of reason in the polarizing debate between the yellow and blue ribbons. The group was forced to change its name to "Green Harmony" after Greenpeace, the global environmental organization, took legal action against it for trademark infringement.

coined a new derogatory term "***gong chu***" (literally, a Hong Kong pig) to describe those who act like farm animals: thankful to be fed a few times a day despite being locked up in a sty.

The contempt was mutual. To the silent majority, the suffragists were naïve, unrealistic and selfish. They sat on their moral high horse and shoved their political ideals down everyone else's throat. They forgot how hard their parents and grandparents had worked to build the city from the ground up. They refused to accept the fact that Hong Kong was now part of China, whether they liked it or not. If the fence-sitters were the *gong chu*, then these headstrong students were the "***fai ching***" (literally, a useless youth) – people in their 20s who milled around at home and lacked the basic motivation to apply themselves in the real world.

Who was right – the *gong chu* or the *fai ching* – depends on your politics. As my brother Dan likes to say: "a government is only as good as the people it governs." In the case of the silent majority, perhaps they don't deserve to have true democracy. Perhaps the status quo, however unjust and grotesque it seems to some of us, suits them just right. Perhaps it is a collective case of Stockholm Syndrome that makes the abused develop an emotional attachment to the abusers. Perhaps that's why Dan and his family prefer to live in New York City instead of their native Hong Kong.

The Dynamics Within

The word "protesters" is a loose term. Participants in the Umbrella Movement were not a single, monolithic group. Whereas a large portion of them were students, the cast of ten thousand also included volunteers and sympathizers from all walks of life: politicians, journalists, teachers, bankers, artists, retirees, parents and grandparents. Some made the protest sites their new home and built a life around their tents. Others showed up after work and spent hours or just a few minutes there. The occupied areas had no gates or proper entrances. Anyone could come and go as they pleased.

Even though participants were united by their demand for universal suffrage, the porosity of the physical venues and the open-endedness of the campaign at times made the occupy movement disjointed and even incoherent. Each person went there for a different reason, guided by a unique set of motives and political views.

Some found this divergence healthy and inclusive. They argued that "unity for the sake of unity" was not necessarily a good thing. Critics, however, felt that the fragmentation significantly undermined the movement's leverage against Beijing. In an attempt to inject coherence into the leadership, a loose coalition called the "**Five-party Platform**" was formed in mid-October consisting of the Occupy Trio, the pan-dems, the HKFS, Scholarism, and a contingent of community leaders.

The Occupy Trio

Every time government officers urged Benny Tai to put an end to the mass sit-ins, the law professor would respond, "The only one who can make the students go home is you – the government."

Tai was correct on two levels. First, the SAR government was in a better position than anyone to find a way out of the political impasse. It alone had access to the decision makers in Beijing and knew what buttons to push when advising them. Second, Tai had neither the clout nor the authority to call the shots in Admiralty. It wasn't up to him to decide whether the protesters would stay or go. His campaign was over almost as soon as it began – OCLP ended when the first shot of tear gas was fired on September 28th.

In fact, Tai had tried to extricate himself from the occupy movement from the outset. His original plan had been to take over Chater Garden for two to three days, get arrested and spend a few hours in police custody. He and his co-organizers would hold a press conference, give a few interviews and be done with it. The Occupy Trio never intended to engage in a drawn-out war of attrition. They also never intended to engage in any form of resistance. Throughout the occupy movement, they stuck to their mantra of "love and peace" and opposed plans to breach police barricades or take over government buildings. They didn't have the stomach for that sort of thing, nor had they signed up for it.

The trio made no secret of their desire to walk away. As a result, every suggestion they made was second guessed by escalation-prone students. On October 23rd, for instance, Benny Tai and the rest of the Five-party Platform proposed a two-day electronic referendum at all three protest sites to determine the direction of the movement. Hardcore protesters lambasted the idea as a thinly veiled ploy for the leadership to abandon ship. The referendum was ultimately aborted, due to a lack of support and consensus on the ballot questions.

On October 28th, the one-month anniversary of the 9/28 Crackdown, Benny Tai and Chan Kin-man announced that they would spend their last night in Admiralty and would shortly resume teaching at HKU and CUHK. That was their way of resigning from the occupy movement. Then, on December 3rd, a week before the Admiralty protest site was cleared, the Occupy Trio, together with more than 60 other pro-democracy activists, turned themselves in to police, thereby taking responsibility for organizing an unlawful assembly and completing the final step of their civil disobedience campaign. It was an honorable thing to do, and a big sigh of relief for Tai and his friends.

The pan-dems

Like the Occupy Trio, the pan-dems kept a low profile during much of the movement, although for the latter it was more by circumstance than by choice. As much as the movement had caught the authorities off guard, it had also stupefied the pan-dems and thwarted their original plan to use OCLP as a bargaining chip to haggle with Beijing over electoral reform. There was very little appetite for compromise at the protest sites, least of all one that was brokered by these political old-timers. Protesters had always viewed career politicians with distrust and disdain, for fear that these perceived wolves in sheep's clothing would usurp their power and hijack the campaign.

In deference to the students, members of the Democratic Party, the Civic Party, People Power and the LSD all took a backseat. They stepped away from the limelight and provided legal, medical and other assistance to protesters only when sought. None of them participated in – or was invited to – the high-profile 10/21 Talks with senior government officials. When political heavyweights like Martin Lee and Audrey Eu were asked to the address the crowds in Admiralty, they kept their speeches short and punchy to avoid overstaying their welcome. That kind of self-restraint was sensible. Considering that many of the old-timers still had a full-time law practice or Legco drudgery to attend to, warming the bench probably wasn't such a bad thing either.

Like the Occupy Trio, the pan-dems disapproved of escalation. The four tenets of political moderation – peace, rationality, non-violence and no profanity – were never far from their lips. Those words were simply another permutation of Benny Tai's "love and peace" mantra. Their conservative approach to the fight for democracy became the *bête noire* of many protesters and especially the radical splinter groups. The tension was captured by the derisive catch phrase "**wo lay fay fay**," the Cantonese acronym for those four precepts repeated daily at the protest sites by pan-dem lawmakers like Emily Lau and **Alan Leong**.

Team Alexter and G-phone

With both the Occupy Trio and the pan-dems sitting out, the burden of leadership fell on the chief architects of the 9/22 Class Boycott. The HKFS's dynamic duo Alex Chow and Lester Shum, together with

Scholarism's Joshua Wong, assumed de facto control and became the vanguard of the occupy movement.

After the HKFS's stellar performance at the 10/21 Talks, Chow and Shum – affectionately referred to by their female fans as "Alexter" – became the latest social media sensation. Their winning good looks only added to the public infatuation. Numerous Facebook and Instagram fan pages were created to track their every move, whether it was eating lunch, taking a nap or exchanging a sideways glance. More importantly, the duo was granted custody of the **Grand Stage**, the main command center in Admiralty for speeches and important messages. At one point, the HKFS was voted the most popular political group in the city.

Nevertheless, Alexter's charm offensives only carried them so far. After the honeymoon period was over, many organizational problems began to surface, and their halos started to fade. By late October, the movement had hit a snag. Protesters had been camping out on the streets for nearly a month, all the while asking what was to happen next. Even though stories of students doing homework at makeshift libraries and volunteers recycling water bottles into handicrafts were commendable, the core participants felt that the campaign was veering off track. The pressure coming from within, coupled with a reversal of public opinion, left the student leaders with three options: vacate, negotiate, or escalate.

Option one was the most sensible alternative to the pro-democracy camp. Exit at a high point, then regroup, re-strategize and return if necessary. To the hardcore protester, however, it was a non-starter. They viewed it as political self-mutilation – the equivalent of pressing the self-destruct button. Packing it in without any concessions from Beijing would undo everything that everyone had worked so hard for in the past weeks. Call it ego or the fear of losing face, but no one wanted to go home empty-handed.

Option two seemed equally sensible, except that the government and the HKFS had not been on speaking terms since the 10/21 Talks. Given their mutually exclusive positions, there wasn't much to discuss, let alone agree on. To the suffragists, any proposal without a civil nomination option would be considered a compromise on principles. To the authorities, Beijing had made up its mind and dug its heels in. Possible concessions, such as allowing nomination by political parties instead of individual citizens or accepting the 1,200-member Nominating Committee but lowering the nominating threshold from one-half to one-eighth (the way it had been in prior Chief Executive elections), fell on deaf ears on both sides.

Team Alexter: Lester Shum (left) and Alex Chow

That left the student leaders with option three. As is the case for many anti-government uprisings, there is nowhere to go but up. To raise the stakes, the HKFS and Scholarism could take a page from the classic student activism manual: picket, besiege or commandeer government buildings. To pull off a major operation like that requires careful planning, skillful execution and, most of all, public support. Absent a catalyst like the September 28th deployment of tear gas to galvanize the city, any attempt to up the ante would alienate the silent majority and be doomed to fail.

The pros and cons of the three options[46] are summarized in Table 9 overleaf. The student leaders were being pulled in different directions and toggling between competing strategies. They knew full well that no matter which course they chose, they would not be able to please everybody. They just had to choose carefully who they wanted to upset.

---

46 – For the sake of completeness, there were also talks of an "Option 1½" – partial evacuation – to minimize disruption to the city without giving up too much ground. This option involved protesters voluntarily vacating Mongkok and Causeway Bay and focusing on Admiralty. They would also open one lane on Harcourt Road to allow limited traffic to flow through. Option 1½ was considered a cop-out among the core protesters and failed to gain traction.

Option	Pros	Cons	Favored by
Vacate: Bow out voluntarily and gracefully	• Would allow an exit at a high point and on the protesters' own terms. • Would provide a bloodless end to a drawn-out campaign. • Would give protesters a chance to recuperate, reflect and regroup before launching the next pro-democracy campaign.	• Failure to make any tangible political gains. • Fear that the occupy movement was a "now or never" proposition, and that citizens would unlikely return in the same numbers and with the same passion the next time around.	• Occupy Trio and the pan-dems • The general public • The SAR government and Beijing
Negotiate: Discuss compromise solutions, such as nomination by political parties or lowering the nominating threshold	• Non-violent. • Would have the highest chance of achieving tangible political results.	• Been there, done that: the 10/21 Talks did not result in any actionable plans. • The SAR government was not authorized to make meaningful concessions. • Any concession made by the student leaders would be considered a compromise on principles.	• Academics • Political commentators

| *Escalate:* | • Would offer the most leverage against Beijing. | • Would lose wider public support. | • Core protesters |
| Raise the stakes with a concrete plan of attack, e.g. picketing government offices or taking over the Legco | • Would energize the occupy movement. • Would give a legitimate reason to end the movement if efforts failed. | • Might involve violence and casualties. • Would increase the chance of arrest and criminal conviction. • Had a low chance of success given police presence and lack of public support. | • Radical splinter groups |

Table 9. Pros and cons of each of the three options facing the student leaders

The core

They were the backbone and they were the limbs. They were the warriors and they were the villagers. They were the people everyone referred to as the "protesters" – people who varied as much in age and education level as they did in motivation and aspirations (see Figure 8).

The core was made up of self-organized and self-governing students and volunteers who took up odd jobs in the occupied areas: manning a supply station, keeping watch on a frontline or making furniture from scrap wood and metal. Those with specific skills were given badges and walkie-talkies to be medics or marshals. As individuals, they were anonymous and vulnerable; but together, they were a formidable force to reckon with. Unity gave them the strength to keep both police officers and Triad members at bay and put pressure on the Grand Stage to stay on message.

The media frenzy surrounding the Umbrella Movement attracted not only reporters and paparazzi, but also special interest groups each clamoring for attention and wanting its pound of flesh. Admiralty became an ersatz people's court to address a hodgepodge of political grievances, from racial inequality and lack of disability rights to ending one-party rule in China. Wary of mission creep, core protesters reminded each other to focus on nothing else but the one thing that truly mattered – electoral reform in

Hong Kong. There was a poignant refrain at the protest sites: "Forget not why you are here!"

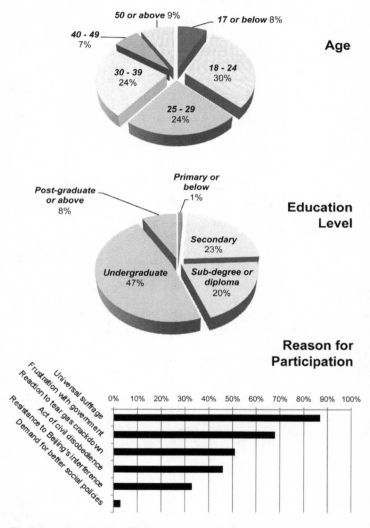

Based on surveys conducted by political science researchers Edmund Cheng and Samson Yuen at all three encampments between October 20th and 26th, 2014.

Figure 8. Demographic breakdown of the protesters

The core was particularly leery of politicians coming in and offering advice and assistance. Protesters made clear to the pan-dems that they would not be told what to do or made political pawns of. The merger between OCLP and the 9/22 Class Boycott on September 28th made strange bedfellows of veteran politicians and headstrong students. The arrival of the Occupy Trio at Tamar that night angered half the student protesters, who threatened to quit the campaign and prompted Long Hair to prostrate himself in public and beg them to stay. At various stages of the movement, strategists repeatedly advised a dignified withdrawal so protesters could regroup and re-launch the campaign on another day. The core group did not want to hear any of it. They did not believe in incremental wins, or that victory came in phases.

Furthermore, protesters fundamentally disagreed with the old timers' *wo lay fay fay* approach. To be fair, the pan-dems had been in the fight for democracy since the 1980s, but none of them had much to show for it. What the students achieved in terms of media buzz and civic education in a few weeks far exceeded what the well-funded, well-organized political parties had accomplished in decades. The pan-dems' finger-wagging and high school debate team tactics on the Legco floor, hamstrung by their innate risk aversion and hidden political calculations, were perpetuating the status quo rather than dismantling it.

The core was also growing impatient with the student leadership. Protesters believed that escalation – operations that involved a tolerable level of violence and causalities – was the only real leverage they had against Beijing. But they needed someone to lead them. With the student leaders dragging their feet and looking increasingly disoriented, the core group felt more alone and restless than ever, and their emotional void would soon be filled by a new political force.

The splinter groups

The Communists were not the only ones grappling with factional infighting – there was plenty of that going around in Admiralty also. The term "splinter groups" refers to a concoction of loosely organized radical coalitions, many of whom have broken away from the pan-dem parties. Like the right-wing populist movement in Europe, these new opposition voices – known as the **localists** – are anti-immigration, anti-government and pro-independence.

Among the many groups that fall within that category, the best-known and most active at the time of the occupy movement was **Civic Passion**, headed by provocateur and ex-People Power member **Wong Yeung-tat**. Their mission is to resist the growing mainland influence in the city, protect Hong Kong's autonomy, and eventually establish an independent city-state (even though the third prong has nearly zero support from mainstream society). The localists systematically go after their enemies, and their targets run the gamut of parallel traders, Chinese immigrants, government officials, anyone in the pro-Beijing camp, and the pan-dems who get in their way.

Splinter groups are known to cyber-bully opponents, heckle at Mandarin-speaking tourists, and fly the Union Jack at street rallies to spite the Communists. Reasoned debate is not for them; effigy burning is more their thing. To their supporters, they are freedom fighters and the best hope for Hong Kong. To their critics, they are insidious, irresponsible and dangerous – for they will always choose scorched earth over common ground.

One of the localists' favorite words is "**leftard**" – left-wing to the point of stupidity and self-delusion – and they use it to alternately denigrate and denounce the pan-dems. Every old trick in the pan-dems' playbook, from shouting slogans and singing pro-democracy songs to organizing commemorations of the Tiananmen Square Massacre, is pointless in the eyes of the localists, because these activities achieve nothing other than making the leftards feel good about themselves. By contrast, the only people who aren't leftards are the localists: real warriors who take real action, such as hurling water bottles at police officers and harassing mainlanders.

In the early hours of November 19th, Day 53, a small army of masked men gathered outside the Legco Building in protest of a copyright amendment bill that they feared would limit freedom of expression on the Internet. The angry men, some of them members of Civic Passion, smashed a pair of glass doors at the building's north entrance and urged other protesters nearby to occupy the legislature. Not sure whether to take orders from these strangers, the students notified the site marshals instead. Minutes later, police moved in with pepper spray and batons, and the agitators fled the scene.

The clumsy **11/19 Wreck-and-run** touched off a political firestorm for the occupy movement. After the incident, localist groups began showing up in Admiralty every night to settle the scores for what happened that night. The challengers questioned the HKFS's ability to lead and the marshals' legitimacy to thwart their operations. They argued that Alex Chow and his college buddies were all leftards just like the pan-dems – they had grown far too comfortable sleeping in their tents and were standing in the way of the fight for democracy. The rhetoric resonated with many (albeit not all) within the core group, who had waited long enough for someone to take the movement up a notch.

The emergence of localism created a protest within the protest, and a revolution within the revolution. If unity had been the suffragists' greatest strength, then it proved to be elusive and, if obtained, short-lived. The splinter groups laid bare a critical question facing the core protesters: *how will it all end?*

The final showdown

Feeling the heat from the core group, on the evening of November 30th, Day 64, the HKFS finally made the long-awaited announcement about an escalation plan. That evening, student leader Nathan Law called on protesters to breach police barricades on Lung Wo Road and lay siege to the Tamar Government Headquarters. Thousands came out in force and assembled at Tamar Park ready for battle. Protesters knew it would be their last opportunity to make something happen. They had to make it count.

Without a proper plan of attack or clear instructions from the HKFS, the 4,000 protesters were quickly overrun by an equal number of police officers mobilized to foil the operation. The latter responded with pepper spray, batons and water cannons. Outgunned and outplayed, the **11/30 Tamar Siege** was an utter disaster for the HKFS. The following day, Alex Chow was asked by a reporter to explain himself. Chow replied, rather blithely, "I did it to prove to the radicals that escalation doesn't always work." Bad idea.

The 11/30 Tamar Siege represented the HKFS's last ditch attempt to revive a languishing campaign. Instead, the movement's final throes left the core group feeling disillusioned and betrayed. The political stardom of Alex Chow and Lester Shum, however promising at first, proved to be just 15 minutes of fame. Some of the criticism leveled against them was clearly justified, such as the botched Tamar siege and the insensitive remark the following day. Nevertheless, it is easy to forget that these de facto leaders were university students without any political, much less combat, training. They were sailing into uncharted waters just like everyone else, but were suddenly thrown into the cockpit to pilot a massive political movement with impossible expectations. Just the same, in the age of keyboard activism and online shaming, public opinion – like the sea wind – can change direction in the blink of an eye. One minute you are the people's hero; the next, a villain.

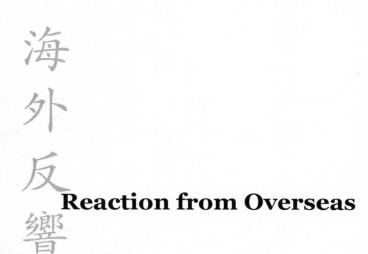

Reaction from Overseas

The Umbrella Movement was the largest pro-democracy uprising on Chinese soil since the Tiananmen Square Protests. Shock waves emanating from this tiny coastal city were felt around the globe, from protest-prone Thailand to Ukraine and Turkey, where the wounds of a popular revolt were still fresh. Rallies and candlelight vigils in support of the suffragists in Hong Kong were held in an estimated 64 cities worldwide, including New York, Los Angeles, London, Paris, Copenhagen, Sydney, Taipei and Kuala Lumpur. The movement even resonated with people half the world away in Ferguson, Missouri, where only two months earlier the shooting death of an African American teenage boy by a police officer had sparked weeks of street violence.

During those fateful months in 2014, ordinary citizens in Hong Kong were bombarded with a barrage of email and text messages from overseas – friends, co-workers and long-lost schoolmates – asking them what was happening and offering words of encouragement. Not since the SARS outbreak in 2003 had the city experienced such an outpouring of support from abroad. Well-wishers were always appreciated, and sometimes also amusing, with advice such as "Don't be a hero and stand in front of a tank."

But it was a shout-out on the least expected of occasions that drew the most praise from citizens. At the 87th Academy Awards ceremony (which was held two months after the movement ended), singer-songwriter John Legend and rapper Common made an explicit reference to the struggles in Hong Kong, when the duo recalled a chapter of the American Civil Rights Movement that unfolded on the Edmund Pettus Bridge in Selma, Alabama:

*"The spirit of this bridge connects the kid from the south side of Chicago dreaming of a better life to those in France standing up for their freedom of expression to **the people in Hong Kong protesting for democracy**."* (emphasis added)

Those eight simple words, uttered in no more than three seconds, were enough to move half the city to tears.

Mainland China

While the international community rallied behind the Umbrella Movement, China joined a handful of autocratic regimes in the world – countries like North Korea and Singapore – in condemning the unlawful protests.

Years of practice from suppressing Tibetan and Uighur separatists have made the CCP exceedingly efficient in snuffing out organized protests on the mainland before they begin. With state-controlled Internet service providers and the "Great Firewall of China" at full throttle, the Chinese government can block website content and intercept search engines at the push of a button, especially on politically sensitive days like June 4th or anniversaries of mishandled natural disasters. The regime commands an army of Internet police who work around the clock to monitor blogs, chat rooms and instant messaging sites. The annual budget for homeland security – or euphemistically called "**stability maintenance projects**" – topped RMB200 billion (US$32 billion) in 2014.

During the 2011 Jasmine Revolution in Egypt, pro-democracy activists in mainland China who attempted to replicate the campaign back home were summarily arrested. Public gatherings were dispersed and flower markets in major cities forbidden from selling jasmines altogether. Searches on Baidu – China's version of Google – using any sensitive words such as "Egypt," "Cairo" or "jasmine" would come back with a "no results found" blank screen.

Three years later, Big Brother was once again at the ready to crush any copycat uprisings on the mainland. Words like "umbrella," "occupy" and "tear gas" were filtered and Instagram was disabled, joining Facebook and Twitter on the long list of social media sites blocked by the Great Firewall. WeChat and Weibo – China's version of WhatsApp and Twitter, respectively – were interrupted frequently to prevent mainlanders working or studying in Hong Kong from sending home "harmful information" such as snapshots and updates from the protest sites.

Amnesty International reported that dozens of Chinese citizens across the country had been arrested for openly supporting the uprising in Hong Kong[47]. In the case of one Wang Li, a protest-inspired poetry reading and a few selfies with an umbrella were enough to get his home ransacked and family members harassed. Stories like that put everyone on guard, prompting mainland tourists in Hong Kong to speak in code if they wanted to visit one of the protest sites out of curiosity. Before heading to Harcourt Road or Yee Wo Street, they would tell friends and family that they were going to "shop for an iPhone 6[48]."

In the meantime, state-owned media on the mainland went on the offensive. The *People's Daily* put out vitriolic editorials, condemning the occupy movement as a "criminal activity" and a "color revolution," and warned Hong Kongers of "deaths and injuries" and other "unimaginable consequences." CCP-controlled *Global Times* took it one step further and called the protesters "enemies of the State."

Apart from rhetoric, state media echoed pro-Beijing newspapers in Hong Kong and published unsubstantiated predictions of property market crashes (citizens' worst nightmare) and economic losses (in the billions of U.S. dollars). They flung out baseless allegations that student leaders and the Occupy Trio were tools of foreign governments employed to subvert the Chinese government. On the CCTV evening news, a reporter interviewed an impostor Hong Kong citizen on Harcourt Road who, in Mandarin-inflected Cantonese, confessed that she had accepted a HK$2,500 (US$320) payment to participate in the sit-in.

With the state propaganda machine in overdrive, the average mainlander was led to believe that Hong Kong had descended into an anarchy where rebels were running around the city attacking police officers in broad

---

47 – Depending on the subject matter and local practice, the mainland authorities are known to operate on a "three strikes, you're out" protocol toward keyboard activists. Those who post politically sensitive materials on social media will have the contents taken down by the service provider – that's a cue for them to cease and desist. The second offense will invite a phone call or personal visit from a community leader or the *gong'an* to "encourage" discretion. The third offense will bring harassment, beating or detention.

48 – Like freedom of assembly, the new iPhone 6 was available in Hong Kong but not elsewhere in China when it was first launched in September 2014.

daylight. The cause? Jealousy and insecurity, of course. State media portrayed the suffragists as spoiled brats who felt increasingly threatened by China's economic ascent and decided to take out their frustration on the authorities.

All that Orwellian newspeak matched up perfectly with what many mainlanders already thought of their Hong Kong cousins: arrogant worshippers of the West. In their minds, people in the SAR enjoyed far more freedoms than anyone else in China, but they wanted still more. Such perceived ingratitude, combined with damning evidence of the frequent harassment of mainland tourists by fringe radicals on the streets of Hong Kong, corroborated the state media's smear campaign. That's why critics of the localism movement, including Benny Tai, argued that those anti-mainlander rallies were not only racist and disgraceful, they were also hurting the pro-democracy efforts in Hong Kong. Had there not been so much hostility and distrust between the two peoples, mainlanders might have reacted more sympathetically toward the protesters in Hong Kong. And if enough of them had organized themselves and come out in solidarity, the Umbrella Movement might have had a very different outcome.

Taiwan

Across the strait, on the island of Formosa, 23 million people watched with great personal interest the unfolding events in Hong Kong. A single thought was on everyone's mind: *Hong Kong today will be Taiwan tomorrow.*

Only a few months earlier, Taiwanese students went through a political uprising of their own. In March 2014, scores of university students stormed the legislature in Taipei and commandeered the entire building. They were angry about the way the KMT, the country's ruling party, had tried to hastily pass a controversial trade agreement with mainland China without proper vetting by legislators. Over 10,000 students and volunteers participated in the so-called **Sunflower Movement**, the largest student-led protest in the country's 65-year history.

Many Taiwanese people viewed the trade agreement, known as **CSSTA**, as another step in Beijing's gradual annexation of the island. They feared that mainland Chinese companies backed by the Communist machine would slowly buy up Taiwanese assets and put the country's economy and national security at risk. They didn't need to look far. That kind of creeping economic imperialism was already happening in Hong Kong.

After weeks of standoff, **Ma Ying-jeou**, Taiwan's President and the KMT's Chairman at the time, eventually caved in to public pressure and withdrew CSSTA from the legislature. The Sunflower Movement was considered a major victory for student activism in Taiwan. It also made the two young leaders, Lin Fei-fan and Chen Wei-ting, national heroes and pop idols.

The student-led movement in Taiwan prompted Chinese President Xi Jinping to ratchet up the reunification rhetoric, something that party leaders had not done in many years. Just weeks before the Umbrella Movement erupted, Xi issued a statement about Beijing's unwavering determination to replicate the "one country, two systems" formula for Taiwan. The statement was not only poorly timed given the looming political showdown in Hong Kong, but it also put his Taiwanese counterpart Ma in a tight spot at a time when he was still struggling to heal the wounds of the Sunflower Movement.

On September 29th, the day after the 9/28 Crackdown in Admiralty, Lin Fei-fan and Chen Wei-ting organized a demonstration in Taipei in support of their Hong Kong comrades. As early as June, the SAR government had already denied them entry to Hong Kong for fear that their star power would add fuel to OCLP or related activities. The government's worries were well-placed – before there was Team Alexter, Team Lin-Chen had already captured the hearts of many young girls in Hong Kong.

The impact of the Umbrella Movement on Taiwanese politics was profound. It was a searing reminder to the CCP that what they did on one island could have serious ramifications on another. On November 29th, voters in Taiwan went to the polls to elect their mayors and other local representatives. The results of the so-called "9-in-1 elections" were devastating for the KMT, which lost many of its traditional strongholds to the main opposition. The elections were widely regarded as a referendum on Ma's administration and his mainland-friendly policies. They were also an important predictor for the Taiwanese presidential elections in 2016. The KMT's bruising defeat in the municipal elections underscored the growing Sinophobia in Taiwan as a result of Beijing's mishandling of the electoral reform in Hong Kong. Jiho Chang, a prominent Taiwanese activist and one of the leaders the Sunflower Movement, put it best: "What is happening in Hong Kong has torn China and Taiwan asunder. We now know that Beijing will break its promises on anything."

International response

People around the world embraced the Umbrella Movement without hesitation or reservation. To many of them, China was guilty until proven innocent because of its tattered human rights record. When they thought about the country, they associated it with the Tiananmen Square Massacre and the invasion of Tibet. The more informed individuals knew the harrowing stories of dissidents like Ai Weiwei, Liu Xiaobo and Chen Guangcheng[49]. It didn't take a Sinophobe to believe that the Chinese government would stop at nothing to sabotage the right to free elections in Hong Kong. The only question was how hard the authorities would come down on those who dared fight for it.

The international community also took to the student protesters right away. Those nerdy, scrawny kids went from zeroes to heroes overnight, rebranding themselves as role models for young activists around the world. They braved police crackdowns for their political ideals, but were never too busy to clean up after themselves or keep each other well-fed. The occupy movement was bloodless, but it was also spotless and selfless. No wonder the foreign press called this "the most civilized street protest in the world." The international handbook on how to stage a peaceful political movement will likely have pictures of Harcourt Road in its next 50 editions.

Nevertheless, reaction at the diplomatic level was far from enthusiastic. Foreign governments had no interest in ruffling China's feathers and jeopardizing important trade relations, not least over an Asian city that they could barely locate on the map. In the United States, then Secretary of State John Kerry muttered something about having "high hopes" that the Hong Kong government would exercise restraint toward suffragists. When then President Barack Obama attended the APEC Summit in Beijing, he denied any American involvement in the occupy movement, and did not explicitly offer his support for the students. "These are issues ultimately for the people of Hong Kong and China to decide," Obama punted.

Across the Atlantic in Germany, Chancellor Angela Merkel rolled out the red carpet for Premier Li Keqiang and received him in Berlin with great fanfare. To avoid offending her guest, Merkel made only a short, generic remark about the importance of freedom of speech but otherwise kept her lips sealed. The other G7 members – France, Italy, Canada

---

49 – Ai Weiwei is an internationally renowned artist-provocateur who has been the subject of constant harassment by the authorities for speaking out against social injustices, including shoddy building construction that killed tens of thousands during the 2008 Sichuan Earthquake. Liu Xiaobo, human rights activist and winner of the 2010 Nobel Peace Prize, was sentenced to 11 years in prison for co-authoring a manifesto calling for political pluralism in China. He died from liver cancer in 2017 while incarcerated. Chen Guangcheng, a blind self-taught lawyer, was placed under house arrest for helping women subject to forced abortions and sterilizations, before he fled to the United States in 2012.

and Japan – were equally muted, with the exception of Britain, which perhaps felt a pang of guilt toward its former colony. When addressing his parliament, then Prime Minister David Cameron invoked the Joint Declaration and urged legislators to "stand up for the rights of Hong Kong people." Chris Patten, the beloved last Governor of Hong Kong who went by the endearing nickname "Fat Pat," also jumped into the fray. He referred to the electoral design stipulated in the 8/31 Framework as "Iranian-style," and maintained that the British Parliament had "a moral obligation to continue to check on whether China [was] keeping its side of the bargain."

A CNN cameraman films a pair of protesters

For the first few weeks of the occupy movement, attention from the international press was overwhelming. Mere hours after the 9/28 Crackdown, correspondents from around the world descended on Admiralty and Mongkok like moths drawn to the flame. The alphabet soup of foreign media – CNN, BBC, NHK, AP and VoA – all set up reporting stations on footbridges and other elevated places in the occupied zones. In the days that followed, news crews from Tokyo, Seoul, Bangkok, Manila, Toronto and São Paulo were spotted all along Harcourt Road. It seemed that the whole world suddenly cared about Hong Kong.

As the protests dragged on, however, the novelty wore off and interest started to fade. Other headlines such as the Ebola outbreak in West Africa and American comedian Bill Crosby's rape scandal took over. Moreover, the Western media – in particular the American press – needed to spin a story that was easily understood by their readers. That meant coverage had to be dumbed down to a simple David-versus-Goliath Hollywood plot starring umbrella-brandishing teenage heroes. The fact that the protesters were not a unified group, or that the movement received limited popular support, was conveniently left out to avoid complicating the narrative. In the age of sensationalist journalism, the absence of bloodshed or an all-out regime change (like the ones in Egypt and Ukraine) also made it difficult to sell papers or excite primetime viewers. Eventually, the news cycle passed and the news story fizzled out.

Hong Kong people are pragmatic and we understand pragmatism better than anyone else. We understand that foreign governments and the international press have their own constituencies and viewership to appeal to, as well as political and financial calculations to consider. At the end of the day, these so-called "strategic moralists" are more interested in attacking China than rooting for Hong Kong. Their support is a nice-to-have but not something we can or should count on. That's why there was another popular refrain at the protest sites: "This is our problem and we will solve it ourselves!"

Part 3

Full Bloom

"To each there comes in their lifetime a special moment
when they are figuratively tapped on the shoulder
and offered the chance to do a very special thing."

– Winston S. Churchill

A Tale of Three Villages

They call it the "Global Village." The three great inventions of the 21st century – smart phones, wireless networks, and social media – are meant to bring everyone closer together. In truth, people today feel more alienated and disconnected than previous generations that didn't have any of those things. In an alpha city like Hong Kong, where the rat race is our national sport and moneymaking a favorite pastime, the word "community" no longer means neighbors and friendly hellos, but chat groups and business networks. Phone calls and business cards are so last century when WhatsApp and LinkedIn are a finger tap away.

But then, a change.

We called it the "Umbrella Village." The three occupied areas[50] – Admiralty, Mongkok and Causeway Bay – were summed up in a single phrase. Its very name was a term of endearment, and the mere sound of it conjured up grainy images of old sampans and rusted tricycles. Long before there were skyscrapers and highways, we had communities. And therein lived the people.

---

50 – At its height, the Umbrella Movement saw protesters blocking major thoroughfares across Hong Kong Island and Kowloon Peninsula, creating pockets of community not only in the three main sites but also in Tsim Sha Tsui and Wanchai, in each case only for a day or two.

Harcourt Village

Admiralty was where the movement began on the fateful day of September 28th. By square footage and the level of organization, it was the big brother of the three siblings. In the heart of downtown Hong Kong, the area stretched along Harcourt Road and Connaught Road, bordered by Pedder Street to the west, Arsenal Street to the east, Queensway to the south and Lung Wo Road to the north (see Figure 9). The perimeter was not static and continued to be chipped away by law enforcement over the course of the movement. For instance, Queensway – a tram-tracked artery that connects Central to Wanchai – was reopened by police in mid-October.

Three protest sites, unique in their own ways

The hilly landscape provided by the arched Harcourt Road expressway added drama to the village and created impressive lookout points for both the media and visitors. The site was also strategic in a military sense. There were footbridges and highlands – such as Tamar Park – where protesters could keep watch of advancing police and thugs. Unlike the dense city grids in Mongkok and Causeway Bay, the Admiralty area was open and porous, which in turn provided numerous escape routes for protesters to evacuate and spread out in the event of a mass arrest.

Finally, its proximity to Central attracted droves of office workers to pop by and hang out during lunch time and after hours.

Admiralty also boasted the largest tent city, thanks to Joshua Wong who in the second week called on protesters to bring their camping gear in preparation for a prolonged struggle. If the umbrellas were likened to flower blossoms, then the dome-shaped tents would be like wild mushrooms – hundreds of them springing up all over Harcourt Road and around the Tamar Government Headquarters.

The critical mass of overnight campers helped to spawn a thriving community, and the campground gradually evolved into a self-sufficient town. There was a study room and library, several public bathrooms, makeshift shower facilities, a barber shop, outdoor galleries of umbrella-inspired art, phone-charging service centers, first-aid triages, and numerous supply stations that rationed food, drinks and other daily necessities free of charge. In the heart of the village stood the Grand Stage, which functioned as a command center and a town square for speeches and public announcements. To put a cherry on top, there was even an organic farm converted from a dug up sidewalk.

Admiralty was a city within a city. Villagers could spend weeks there without ever setting foot beyond its borders. The area was so vast and complex that a billboard-sized wall map was created to guide visitors. The map was affectionately titled *Along the River in Admiralty*, named after the iconic 11th century Chinese scroll painting *Along the River During the Qingming Festival*.

Nathan Village

Mongkok, or MK for short, is a rough neighborhood on a good day, a cross between Harajuku in Tokyo and the Bronx in New York City. It is where shopping malls tower over decades-old tenement buildings, where young buskers belt out Cantopop hits next to a 55-year-old hula-hooper, and where mafia bosses patrol the streets to check on their seedy bars, nightclubs and massage parlors. Former Security Secretary Regina Ip called it a "very sleazy part of Hong Kong."

The occupied area in this working class neighborhood took the shape of a cross formed by the intersecting Nathan Road and Argyle Street. It took up a half dozen city blocks on Nathan Road between Mongkok Road to the north and Shantung Street to south, and four blocks of Argyle Street between Shanghai Street to the west and Tung Choi Street to the east (see Figure 10). The long and narrow geographical configuration was not conducive to a sprawling tent city like the one in Admiralty. Instead,

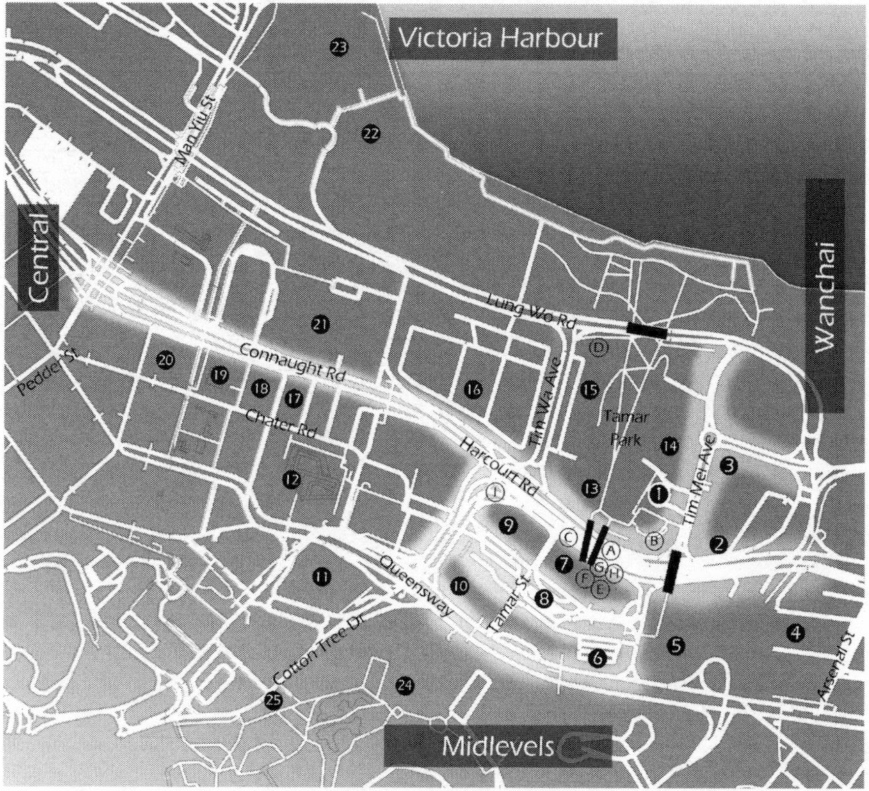

Ⓐ Grand Stage
Ⓑ Lennon Wall
Ⓒ Study Corner
Ⓓ Dark Corner
Beating
Ⓔ KFC
Ⓕ McDonald's
Ⓖ G1 Supply Station
Ⓗ Admiralty Centre
Medical Station
Ⓘ A7 First Aid Booth

▮ Bridge/Tunnel

❶ Civic Square
❷ Red Cross Building
❸ CITIC Tower
❹ Police Headquarters
❺ Harcourt Garden
❻ United Centre
❼ Admiralty Centre
❽ Queensway Plaza
❾ Far East Finance Centre
❿ Lippo Centre
⓫ Bank of China Tower
⓬ Chater Garden
⓭ Tamar Government Headquarters
⓮ Legco Building
⓯ Chief Executive's Office
⓰ PLA Barracks
⓱ Hong Kong Club
⓲ World War II Memorial
⓳ Statue Square
⓴ Mandarin Oriental Hotel
㉑ City Hall
㉒ AIA Carnival
㉓ Hong Kong Observation Wheel
㉔ Hong Kong Park
㉕ Hong Kong Park Sports Centre

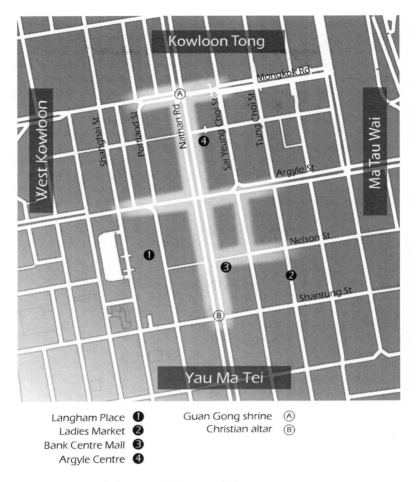

Langham Place ❶   Guan Gong shrine Ⓐ
Ladies Market ❷   Christian altar Ⓑ
Bank Centre Mall ❸
Argyle Centre ❹

Figure 9 (opposite). Map of Harcourt Village
Figure 10 (above). Map of Nathan Village

there was a cluster of sofas, bunk beds and makeshift sleeping quarters covered by tarpaulins.

If Admiralty was the big brother among the three villages, then MK was the tough middle child. It did not receive the same level of media attention, and sightings of political celebrities were rare. There was no Grand Stage, just a speakers' corner with two microphones for street debates. The area, having long been associated with Triad activities, bore the brunt of the thug attacks during much of the occupy movement.

While campers in Admiralty hung out in hoodies and cargo pants, MK fighters wore hard hats and body armor made from foam mats. While college students hunkered down at night to do homework on Harcourt Road, topless tattooed men climbed on top of subway station exits to keep the night watch. And while student leaders addressed a cheering crowd on the Grand Stage every night at 8:00, they held little sway with protesters on Nathan Road. There were "HKFS doesn't represent me" posters all over MK, compliments of the many splinter groups active in the area.

Nathan Village had a cult following. Hardcore protesters preferred it to the other two sites because of its rawness, grit and diversity. Compared to the prim and proper Harcourt Villagers, their Mongkok counterparts cut a different figure and ran the gamut from storekeepers and retirees to hardened gang members[51]. Some of the characters were lifted straight out of the bar scene from *Star Wars*. Whereas police and organized thugs only occasionally set foot in Admiralty, violent clashes happened nearly daily around the Nathan-Argyle intersection. One of the bloodiest confrontations took place on the weekend of October 17th, Day 20, when protesters tried to reoccupy a section of Shantung Street that was cleared by the police the night before. During the three-day **10/17 Mongkok Operation**, baton-wielding officers came down on the students with all the strength they could muster – on the head, on the limb, and on the back – like a birthday boy with his piñata. MK was not for the faint of heart; it was the real deal.

Yee Wo Village

The littlest of the three, the area in the heart of a bustling shopping district was the size of a standard swimming pool. It took up a small section of Hennessy Road and Yee Wo Street in Causeway Bay, between Percival Street to the west and Sugar Street to the east (see Figure 11). The village had a few bookshelves, a handicraft studio, a supply booth and a few dozen tents. A speakers' corner, minuscule compared to the one in Mongkok, was set up outside Sogo department store where activists held teach-ins to a thin crowd. Later in the movement, there was a modest outdoor exhibition featuring protest-themed photography.

Yee Wo Village had the advantage of being a stone's throw away from megamalls such as Times Square and Hysan Place, where protesters could find food and use the bathroom. Its location in the heart of a shopping mecca allowed it to reach an audience of mainland Chinese

---

51 – Not all gang members were blue ribbons or hired thugs. Many supported the student protesters out of a sense of social justice despite their affiliation with organized crime rings.

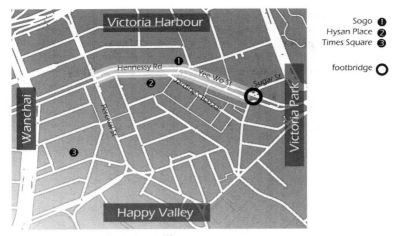

Figure 11. Map of Yee Wo Village

tourists, to whom the idea of an anti-government uprising remained foreign, if not altogether unthinkable. While most of them took pictures and walked away, a few would lean in to read some of the placards and confer with one another in hushed tone. Despite its diminutive size, the enclave echoed a loud message of dissent and defiance to those who kept to themselves back home.

Causeway Bay was dubbed the "forgotten site" because its crowds were small and media attention was close to zero. Sometimes a low profile has its benefits: Yee Wo Village ended up outlasting the other two – it held its ground for four more days after Admiralty was cleared on Day 75.

*   *   *

To use a New York City analogy, Admiralty, Mongkok and Causeway Bay were the equivalent of Midtown, the Bronx and Times Square. Each site had its own quirks, character and strategic importance. Admiralty was the nucleus, Mongkok the battleground, and Causeway Bay an outdoor classroom for the tens of thousands of mainland tourists who passed through every day.

Protesters defended all three encampments with equal fervor, treating them as links in a chain that united the occupy movement. The rupture of one would spell trouble for all. Villagers believed in a prophecy: *when one site falls, so will the others.*

Hong Kong 2.0

For tens of thousands of Hong Kong teenagers, childhood was canceled in the fall of 2014. They had to grow up overnight to lead a hard-fought and at times violent struggle for true democracy. Still, the Umbrella Movement was more than just police standoffs and sleepless nights. By taking over large swaths of the city center, these young warriors reenacted a way of life known only to their grandparents – a slower, sleepier, more romantic Hong Kong.

Harcourt Village – or Umbrellaville as I preferred to call it to give it more panache – was easily the most beautiful place in Hong Kong. It was where I spent nearly every evening during the week and all day on the weekend. It was where I ate and frequently slept, observed and reported, taught and learned, saw old friends and met new ones. For 11 weeks, it was my primary residence.

A new way of living

As an author who writes almost exclusively about Hong Kong, who makes a living from pointing out the proverbial elephants in the room, I am the city's biggest fan and its harshest critic. I have said that people in Hong Kong can be divided into two broad categories: selfish and very selfish. I have written about the double trouble of ***gong hai*** – the trophy generation raised by domestic workers and spoiled rotten by middle class parents – and *fai ching* – people born after the 1990s who live off their family and lack direction in life.

If everyone has two sides to his personality, then for 79 days in 2014, it appeared that our good side – the part of us that is suppressed by life's demands – broke loose. Everything that every cynic has ever written about the people of Hong Kong, every indictment and criticism ever leveled against its youth, demanded a rewrite.

Volunteerism – The slogan "If not me, who? If not now, when?" summed up the can-do spirit in Umbrellaville. Villagers distributed supplies, directed pedestrian traffic and even cleaned public toilets, without being asked or prompted. If someone saw so much as a chewing gum splotch on the sidewalk, he would quietly pick up a putty knife and start scraping. Soon, two others like him would join in and a fledgling gum removal team would spring to life.

Across the three villages, everyone pitched in whatever way they could. Doctors treated the injured, lawyers advised the arrested, carpenters made furniture, construction workers built bamboo scaffolding[52], musicians played music, bankers gave money, teachers taught, counselors counseled, mothers cooked, grandmothers knitted. Outside the villages in mountains far far away, climbers risked their lives and hung giant pro-democracy banners from cloud-hugging cliffs.

Inclusiveness – In Umbrellaville, age was no indication of rank, and being different was no barrier to social acceptance. On the Grand Stage, student leaders commanded more clout than political veterans. Off the stage, people of all races and creeds sat side by side in discussion groups, turning Harcourt Road into the cover of a liberal college's recruitment brochure. Cantopop stars Anthony Wong and Denise Ho, both of whom happen to be openly gay, attracted bigger crowds than other celebrities.

The Hong Kong Pride Parade held every early November typically draws less than 100 participants. In 2014, however, the turnout surged to several thousand, in large part because of two new heterosexual supporters: Alex Chow and Lester Shum. Their famous bromance – thanks to G-phone's tireless matchmaking – was a favorite topic in Admiralty. The good-natured tease about their so-called "hehe" relationship (a concatenation of two masculine pronouns) was remarkable considering that the subject matter of sexual orientation remains taboo in socially conservative Hong Kong. Homophobia – and other kinds of prejudice – appeared to have no place in Umbrellaville.

---

52 – Bamboo scaffolding is an age-old construction technique in southern China, dating back centuries. Even today, bamboo scaffolds are widely used in lieu of steel structures in property development projects across Hong Kong. During the occupy movement, volunteer construction workers used their time-tested skill to build barricades, many of them several stories high, to reinforce protest zone borders.

Sense of community – Umbrellaville harkened back to the old Hong Kong we loved and missed. All along Harcourt Road, micro-communities emerged where people smiled, the streets were inviting, and the nights – the nights were just beautiful. There were no colleagues to compete with, no bosses to impress, and no bank statements to measure one's self-worth. The occupy movement forced all of us to take a long, hard look at our way of life, and to challenge the conventional wisdom that social progress is achievable only through greater affluence and more development. There is a simpler, easier way that doesn't require either a credit card or a fast car.

Indeed, carlessness has its perks. In Admiralty and Mongkok, we saw people riding their bicycles and scooters on main roads and highways. We couldn't remember the last time we saw bicycles and scooters on main roads and highways. When night fell, we saw strangers sitting in circles and chatting on the street. We couldn't remember the last time we saw strangers sitting in circles and chatting on the street. These simple activities may be commonplace anywhere else in the world, but they have all but gone extinct in emotionally unavailable and socially awkward Hong Kong since it transformed from a cottage industry economy into a global financial center.

A renewed sense of community in Umbrellaville

Sex and the city – It was said that more condoms were sold in Admiralty than anywhere else in the city and during those 11 weeks than the rest of 2014 combined. That's a remarkable feat given that Hong Kong is often called the sexless city – a recent study ranked it the third lowest in sexual satisfaction out of two dozen territories surveyed. The tent city in Umbrellaville – and the scenic waterfront nearby – proved to be highly conducive to love and romance, especially for young people with raging hormones and a sense of adventure. The equal parts Woodstock and spring break atmosphere set the mood for casual encounters, new relationships and even marriage proposals. Some joked about a cohort of "Umbrella babies" conceived in Admiralty who would grow up to be the next generation of freedom fighters.

A new way of thinking

Hong Kong is a city that doesn't read, never writes and barely wants to think. In our so-called "instant noodle culture," the only mental stimulation we get is soap opera on television, celebrity gossip in tabloid magazines and the sound of cash registers at shopping malls. Garbage in, garbage out.

The Umbrella Movement changed that, however temporarily. It did more than just bring out the citizens' good side and show them an alternate way of life; it also sparked a cultural renaissance. 79 days of immersion learning elevated the intellect of an entire generation. During that period, many believed that the future of Hong Kong would no longer be forged on university campuses but at each of the three encampments.

Anti-materialism – Sitting at the makeshift library on Harcourt Road one evening, it suddenly dawned on me that I hadn't spent any money in days. The only reason to open my wallet was to buy lunch boxes for the volunteers or take a taxi home after the last subway train had left Admiralty. I hadn't swiped any of my half-dozen credit cards since the movement began.

Shopping – Hong Kongers' favorite pastime after moneymaking – was the furthest thing from any villager's mind. Retailers complained about dismal sales because of snarled traffic and vanished tourists, but the real culprit might have been a loss of libido for material gratification. At a time when citizens had the future of their city in their hands, trifles like designer jeans, name brand handbags and expensive watches all started to look a little, well, immaterial.

Before September 28th, young people – and many adults – couldn't tell Martin Luther from Martin Luther King, Jr., Mahatma Gandhi from Mohammad Ali. On September 28th, it was as if Peter Pan had grown up overnight to self-organize, self-sustain and self-determine. What was once a talk-of-the-town topic like the release of a new iPhone or a soap opera's season finale became completely irrelevant. Even Facebook walls received a facelift: food porn, selfies and narcissistic rants had all given way to protest updates and stories of random acts of kindness. Protesters were reading Karl Marx and debating Georg Hegel one moment, and dodging pepper spray and pushing back angry thugs the next. It was the best "moral and national education" there ever was.

Inventiveness – Cynics call Hong Kong a cultural desert, and for good reason. Rampant materialism and cut-throat peer competition have drained the last drop of creative juice out of citizens. Talented men and women trade their paintbrushes and dance shoes for briefcases and pinstriped suits. But you wouldn't know that from visiting the Umbrella Village. Decades of pent-up creativity suddenly burst out of the Genie's bottle, releasing the Henri Matisse and Martha Graham in us and turning the protest sites into galleries and theaters.

They say necessity is the mother of innovation. Umbrellaville was full of outside-the-box ideas such as charging booths for smart phones and Wi-Fi routers powered by car batteries. The greatest invention was a 24-hour study corner that was a library, classroom, cafeteria, town center and storm shelter wrapped into one. The facility was like a living, breathing animal – it grew in size and new features nearly every day.

For over a decade, the SAR government has tried but failed to promote recycling and combat air pollution[53]. Protesters succeeded on both fronts in a matter of weeks. Together, the three villages ran the city's largest recycling program, with volunteers diligently sorting papers, water bottles, soda cans and even leftover food. During the 79 days, the Hong Kong Observatory consistently ranked Admiralty the least polluted area in the city. The air quality ratings of all three protest zones went from "serious" or "very high" to an unprecedented "low." It was due in large part to the absence of vehicular traffic but also a result of the villagers' discipline and ingenuity.

Political engagement – For generations, young people have been told to focus on their studies. They have been taught by parents and teachers to stay away from politics because it is "dirty" and that it has nothing to do them. But the ghastly whistle of tear gas has jolted our youth out of their political apathy. Many realized that politics affects them personally and directly. Every decision from the minimum wage and housing policy to how their tax dollars are spent, right down to the number of bus routes in their local district, is made by partisan politicians who work the political system.

---

53 – Survey after survey has shown that the poor air quality in Hong Kong is the leading reason why many highly skilled expatriates are relocating to Singapore, Tokyo and other Asian cities.

Many also realized that video games, karaoke and television shows might have been social anesthesia prescribed by the ruling elite to divert their attention from what really matters. Oblivion and non-participation are the reason that gross injustices inflicted by the functional constituencies are allowed to fly under the radar for so many years. Once awoken, this so-called "Umbrella Generation" would never relapse into their existential coma. Instead, they are armed with a new sense of purpose and ready to make up for lost time.

Lion Rock Spirit rekindled

On October 28th marking the one-month anniversary of the occupy movement, tens of thousands of citizens gathered on Harcourt Road to observe 87 seconds of silence, one for each shot of tear gas fired by riot police. At the precise moment of 5:57pm, they pop-opened their umbrellas in unison, a sight that resembled a time-lapse video of flower blossoms in a rainforest.

The 11 weeks I spent in Umbrellaville were the happiest in all my years in Hong Kong. I alternated between euphoria and tears of joy, gratitude and amazement. Protesters occupied city streets, but by displaying exemplary discipline and world class charisma, they also occupied our hearts. I felt sorry for friends and family who weren't in Hong Kong to experience it themselves, because so much of what went on had to be seen to be believed.

If the old Lion Rock Spirit was premised on hunkering down for trickle-down economic benefit, then the new Lion Rock Spirit would be about social justice and civic participation. Who could have predicted that the biggest political crisis of our time would renew our age-old ethos and bring out the absolute best in us? No one knew whether the new way of life and intellectual rebirth would last beyond the occupy movement. What we did know was that a seed had been planted in each of the protester's head, and that the seed would germinate when the conditions were ripe.

Harcourt Academy

Students belong to the classroom, not the streets.

Although not every protester opted to participate in the 9/22 Class Boycott, enough of them did. High school kids would sit on the playground to do "self-study," while college students would cut class and spend the day at various campus demonstrations or volunteer in one of the villages.

The Hong Kong education system did not slow down for anyone, not even when half the city was paralyzed by a political crisis. Class or no class, there would still be essays to write and term exams to study for. Teachers would continue to post assignments on school websites or send them out by email. That led to one of the most talked about features of the Umbrella Movement: protesters in full protective gear doing homework with pencils and highlighters. The phenomenon was bizarre, inspiring, and so very Hong Kong.

A humble start

On October 2ⁿᵈ, Day 5 of the Umbrella Movement, I had a eureka moment. The idea never would have crossed my mind if it weren't for the volunteerism I had witnessed in Umbrellaville. That day, I grabbed a piece of cardboard from the sidewalk outside the Hong Kong Club Building and made a sign. The sign read:

> "*FREE help with homework*
> *English, essay writing, law*"

Tutoring is a big business in Hong Kong. Parents spend thousands of dollars each month to send their children to cram schools, where students of all ages are taught ways to beat the education system. The industry is based on fear: no one wants to find out the consequence of *not* getting a tutor when everyone else does. So the lemmings all head for the cliff. Leading the children are the Pied Pipers of Hong Kong – the so-called "celebrity tutors" who appear on life-size billboards and get paid millions for doling out exam-taking tips[54].

I, too, have been a tutor – minus the billboards and the million-dollar contracts. For almost 10 years, I have been teaching literature and creative writing every Sunday morning at a center in Central. Putting two and two together, I decided to offer pro bono roadside homework assistance in Admiralty to whoever needed it. I've always considered the most beautiful words in the English language after "mother" to be "teacher" and "journalist." In Umbrellaville, I could be both.

With the help of social media, I posted my location and office hours on Facebook, Instagram and Twitter. I had initially planned to teach for a couple of hours on a few odd nights each week. I had no idea that I would end up spending four to five hours *every* night, interrupted only by bathroom breaks and the loud broadcast of the 8:00pm nightly speech on the Grand Stage. Long hours and no pay notwithstanding, it was the best teaching gig I ever had.

On my first day of teaching, I sat on the street with nothing but my homemade cardboard sign and a bottle of water. My "office" was on the downhill slope of the Harcourt Road expressway. I chose that spot for its sweeping views and heavy pedestrian traffic. It felt a bit awkward at first: I wasn't sure if anyone would take up my offer. A few passersby slowed to read my sign, took pictures of it and walked on. Others said to each other, "Okay wor[55]!" and giggled together. The more vocal ones gave me a thumbs up and offered words of encouragement. Then, suddenly, a young girl walked over and sat next to me. My first student, Cathy, was a high school student who needed help with English grammar. I answered her questions; she smiled, thanked me and left.

---

54 – Y.Y. Lam, one of the highest paid star tutors in Hong Kong, was once offered an annual salary of HK$85 million (US$11 million) to join a rival tutoring center.

55 – Chinglish for "Not a bad idea!"

Everything seemed easier after Cathy. More students came, most of them needed a crash course on local politics or just wanted to share their thoughts on the occupy movement. Some came alone, while others brought friends and even their parents. A group of teenage girls from an international school in Shatin stopped by and offered me freshly baked cookies. "Can you come to our school and give us a talk?" they asked.

By 10:30pm, my legs were completely numb. I made a mental note to bring two other things the next day: a hand towel to sit on and a sign in Chinese. In all, I had about 30 takers within the four-hour window. Not bad for a first night.

A roving teacher

By the second day of teaching, I had my routine down pat – the same routine I would follow for the next two months.

I would leave my office in Central at 6:30 each night and go to my *other* office in Admiralty. I would put out my bilingual signs and sit in my usual spot until 11:00pm. On weekends when the crowds were bigger, I would spend nearly the whole day there. In between talking to my students, I would read a book or work on my next news article. Friends would pop by to say hello, and leave when they saw a student waiting. When "business" was slow, I would yell "Anyone need help with homework?" at the top of my lungs, like a roasted chestnut hawker in the old days. Students would come and go; people would thank me and I would thank them. Time would go by very quickly.

Every so often, a foreign press crew would be drawn by my cardboard signs and approach me for an interview. I spoke to, among other organizations, the Associated Press, BBC News, Bloomberg News, the Voice of America, *Maclean's* (a Canadian newsmagazine) and *de Volkskrant* (a Dutch newspaper). They would ask similar questions[56]: "Why are the students here?" "What made you want to volunteer?" "What's the end game?"

Out of the two dozen interviews I took from the overseas press, the most memorable one was with a Bangkok television station. I greeted the crew with the *wai* – a hand gesture to signal respect in Thai culture by bringing together of the hands with the thumbs placed just below the mouth – and proceeded to answer their questions. Off camera, the producer, Khun Somchai, told me how impressed he was with the peaceful suffragists in Hong Kong. "In Thailand, we have the Red Shirts and the Yellow Shirts.

---

56 – A list of these frequently asked questions and my responses to them can be found in *Part 3 – Out of the Village, Into the World.*

We have snipers and homemade bombs, and people die," Somchai sighed. "We have so much to learn from you Hong Kong people." The crew sat with me for another two hours that night as we chatted under the moonlit sky.

My cardboard signs were a magnet for colorful characters in Umbrellaville. From time to time, a blue ribbon would approach me looking to start an argument, but he would back off when he found out I was a lawyer. Sometimes strangers would talk to me for hours about their grand political theories and profound life philosophy.

There was one old man, whose name now escapes me, who would walk up and down Harcourt Road with a bullhorn. One night, he sat down next to me and told me his entire life story from the day he was born: how he grew up in a wealthy landowner family in Guangdong, fled the Communists, moved to Vancouver, Canada, ran a successful import-export business and recently divorced his wife. Or was it his son who did all that? I wasn't quite sure because he wasn't always coherent. The man with the bullhorn ended his hour-long autobiography with a stern warning: never believe a word the Communists say. "They killed our men and raped our women in the 50s and 60s and they will do it again and again," he said, his cheeks twitching with anger.

Being out on the streets exposed me to the elements. I would feel the summer heat emanating from the asphalt beneath me. When it rained, I would scramble to protect my cardboard signs and camera. Once it stopped raining, there would be fleas to reckon with. Who knew there would be fleas on a highway? But none of the minor nuisances compared to the bounty of generosity I received. Tennessee Williams was right about the kindness of strangers. Every night I was offered sandwiches, cold drinks, tissue paper and umbrellas. I once accepted a hotdog from an Australian couple, a peeled pear from a Korean teacher, and an autographed novella from a Bangkok-based author.

I also got to know the students at the nearby supply tents fairly well. They were the good Samaritans who ran to my rescue with raingear whenever it rained. Noticing that I kept shifting positions when I crouched on the street, they upgraded me from a hand towel to an alphabet play mat – the type that people used in kindergarten playgroups. After spending days sitting on a piece of rag, that tiny square of foam mat felt like a Sealy Posturepedic mattress.

The first-generation Study Corner

The Study Corner

On October 9th, Day 12, a new feature emerged in Admiralty. A team of handymen put their carpentry skills to use and built trestles that straddled a section of concrete highway divider on Harcourt Road. They then placed planks of plywood on top, lined up donated chairs and homemade benches on either side, and hung battery-operated LED lamps overhead. Finally, the finishing touch: a giant "do not disturb" sign to remind visitors to keep their voices down and refrain from flash photography.

Tear gas crackdown by riot police outside the Tamar Government Headquarters on September 28th (photo credit: *Apple Daily*)

Heavy-handed police response draws tens of thousands more to Admiralty (photo credit: Joel Odesser)

The Occupy Trio: Reverend Chu Yiu-ming (left), Benny Tai (middle) and Chan Kin-man (photo credit: Tom Grundy)

Lester Shum (left), Alex Chow (middle) and Joshua Wong address a cheering crowd on the Grand Stage (photo credit: *Apple Daily*)

Protesters face off with police inside the Lung Wo Road tunnel
(photo credit: Tom Grundy)

Protesters gather at one of the Mongkok subway station exits on Nathan
Road (photo credit: Tom Grundy)

Teenagers lie on the Harcourt Road expressway with nothing but the clothes on their backs – and their smart phones

A pair of demonstrators take a break next to a fortress of steel barriers outside the Legco Building (photo credit: Tom Grundy)

Tent city on the arched Harcourt Road expressway

Village life in Umbrellaville

The main speakers' corner at the Nathan Road and Argyle Street intersection in Mongkok

A roadblock on Yee Wo Street in Causeway Bay

Under the giant Mandarin Oriental billboard next to City Hall

A volunteer hands out food and drinks to passers-by

Volunteers keep the streets clean

A 92 by 20 feet banner on Lion Rock bears the words "We demand real universal suffrage"

The author and his cardboard signs during his "office hours"

Core members of the Water Blowers' Society

The first-generation Study Corner

The next-generation Study Corner

Lion Rock Villas at the peak of Harcourt Road

A few good men do a lunch run at Maxim's fast food restaurant

The Lennon Wall on Tim Mei Avenue

The Umbrella Man sculpture

President Xi's cut-out figure

A papier-mâché coffin custom-made for C.Y. Leung

The Guan Gong shrine at the Nathan Road and Mongkok Road intersection in Mongkok

A crowd of gouwu shoppers give police the three-finger salute
(photo credit: Tom Grundy)

Bailiffs, lawyers and their removal crew ready for clearance
(photo credit: Tom Grundy)

Harcourt Road (above) and the Lennon Wall (below); upper pictures show the morning after clearance and lower pictures show the movement in full bloom a few weeks earlier

Next to the trestle desks, knee-high square tables sat atop yoga mats and area rugs, creating a Japanese-style *ima* living space that seated about 20. There were more signs: "Please remove your shoes, "Help keep the area clean," "Study hard and you just may sit next to *him* in class." The last sign had an arrow pointing at a headshot of Lester Shum.

The Study Corner was the greatest invention since sliced bread. It didn't take much persuasion for me to move out of my crummy outdoor office into the Grade A office space. I found an empty spot at one of the low tables, propped up my cardboard signs and resumed teaching. It was night and day compared to crouching on hard asphalt for hours on end. I immediately posted my new location on social media. I could barely contain my excitement when I tweeted, "Come one, come all! Check out the new study hall!"

The Study Corner was extremely popular among the students. It ran out of room within the first few days of operation. Carpenters worked over time to expand the area, churning out more tables and benches. The squeals of chainsaws and electric screwdrivers pierced the quiet nights. There were now two full time staffers at the facility in charge of distributing food, sourcing supplies and keeping the peace. I became friends with one of them. Christie, a recent university graduate and a freelance graphic designer, took the night shift from 5:00pm to midnight. She carried a badge and a bullhorn, and would announce my presence each time I showed up so that students would know to look for me.

In addition to Christie's public announcements, there was a white board near the entrance for tutors to write down their names, the subjects they taught, and their check-in and check-out times. That was how I discovered there were other volunteer tutors like me. Each night, there were at least a half-dozen names scribbled on the board, offering help with anything from liberal studies, math and chemistry to foreign languages including French, Japanese and Korean. The Study Corner was a meeting place that connected students and teachers from all over the village.

My teaching role continued to evolve with time. In addition to English, essay writing and law, I added journalism and multimedia studies to the list of subjects I tutored, in response to the growing demand for help with film projects and school newspaper reports. Most of the help-seekers were journalism and communications majors at universities and community colleges.

I had seriously considered adding "counselor" to the list as well. Many students were having family problems, either because their parents were diehard blue ribbons, or because they were forbidden from going to the protest zones out of safety concerns. Some had not spoken to their families for days, while others had stopped going home altogether. Like a bartender who absent-mindedly wipes down the counter and coaxes the woes out of his troubled patrons, I sat there and listened. Most of the time I refrained from dispensing advice, except for a simple suggestion, "At least send your mom a text message and tell her you are okay."

When I wasn't teaching or counseling, I would have my own work to do. I would bring out my laptop and work on a news article or blog entry. The Study Corner might have been fraught with distractions like free food and endless chitchat, but there was no shortage of inspiration for a freelance reporter. It was there I wrote the dozen articles or so for the *SCMP* and other publications, including *Worst of Times, Best of Times* (about the protesters' discipline and volunteerism), *Darkest Before Dawn* (chronicling the 10/3 Mob Attacks), *Searching for Umbrella Man* (comparing the Umbrella Movement with the Tiananmen Square Protests), *A Season of Discontent* (analyzing the social frustrations that had engendered the protests), *15 Minutes with Mr. Lau* (debunking the myth that the movement had destroyed the livelihood of all taxi drivers), *Mobile Occupy* (tracking the flash mob operations outside the encampments), and *What's Next for the Umbrella Movement?* (the title is self-explanatory)[57].

By the end of October, the study room had more than tripled its original size. The entire area was covered by blue marquees with side curtains to keep out the sun and the rain. There were a small library, a concierge desk, drainage pipes, and exercise bikes that doubled as power generators. In early December, despite the looming threats of police clearance, protesters showed their defiance and optimism by putting up a Christmas tree and decorating the area with tinsel and snow spray.

---

57 – These articles can be found at *www.scmp.com/author/jason-y-ng-1*. In May 2015, the *SCMP* won the Amnesty International Human Rights Press Award for its coverage of the occupy movement.

Water Blowers' Society

There was more to the Study Corner than homework and tutorials; it was also a neighborhood pub – minus the alcohol – where everybody knew your name. I had friends, colleagues and Facebook followers regularly drop in to say hello. For two months, I lived the life of a college student shooting the breeze on the campus lawn, or, at my age, more like an over-zealous professor who lingers in the hallway long after the lecture is over. Like the blue tarps and wooden benches, I was part of the furniture.

I quickly developed friendships with a stable coterie of teenagers who showed up every night at roughly the same time. I called them "my students" because the founding members of the group – which we self-deprecatingly called the "Water Blowers' Society[58]" – had asked for my help with their English assignments. The ones who joined in later were friends of friends I had never taught. During club hours, we debated the direction of the occupy movement and traded war stories from the frontlines. Sometimes our symposium on local politics got so loud that Christie had to come over to shush us. Other times, passersby would poke their heads in and listen, and occasionally add their two cents.

My students came from a cross-section of the city. Their views and aspirations were as diverse as their backgrounds. We created a WhatsApp group to keep each other informed of our whereabouts, which was especially handy on nights when the confrontation with police got violent and club members were drafted as reinforcements. The chat

58 – "Blowing water" is Cantonese slang for talking nonsense.

group remains active today, and we use it to stay in touch and continue our never-ending debate.

Club membership was hardly exclusive – it required neither a fee nor an application. The only prerequisite was the ability to speak your mind. Everyone in the Water Blowers' Society, without exception, was outspoken, opinionated and full of witty comebacks. Among the 15 or so members, I had gotten to know a few of them better than others and vice versa. Their stories intertwined with the narrative of the Umbrella Movement as I saw it, and provided a window on – and filled the gaps in – aspects of village life I did not personally experience. Their voices needed to be heard, recorded and broadcast. This was, after all, *their* movement.

Kent

The 19-year-old was at the time a freshman at City University majoring in aviation. Kent's parents separated when he was 8, and he lived with his mother and a girl cousin in Tai Wai in the heart of the New Territories. Since the divorce, his mom had taught herself to be a beautician and kept the household on an even keel.

Although mother and son shared a small public housing apartment, their views were worlds apart. Kent's mom was a blue ribbon – she was against the occupy movement and disapproved of his son's active participation in it. She believed young people complained too much and should learn to roll up their sleeves to make a living – as she did after she became a single parent. The two barely talked and when they did they fought. That was why Kent tried to spend as much time as he could in Admiralty and Mongkok during those 11 weeks.

Political differences were not the only wedge between parent and child. According to Kent, his mother was a typical Chinese parent who practiced tough love. Her idea of motivation was a daily dose of cutting criticisms: she often lamented, to her son's face, what a *fai ching* he was, and that his lack of good looks and good grades would bring a lifetime of celibacy. Her curse had become something of a self-fulfilling prophecy. Kent remained an "apartment male" – single guys who shut themselves in their bedrooms in front of their computers all day – and didn't have much interaction with the opposite sex or with anyone else for that matter. On social media, boys like him are assigned the relationship status "A0": A stands for "available" and the big zero denotes the number of girls they have dated.

Kent and I became friends after our animated discussion about the economic wisdom of building a third runway at the Hong Kong International Airport. An aviation enthusiast, Kent argued that the HK$142 billion (US$18 billion) infrastructure project was a white elephant designed to enrich big construction companies. The project made no sense because our congested air space was caused by the city's mountainous terrain and the irresolvable incompatibility between the Hong Kong and mainland Chinese air traffic control systems. Adding a new landing strip, Kent concluded, would do nothing to improve the airport's capacity. The conversation impressed me deeply and cemented our friendship. It taught me that there was as much for me to learn from these young people as they did from me.

Renee

When I met the 17-year-old, she was a Form 6 (12th grade) student at Bishop Hall Jubilee School in Kowloon Tong. Renee lived with her family in Tsuen Wan in western New Territories, and commuted daily to Kowloon by double-decker bus. Her father ran a small family business importing machinery parts from overseas, and her mother was a homemaker. She had two brothers, one of them was studying animation in the UK.

Renee first came to me for help with a writing assignment. She also had questions about the electoral system in Hong Kong – knowledge she needed to fend off her anti-protest parents and friends. For a teenager girl, she was feisty and straight-talking. Her assertiveness and good command of the English language made her a popular target for the foreign media. She was interviewed by Italy's Rai Television and, through my referral, Brazil's RedeTV!. Her two-minute tirade against Priscilla Leung (a pro-Beijing lawmaker) during an on-camera interview with the *Apple Daily* won her praise on social media. Leung had previously proposed to remove liberal studies from the secondary school curriculum because it "encourages students to protest."

Renee was different from most teenage girls her age. Instead of chirping over fashion, make-up and boys, she played techno music, a rarefied pursuit in a materialistic city. She performed as a vocalist in a two-person band at underground shows in warehouses and industrial buildings. She never quite blended in with her classmates, both by choice and by circumstance. To her, Umbrellaville was not only a protest site but also a sanctuary from peer pressure and petty conflicts at school. As soon as classes were over, she would take the subway from Kowloon Tong to Admiralty, and stay in the village until the last train departed at 1:00am. That was why Renee was always seen in the village in her white school uniform.

Hinson

Like Renee, Hinson was born in the spring of 1997 just before the Handover. At the time of the protests, he was a Form 6 student at La Salle College, one of the city's elite all-boys high schools. He came from a well-off family – they lived in Kowloon Tong, a traditional upper middle class neighborhood not far from his school. Hinson's father was a business owner and his mother a homemaker. He had an older sister who worked for an insurance company.

I got to know Hinson through Kent and Renee. I quickly learned that the La Salle kid – as he was often called in the village – was a popular man among villagers. He was a medic on one of the first aid teams, which meant he got to wear a staff vest and carry a walkie-talkie that at all time hissed noisy conversations between his teammates and other support units. His popularity earned him many friends, a few groupies, and to his dismay, an occasional stalker.

Hinson had been a volunteer with St. John Ambulance Brigade since the age of 13. He became a first aider in Admiralty on September 28th, and continued his service for the entirety of the occupy movement. Hinson started off volunteering at the official OCLP medical station, but he left a few days later after the convener of the medical team Dr. Au forbade medics from going to the frontlines for safety reasons. Hinson quit to join a more progressive first aid unit, nicknamed the Peak General Hospital for its location at the top of the windswept Harcourt Road expressway. He and his 15 or so teammates provided medical support to protesters on the Lung Wo Road border as well as backup services to the warriors in Mongkok.

Ken

The 21-year-old was a sophomore at the Hang Seng Management College studying journalism and communications. Ken grew up in Sai Wan on the west end of Hong Kong Island, where his father had owned and run a small Chinese dried seafood store until he was forced to shut it down a few years earlier due to high rent and become a security guard. His mother used to be a seamstress, but she also switched jobs recently to work as a janitor at a local school.

I met Ken at the Study Corner when he approached me with two of his friends. The trio were working on an assignment for their "Reporting and Writing in English" class and were looking for journalists to talk to. After our interview, I gave each of them a reporter's notebook from the Foreign Correspondents' Club as a keepsake. They thanked me for the

From left: Kent, the author, Renee and Hinson

gift and promised me that they would work hard so that one day they would become a member there too.

Ken was not the most popular member in our group, mostly because he lacked an edit switch and had the tendency to drone on. Listening to him talk could feel like watching paint dry. In a place like the Study Corner, social skills were of great importance – talk too little and people find you passive and uninteresting; talk too much and they avoid you like a plague. In that sense, Umbrellaville was perhaps not that dissimilar to your average local high school. It goes to show that you can take the kids out of a schoolyard, but you can't take the schoolyard out of the kids.

Yoko

An honorary member of the Water Blowers' Society, the 31-year-old was also a VIP. Yoko was the manager of Station G1, the largest supply unit in Admiralty located on Harcourt Road outside McDonald's. The steel magnolia oversaw the collection and distribution of everything from tents and bottled water to fresh fruits by the crate. She was my go-to person for blankets, foam mats, and other items for a comfortable sleepover in the tent city.

Before the occupy movement, Yoko was a typical single woman who worked at a bank and spent her paychecks at shopping malls and nail salons. After the 9/28 Crackdown, she took an extended leave (thanks to a sympathetic boss) and began her new life in Umbrellaville. The self-proclaimed "princess" was an accidental volunteer. Her involvement started with a few cases of bottled water and a pile of umbrellas and raincoats she discovered by the roadside. She moved the supplies to a shaded area under a footbridge, and the next thing she knew, everyone started giving her all kinds of things. She began to inventory the goods, recruited students to distribute them, while provisions from business owners and individual donors continued to pour in. That was the genesis of G1, where she worked and slept almost every night until Admiralty was cleared by police in December.

Yoko had a staff. She called them "her kids" – around 30 young volunteers who took turns manning the station around the clock. Everyone at G1 knew me by my name. They recognized me from my tutoring signs and my several interviews in the *Apple Daily*. The kids called me "Ah Sir" or "Jason Gor[59]." Most of the time I called them "Hey, you!" because I am hopeless with names. I had a list on my iPhone with their first names next to simple descriptions such as "smoker with baseball cap" and "skinny girl who loves lemon iced tea."

---

[59] – "Gor" is a Cantonese honorific for a man who is older than the speaker.

Lion Rock Villas

Young people don't sweat the small stuff, like personal comfort and a good rest. At the start of the occupy movement, most of the student protesters slept without a tent, with only the moon and stars above them. In many cases, they just lay on the highway without so much as a foam mat between the hard asphalt and the clothes on their backs. Some used a shoe or folded T-shirt as a pillow, oblivious to the blinding streetlight and noisy conversations all around them. Admiralty might enter the *Guinness Book of Records* as the largest – and certainly the longest and roughest – urban sleepover in modern history.

Another humble start

I spent my first night in Umbrellaville on October 10th, Day 13.

I was better equipped than most villagers. I brought my own yoga mat, ear plugs and eye mask. I also received plenty of provisions from friends. Aviation major Kent had bought a few inflatable travel pillows from a nearby drugstore and insisted that I take one. The supply station volunteers next to my outdoor office (before there was the Study Corner) gave me a blue and white tarp that measured 6 feet by 8 feet – larger than a king-sized bed. They told me that the waterproof material would go a long way to ward off the harmful *chi* – negative energy seeping from the ground that could cause all kinds of long-term health problems. I had two questions for them: *what about the rest of you if I took your tarp?* and *how did a bunch of 17-year-olds learn such old wives' tales about ground* chi?

I had forgotten one important item: a blanket. I naturally turned to Yoko, impresario of Station G1. "No problem," she said, before sending one of her kids into the fortress of supplies. The young man came back with a baby blue beach towel with the famous Japanese *manga* character Doraemon printed on it. Cute and functional.

With a yoga mat, a travel pillow, a tarp and now a cartoon blanket, I was ready for my sleepover. The last time I slept on the street was in my late teens. I was backpacking through Europe one summer, and had wanted to save a night of youth hostel costs by crashing on a bench outside the Florence train station. I was woken up by a *carabinieri* (Italian police) who tapped on my shoulder and growled, "*Via dalla strada!*" (get off the street) This time around it was very different: I was much better prepared and there were thousands of others to keep me company. If the word "luxury" could ever be used to describe homelessness, then this would be the occasion.

I also had my iPhone to post pictures of my meticulously arranged sleeping quarters on Facebook and Instagram. My posts must have caught the eyes of my two best friends Ling and Victor: they turned up by my bedside unannounced just before midnight. We talked and laughed, joked and sobered up when we discussed politics. Victor was the least optimistic of the three. He compared the students to an army of ants and the Communists to a steamroller that could easily pulverize them. In recent weeks, Victor and his wife had been talking about emigrating to Taiwan or Singapore. The city's political deadlock aside, their dreadful experience trying to get their 2-year-old into a neighborhood kindergarten had turned their pessimism into anger. They were asked by the school principal to submit, among other ridiculous things, a portfolio of personal achievements (in the format of a CD-ROM) to demonstrate the toddler's worthiness for a spot. That episode alone was enough proof to the young parents that Hong Kong was an inhospitable environment to raise children.

At 3:00am, Ling and Victor decided to call it a night and went home to their families. I put on my earplugs and eye mask and went to sleep, only to be woken up an hour later by a megaphone on the Grand Stage. "Everybody, please wake up!" yelled whoever was clutching that godforsaken noisemaker. "We need reinforcement on Lung Wo Road right away!" Within seconds, villagers sprang out of bed into full protective gear: hard hats, construction masks and rain ponchos.

I walked down to Station G1 and asked one of Yoko's kids what was happening. "Is this your first time sleeping here?" the boy asked me and I nodded. "This happens every night. Go back to sleep, old man. There are enough of us to push back the police."

He went on to tell me that it was probably just another false alarm, even though things had been a bit tense in the past few days. There were rumors spreading across Admiralty that the police had hired dozens of tour buses for a mass arrest operation. Then again, rumors were in big supply those days, like the ones about undercover Triad members setting up their own tents inside the village or the PLA rolling in armored vehicles across the Shenzhen border. I didn't believe any of it – nor could I believe someone had just called me an old man.

I woke up at 7:30 the next morning. With barely four hours of rest, I was feeling groggy and dry-mouthed. I let out a loud yawn, stretched my body and got out of my cocoon that was Yoko's Doraemon blanket. I felt a sudden euphoria, realizing that I had just woken up in the middle of a highway in Central. The rising sun sent shards of gold through the shimmering buildings from the east. Harcourt Road was a weave of long shadows cast by protesters busily folding up their blankets and unpacking their takeout breakfast. A few joggers dodged a row of late risers and zoomed past me. The morning scene in Umbrellaville brimmed with beauty and life.

I spotted two things next to my pillow that did not belong it me. It was half a loaf of sliced bread and a bottle of mineral water. Someone had left me breakfast in bed while I was sleeping. I had a good idea who the donor was. The night before, while I was talking to Ling and Victor, I spotted the old man with the bullhorn – the strange character who tortured me with his life story just a few nights before – carrying bags of sliced bread as he walked past us. The breakfast might have been a reward for my patience and company. Whatever it was, the simple gesture moved me deeply. As I wolfed down the world's greatest invention, I promised I would think of that old man each time I was about to write someone off because they seemed different or out of place.

From rags to riches

Friday and Saturday were the two nights of the week when I didn't have to go to work the following morning, which meant I could spend the night in the village without worrying about not getting enough sleep or having a bad hair day. I grew accustomed to doing my morning routine in front of hundreds of strangers in broad daylight: making my bed, brushing my teeth, eating breakfast, and returning borrowed items to my benefactors.

The city started to cool down significantly by mid-November. As winter advanced, T-shirts and shorts gradually gave way to hoodies and sweatpants; battery-operated fans and cooling patches were replaced by scarves and thermoses. Tents were now stuffed with blankets and throws from IKEA. The nights got so nippy that I could no longer sleep outdoors without catching a cold. My accommodation needed an upgrade.

Hinson, the first aid medic, told me and Kent that there was an empty tent next to the Peak General Hospital atop the Harcourt Road expressway. The first aid station had a row of well-appointed accommodations reserved for staff only – the tents were generally clean, odor-free and spacious enough for two. The location offered highly coveted harbor views, the kind that deep-pocketed citizens would fork out tens of millions just to get a sliver of. These exclusive residences even had a name and address: Lion Rock Villas, 8 Harcourt Road.

"Villa 3 is available," Hinson said, "I'm at No. 2. We'll be neighbors!" He proceeded to give me a security briefing at Lion Rock. Residents did not lock their doors – or in our case, do up the zipper. There were no intruders or burglars (in fact, I had seen money bills lying around unattended inside some of the tents). The check-in procedure seemed equally straightforward: to signal occupancy, simply flip the card on the outside pocket from "Available" to "Taken." Inside the upscale residence, there was a vestibule by the entrance to store shoes and socks, an air vent for circulation, and a ground sheet to keep out the infamous ground *chi*.

Kent and I gladly took up the offer. By then, he was already quite experienced with tent-sharing, having done so a few times with friends, friends of friends, and sometimes even total strangers. He told me that he once spent the night at the campground outside the Legco Building entrance and, when he woke up the following morning, a nice lady brought him a bowl of steaming hot congee (rice porridge) donated by a restaurant in Wanchai. He also told me that he once shared a tent with Renee the techno singer and her friend Cammie. Cammie loaned each of them HK$200 (US$25) to take a cab home. "Loan" was just a word she used so Kent and Renee wouldn't refuse the gift. Kent would not see that woman in Admiralty again.

I peered into my villa and saw Kent's backpack and pillow already inside. The fact that the two of us kept very different schedules worked out well for our rooming arrangement. I would normally hit the sack at 1:00am and get up at 8:00am the next day. Kent would hang out at the Study Corner till day break and sleep in. We would almost never overlap. My students all suspected that Kent's nocturnal tendencies had to do with some girl he was secretly courting. The boy who was cursed with a perennial "Ao" relationship status was not about to let the Umbrella love boat sail off without him.

Protesters take up residence at one of the "villas"

Just because I was sleeping in a dome tent didn't mean I had to rough it. I told Yoko about my new address and asked for a foam mat to sleep on. She gave me a wink, disappeared into a stack of blankets and came back with a 6-inch thick air mattress. She told me it was a very rare item reserved for the injured – protesters with a broken leg or dislocated shoulder. But since there hadn't been any reported injuries of late, the mattress was mine to have for the weekend. "Are you sure?" I demurred, tempted by the offer but wary of the unwanted attention the big thing would draw when I lugged it up the highway. "Take it before I give it someone else," Yoko said, before tucking a fluffy IKEA comforter under my arm.

With that, I crawled into my not-so-humble abode that was Lion Rock Villa No. 3, an urban sanctuary of rough comfort and redefined luxury. I looked up to the night sky through the A-shaped opening, and remembered the Bing Crosby classic:

> *The moon is for everyone,*
> *the best things in life are free;*
> *The stars are for everyone,*
> *They gleam there for you and me.*

Not all fun and games

All the talk about comfort and luxury makes it easy to forget that sleeping on the street is, no matter how I romanticize it, sleeping on the street. To people like me who spent the night in the village only twice a week, the experience was novel and even entertaining. Nevertheless, the novelty wore off after about six or seven times. By the eighth time, it was done more out of a sense of duty. Showers and clean clothes were hard to come by, and there were mosquitoes, fleas and sometimes cockroaches and other wildlife to fend off; not to mention the torrential rains, deepening cold temperatures and round-the-clock noises as people talked and walked around the tent city at all hours of the day. I could imagine how punishing it must have been to repeat that routine night after night for 70 straight days. But that was exactly what many students and volunteers had to endure.

It was also easy to forget that there was still an anti-government uprising going on. At any of the three protest sites, things could change in an instant and violence could break out at any time without warning. Not a night went by without the entire campsite being woken up by the megaphone at 3 or 4 o'clock in the morning. If it wasn't a call to arms after dubious characters were spotted on the frontlines, it was another false alarm of a police ambush. On a good night, protesters could get about three hours of sleep and spend the rest of the night tossing around or trying to make sense of the commotion outside their tents.

In addition to unpredictability, there was a palpable sense of impermanence in Umbrellaville. Villagers rarely planned more than a few days ahead and things like tents and furniture weren't built to last. People lived from day to day as if every day would be their last – and every day could well be. Before I returned a used blanket to Station G1, I would always have it dry-cleaned. Yoko would take one look at the drycleaner's bag and shake her head. "Seriously, stop wasting your money," she would chastise me. "You and I might not even be here tomorrow." What she said would cut me to the quick, because I knew she was right.

The village experience had left an indelible mark on this generation of Hong Kongers. For the estimated 1.2 million citizens who participated in the protests in one way or another, 79 days of occupation had forever changed the relationship between citizens and city, pedestrians and streets. Long after the movement was over, I would stare at a section of the sidewalk while waiting for a minibus, and my mind would start to drift. My eyes would glance up to check for cover and dart around to spot the nearest bathroom, and then I would conclude, with some satisfaction: "That looks like a good place to set up a tent."

Admiralty Food Bank

Every evening, village life would pick up at around 6:30 when residents started to think about what was for dinner. Mickey-D's or KFC again? Or a free rice box from one of the supply booths? How about grazing on Pringles and Snickers bars? Whatever it was, villagers would put down their textbooks and crawl out of their tents to spend a couple of hours socializing around the Grand Stage.

Soon, the evening sky would dim, before the highway lampposts cast a heavy sheet of amber on the bustling community. Conversations would swell, accompanied by the rustling of plastic bags and the crackling of Styrofoam boxes. The streets, now at their most kinetic, would be redolent with barbecued pork and French fries. The 11th Commandment would be upheld once again: thou shalt not go hungry in Umbrellaville.

Collectivism in action

There were 26 supply units in Admiralty, seven in Mongkok and two in Causeway Bay. Like a convenience store, they each offered food, drinks and basic household items to shoppers. Unlike a convenience store, there were no price tags or cash registers. Anyone could easily spend all day in the village without spending a dime. I once left my wallet in my office and didn't bother to go back to get it.

There were lines just about everywhere: lines to cross the highway divider, lines to get a blanket, lines to get a free lunch box, and lines to refill water bottles from the commercial-sized tank. Villagers shared meals, daily necessities and sleeping quarters like comrades in a Maoist commune. For a city crowned year after year as the most capitalistic territory in the world, Hong Kong suddenly felt remarkably socialist.

Station G1 was the largest of the supply stations and the only one that operated round-the-clock. Two of Yoko's kids would take the graveyard shift every night. The station carried a full range of provisions including distilled water, crackers, candy bars and fresh fruits. Non-food items covered everything a camper needed to spend the night: blankets, foam mats, batteries and toiletries. The station also doubled as a pharmacy with face masks, Band-Aids and disinfectants. If someone asked for an item they didn't have, one of the kids on duty would mumble into his walkie-talkie and, minutes later, a biker would arrive with an object in hand and ask, "Who was looking for a hex-tip screwdriver?"

Every day, delivery trucks would arrive at one of the borders and unload crates of food and supplies onto push carts. The push carts would then make their way to G1 for the goods to be sorted and disseminated across the village. Provisions like cooked food and produce needed to be replenished daily, whereas durables such as bottled water and hygiene products came once a week.

The extraordinary generosity shown by citizens and the equally extraordinary organization it took to manage the donations had fueled rumors of foreign intervention. Perhaps the idea of giving back to the community and wanting nothing in return was too alien a concept to the ruling elite. From the start, there had been conspiracy theories that the CIA was orchestrating the campaign and had offered student leaders iPhones and Ivy League scholarships as bribes. To back up these allegations, former Security Secretary Regina Ip pointed to the constant flow of food supplies in Admiralty. In a radio interview, Ip challenged the host, "Tell me how it's possible for a bunch of teenagers to get their hands on tens of thousands of bottles of water without assistance from foreign governments!"

This was how. The majority of the provisions were donations from pro-movement individuals and business owners. Donors included investment bankers, doctors and other professionals who wrote five-figure checks for a big shipment of tents and blankets. One young lady gave Yoko HK$5,000 (US$650) in McDonald's gift certificates, while another purchased 100 cases of Red Bull for students who needed them to pull all-nighters. One day, an anonymous truck driver dropped off a few hundred director's chairs, because he noticed that volunteers had nothing to sit on. Yoko recalled her happiest moment when a large shipment of ice cubes arrived on an unseasonably hot day, and everyone made lemon iced tea out of them.

There were also more grassroots supporters who did what they could within their means: a few sandwiches here or six cans of soda there. Yoko told me about a 7-year-old boy who came by and fished out of his backpack several packs of cookies and a HK$20 bill. She took the cookies but turned down the cash. She told the boy that money always complicated things.

All-you-can-drink anywhere in the Umbrella Village

Every now and then, I would go from station to station to find out what was needed most – usually tents and other camping gear – and made pleas on Facebook and Twitter to have the items purchased and delivered. Hours after one of my posts, I would get a WhatsApp message from Yoko telling me an anonymous donor who mentioned my name had dropped off 25 yoga mats and 50 lab goggles.

According to insiders, other than the sound systems for the Grand Stage and the printing costs for T-shirts and posters (both paid for with OCLP funds), there weren't that many expenses at all. Everything else came from donors who wanted nothing in return, other than to send a strong message to Ms. Ip that the only foreign intervention present in the protest zones were North Face and IKEA.

The supply booths had attracted a number of elderly citizens who traveled to Admiralty from far flung corners of the city. Old age poverty is a burgeoning social issue in Hong Kong and one needs to look no further than Umbrellaville for proof. Food seekers, many in their 70s and 80s, got word about giveaways and headed to the Admiralty Food Bank. Most of them knew very little about the movement or the politics surrounding it. Yoko told me she didn't mind handing out lunch boxes to senior citizens, even though the food was meant for the students. She said there was enough for everyone.

Lunch box runs

Villagers didn't always have to go to a supply booth for free food. Sometimes free food went to them.

In the morning, volunteers would walk around the village handing out congee – a rice porridge and a breakfast staple for the Cantonese. Yoko told me that a lady delivered 30 bowls of congee every morning for the entire duration of the protests. Kent recalled waking up outside the Legco Building and thinking that he had never tasted better congee in his life than the one he had that morning.

After sundown, teams of volunteers would walk up and down Harcourt Road offering burgers, fried chicken, green tea and latte with skimmed milk. I had seen expats handing out hot dogs, tuna sandwiches and cupcakes. Once, a group of Australians brought their propane barbecue and started grilling sausages and hamburger patties. Site marshals swooped in and kindly asked them to put out the fire. The gas tank posed a safety hazard and might give the authorities an excuse to send in the fire department.

The sense of collectivism in Umbrellaville inspired me for a new campaign. To be honest, I didn't come up with the idea – I stole it from an office worker I ran into outside KFC a few days before. On October 6th, Day 9, I did my first lunch box run. I invited two colleagues from the office (a Texan and an Irishman) to accompany me to Maxim's, a fast food restaurant at City Hall. We bought as many takeout boxes as we could carry, which was around 16 Styrofoam boxes per person, or 48 in total. We ordered the local favorites: barbecued pork over rice, thick-cut pork chop with baked rice, and beef brisket curry with rice. The three of us lugged the bulging plastic bags like Santa's helpers, climbed over the waist-high highway divider, and went from tent to tent in the quarter-mile stretch from City Hall to Station G1.

The reception was overwhelming. We were greeted with cheers everywhere we went. Some students were amused by the exotic sight of foreigners delivering lunch, others offered us free yellow ribbons in return. One young man said, "Hurray! I was getting sick of eating cup noodles!" Another one asked, "How did you get here so fast? The food is still warm!" Most people were too polite to ask what actually was inside the takeout boxes. When I asked them to choose, they would say, "Okay, perhaps the pork chop. But really, we will eat whatever you give us!"

Once I started, it was impossible to stop. So I did the lunch box run every day at noon, work schedule permitting. Each day I would recruit a different pair of co-workers to avoid the exercise becoming a financial burden on any one individual. Curiously, most volunteers were Caucasian expats. Local Hong Kongers were less enthusiastic, perhaps for fear they would have their pictures taken in Admiralty by undercover police and be denied entry to China on their next business trip. They would rather give money instead.

That's how I met Fat Girl (her words, not mine), a volunteer at the Far East Supply Station next to the Study Corner. She screamed each time my colleagues and I showed up with food, as if we were the Beatles on a reunion tour. The bubbly 20-year-old high school graduate had an affinity for Western men and would not hide her disappointment when I showed up by myself on the odd day. In addition to being a beam of sunlight that brightened everyone's day, Fat Girl was also a handy person to know. Rather than lugging my personal belongings in and out of the village every day, I could store them safely in her tent. There was that 12th Commandment in Umbrellaville: thou shalt not mess with Fat Girl and her things.

Over time, I got to know the Maxim's staff well. Whenever the cashier saw me approach the restaurant, she would assign someone else to look after my large order so that I wouldn't hold up the queue. The kitchen staff would spring into action and form an assembly line to chop, ladle and bag, while I would count the number of cutlery sets needed. My coworkers and I would be in and out of the restaurant in less than 15 minutes.

One Friday, I decided to splurge a little and buy lunch from Yung Kee instead of Maxim's. Yung Kee is one of the best known restaurants in Hong Kong that specializes in roast goose. When my coworkers and I arrived on Harcourt Road with those famous burgundy-colored takeout bags, we got a round of applause from the volunteers. Pan-dem lawmaker Raymond Wong, who happened to be in the vicinity, heard the commotion and came over. He looked at the lunch boxes and said, "This is a real treat! We order from Yung Kee only on special occasions when we have to filibuster at the Legco all night!"

Friends and acquaintances who saw my social media posts would offer to give me cash to pay for the lunch boxes, as would colleagues who did not feel comfortable doing the runs in person. I would accept the donations and thank them on behalf of the students. One night, I was teaching at the Study Corner when a complete stranger came up to me and said he had seen my Facebook posts through a friend of a friend. He proceeded to shove a HK$500 bill into my hand and immediately ran away, knowing that the two of us would likely spend the next 30 minutes pushing the money back and forth. The next day, I used the money to buy lunch and extra lemon iced tea.

Toxins and antidotes

For weeks, Harcourt Villagers had been subsisting on whatever was on the menu at the two closest fast food joints: McDonald's and KFC. In between meals, there was a constant supply of potato chips, cookies and candy bars. The "Super Size Me" diet engendered two outcomes: *yit hey* and the Umbrella pounds.

Yit hey is a quintessential Chinese folk belief. The term, which literally means hot energy, refers to the imbalance of *yin* (negative or female energy) and *yang* (positive or male energy) within the body brought on by eating too much deep-fried or junk food. Common symptoms of *yit hey* – when the *yang* overpowers the *yin* – include oral blisters, acne and sore throat. To restore the internal balance, Cantonese people swear by their mother's homemade soup, a tried-and-tested method of detoxification.

Where there is demand there will be supply. Noticing that many villagers were suffering from cold sores and bad skin, an army of mothers descended on Admiralty with big pots of Cantonese soup. The ingredients of choice were water cress, winter melon and jujube (a Chinese date). A few times a week, the soup mamas would come by the Study Corner and insist that everyone drink at least one cup – two, if they wanted to look pretty again. Every now and then, an old lady would show up with cut pears and watermelons – both fruits are believed to be the next best remedy against *yit hey* after homemade soup.

The second unintended consequence of village life was harder to deal with. Having a junk food diet while leading a sedentary life in the tent city did not do service to the waist line. I remember going to a client meeting in early December and was told point blank by an acquaintance, in classic Hong Kong fashion, that I had put on weight. What I wanted to – but didn't – tell him was that I had stopped going to the gym for two months, and that I had been having Big Macs and Coke for dinner for just as long. That same night, I had a salad for dinner instead of McDonald's and ran two laps around the village before I almost cried myself to sleep at Lion Rock Villas.

Umbrella Cultural Center

Villagers went in and out of town so many times that they no longer stopped to marvel at the treasures in their midst.

The gentle slope of Harcourt Road was a gilded promenade of candy-colored placards, handwritten with pro-democracy battle cries in dozens of languages. Past that grand entrance, beyond a foyer of sidewalk chalk graffiti, another visual feast awaited. Local *manhua* comics were a vanishing craft dating back to the late Qing Dynasty, and here at the crest of the highway, they received a new lease on life. Cartoonists used their artistic license to warp the timeless images of Cantonese folklore, and reincarnated heroes of yesteryears into modern day revolutionaries. The result was festoons of laminated prints of *kung fu* warriors with menacing gazes and bulging biceps, their bladed weapons replaced by a yellow umbrella – the ubiquitous symbol of courage and defiance in Umbrellaville.

Down the slope toward the town center, a barefoot guitarist strummed a vallenato tune to an audience of young girls. The crooner played the chords from memory, improvised a bit, and segued into something else. Further into the crowd, a middle-aged woman sang of love and devotion. She might have other Cantopop favorites, but this was the one she knew all the words to: Leslie Cheung's "This Life, This Time."

Welcome to the Umbrella Cultural Center.

An outdoor gallery

Visitors to Umbrellaville would not leave the area without seeing the Lennon Wall. It was the most striking exhibit in the entire village, like the *Mona Lisa* at the Louvre or the *Starry Night* at MoMA. Tens of thousands of fluttering Post-it notes, several layers deep, wallpapered an outdoor stairwell that spiraled from Tim Mei Avenue to the upper level atrium outside the Government Headquarters. On the sticky notes were scribblings of pro-democracy wishes and emoticons of every kind.

The creation was named after the eponymous wall in Prague, which features John Lennon-inspired graffiti and lyrics from his signature song "Imagine." The Hong Kong version was believed to have been created by a group of young social workers on October 1st, taking the idea from a double-decker bus that had been commandeered by Mongkok protesters and turned into a giant bulletin board. Suffragists pinned their political demands and grievances on the sides of the vehicle and changed the bus route to "689" (one of C.Y. Leung's nicknames), destination: "Hell."

My students wanted to leave a mark in history and contribute to the Lennon Wall. Most of them, like Renee and Hinson, went with the usual "Stay strong, Hong Kong!" or "Step down, 689!" Kent preferred something more exotic. A Germanophile, he wrote the words "*wir sind das volks*," which means we are the people.

The second most striking exhibit in Admiralty was the Umbrella Man. The 12-foot-tall sculpture was made from scrap wood by a 22-year-old media graduate who went by the alias Milk. The towering figure symbolized the brave suffragist using an umbrella to fend off rain, tear gas and political oppression. The installation drew inevitable comparisons with the 33-foot-high Goddess of Democracy statue erected on Tiananmen Square by Beijing University students in the spring of 1989, before it was toppled by the PLA during the June 4th crackdown. The Umbrella Man proved

The Umbrella Man sculpture makes a brief appearance in Admiralty

to be equally short-lived: the sculpture was removed a few weeks after its début on October 5th, likely a result of its structural instability. Its whereabouts remain a mystery today.

Everywhere you looked in Umbrellaville, there were huge banners draped from footbridges and rooftops like waterfalls. Near the PLA Barracks on Harcourt Road, a 40-foot-wide banner offered a bold warning to the authorities: "It's just the beginning." Hovering above the Grand Stage, hundreds of broken umbrellas were stitched together to form a giant canopy straddling between a pair of footbridges to shelter the tent city down below, while a woman warrior painted on a 20-foot-long piece of fabric stood guard. The 10-foot-high fence that turned Civic Square into a fortress was transformed into a wall of shame with sharp messages addressed to the Chief Executive.

There were smaller artworks too: umbrella *origami*, umbrella-inspired pendants and bracelets, effigies and "Wanted" posters of unpopular politicians, cut-out figures of President Xi Jinping holding up an umbrella[60], and a papier mâché coffin earmarked for C.Y. Leung; not to mention a ubiquity of oil paintings, watercolor portraits, pencil sketches, sculptures, and photography that blended art with journalism. Traditional visual art was complemented by a deluge of multimedia creations in the form of video diaries, photoblogs, projection art on buildings, and social media campaigns. Suddenly, anybody with a smart phone or camcorder was making their personal documentary to chronicle live events as they unfolded.

Hong Kongers' adaptability is reflected in their penchant for derivative art. At Umbrellaville, secondary creations based on Roger Hargreaves' *Little Miss* series, Japanese manga *Attack on Titans* and *Doraemon*, and Michelangelo's *Creation of Adam* fresco all took on a satirical, pro-democracy bent. Even those hated warning flags used by the police couldn't escape a touch of artistic flourish: protesters made similar banners that read "STOP BULLCRAPPING OR WE SING HAPPY BIRTHDAY" and unfold them to push back blue ribbon troublemakers.

Mongkok and beyond

It didn't take long for folks in Mongkok to come up with their quirky responses to the Lennon Wall and the Umbrella Man. The emergence of a *Guan Gong* shrine, a Christian altar and a statuette of Saint Michael[61] on Nathan Road was a prime example of MK gumption and ingenuity.

---

60 – The cut-outs were a spoof of a famous photograph of Xi, taken on October 21st by Chinese media at the height of the Umbrella Movement. Xi was visiting a shipping terminal in Wuhan, capital city of Hubei province, when it suddenly started to pour. Someone handed the president an umbrella and he held it up to keep off the rain while his shirt was soaked and his pants were hiked up. The picture was meant to show the Paramount Leader's down-to-earth side, and went on to win a photojournalism award on the mainland. But the fact that Xi was pictured with a sensitive symbol of insurgency at a sensitive time sparked widespread rumors that the photo op was actually a setup by his political rivals to embarrass him.

61 – Saint Michael is the patron saint of police officers.

Guan Gong is the Taoist god of justice who governs and protects both the righteous (the "white realm") and the underworld (the "black realm"). In Hong Kong, a *Guan Gong* shrine can be found in every police station, as well as mahjong parlors, go-go bars and gambling pits operated by the Triads. The presence of Taoist and Christian deities in Nathan Village served multiple purposes: they were at once artistic, spiritual and functional. Since members of both the white realm and the black realm are known to be superstitious to the point of fanaticism, the iconography was designed to play up that weakness and make law enforcement and hired thugs think twice before they would desecrate the holy ground.

This led to a rather curious episode on October 17th, Day 20, when a Mongkok police unit was dispatched to clear a part of Nathan Road where the *Guan Gong* shrine sat. A female police superintendent in charge of the operation was caught wearing the colonial hat bearing the British crown (instead of the SAR emblem), a headgear she hadn't worn for 17 years. Reporters spotted the mistake, and the flustered officer was forced to apologize but struggled to come up with a plausible explanation for the mix-up. Many believed that Lady Superstition had put on an old hat before the high-profile raid in order to deflect any bad karma from defiling the *Guan Gong* shrine. Whatever it was, the protesters' little mind games worked, and the adults were once again outwitted by the quick-thinking teenagers.

The explosion of creativity extended far beyond the confines of the encampments. On October 23rd, Day 26, a team of 14 expert climbers who called themselves "Spider-kids" scaled the south face of Lion Rock and draped a 92 by 20 feet yellow banner bearing the words "We demand real universal suffrage." At 1,624 feet above sea level, Lion Rock watches over the city like Christ the Redeemer in Rio de Janeiro and Mount Fuji in Japan. Visible from miles away across the sprawling Kowloon peninsula, the symbol of Hong Kong's can-do spirit was the perfect spot for a political manifesto. Hours after the feat, a "making of" video was posted on YouTube that underscored the mission's danger and the climbers' gallantry. With a beloved Cantopop song playing in the background, the video guaranteed to leave no dry eyes in its audience.

The authorities scrambled to respond to the talk of the town, now another public black eye for all the world to see. Four O'clock Hui Sir called the yellow banner a "serious threat to public safety." He vowed to arrest the perpetrators and warned that copycats would be prosecuted to the fullest extent of the law. The banner was taken down the following day by a government helicopter, but its removal had an unanticipated effect. Countless smaller replicas of the yellow strip began to appear on apartment windows, park benches and lampposts across the city. Some were also sighted on university campuses in Macau with the words "Macau demands real universal suffrage too."

Long before the occupy movement ended, villagers had been discussing ways to preserve all the protest-inspired art for posterity. Academics and preservationists formed groups like the Umbrella Movement Visual Archives & Research Collective to catalog the artworks and identify places to store or exhibit them. The challenge was the quantity and size of many of the pieces. Some believed even structures like the Study Corner and supply tents were themselves a form of installation art that should be protected in their present state.

By December, organizers began evacuating paintings, sculptures and installations from each of the encampments and warehousing them at various local universities – perhaps the biggest rescue effort since Noah's Ark. Not surprisingly, the search for a permanent home was met with resistance and indifference, as few private galleries and none of the government-funded museums were prepared to take the political risk of harboring symbols of subversion. Until Hong Kong has a democratically elected government, a dignified venue to display and celebrate Umbrella art will remain an elusive dream.

The village soundtrack

Even for a city that has long considered classical music a bore, a few minutes of Mozart and Schubert can go a long way to take the mind off the serious subjects of protests and politics. The occupy movement had given students an excuse to dust off their once-hated musical instruments and put on free concerts as a way of giving thanks and showing solidarity. The performers got something in return too. At last they realized that music was not about nailing the fast notes or passing certification exams – as so many young musicians in Hong Kong grew up thinking – and that live performances had less to do with form or technique than connecting with the audience. Years of torturous violin lessons and grueling piano practice foisted upon them by tiger moms and helicopter dads finally paid dividends.

Violin soloists and string quartets were soon followed by brass bands and rock groups. Not to be upstaged, modern dancers joined in to show off their free form moves. The performers were mostly amateurs, but where they lacked in credentials, they made up for in passion and soul. The sound of music was powerful and contagious, enough to inspire Ken the journalism major to bring his guitar to the Study Corner and regale the Water Blowers' Society with oldies from the Simon & Garfunkel songbook.

If the Umbrella Movement were to release a soundtrack album, it would include a few familiar tunes, starting with John Lennon's "Imagine" and "Do You Hear the People Sing" from the revolution-themed musical *Les Misérables*. There would be Chinese staples like "Blood-stained Glory" and "Freedom Flowers" – songs sung every year at the Tiananmen Square Massacre commemoration in Victoria Park. Still, all of them would be mere filler tracks compared to "Under the Vast Sky" by Beyond, a popular local boy band. The 1980s classic swooned about adversity and resilience, and was the closest thing to a national anthem for freedom-loving Hong Kongers. That same song was sung by 100,000 people in Admiralty on the night of September 28th; it was the soundtrack for the Spider-kids' YouTube video; and its familiar piano introduction was enough to make protesters put aside what they were doing and give the famous three-finger salute (from *The Hunger Games* movies) as a show of defiance and unity.

On October 4th, Beyond's ode to freedom finally met its match. The day after the 10/3 Mob Attacks, an ensemble cast of local musicians recorded an official anthem for the Umbrella Movement to buoy the suffragists' spirit in the face of violence and thuggery. "Raise Your Umbrellas" – our answer to Live Aid's "We Are the World" – was written by Lin Xi, the city's best known lyricist, and performed by, among others, outspoken singers Anthony Wong and Denise Ho.

Both Wong and Ho are openly gay entertainers who know a thing or two about oppression, making them apt ambassadors for the occupy movement. They demonstrated their steely backbones by risking their careers for social justice, and at the same time amplified the deafening silence of all the *other* Cantopop stars who had gone missing in action. Too many of them seemed willing to abandon their young fans – who used to buy their albums and scream their names – for fear of losing the lucrative mainland market.

Within weeks, "Raise Your Umbrellas" got close to half a million views on YouTube, many of them sympathizers abroad. At the urging of my friends overseas who don't speak Cantonese, I translated the lyrics and posted them on social media:

> *Sitting quietly in the crowd, we are filled with fear*
>   *of what is to befall us*
> *We have come to a juncture in our destiny*
>   *where the real danger is silence*
>
> *Standing on the frontlines, we are filled with courage*
>   *even though the future is grim*

Who would have guessed that to look through the lies
we must open our eyes in the smoke of tear gas

Together we raise our umbrellas
we may be anxious but we are not alone
Together we raise our umbrellas
we ask for no more than what we were promised

Heavy rains fall, but not our spirit
Umbrellas are in full bloom
like flowers that refuse to wither

We must remember today for the sake of tomorrow
we shall meet what lies ahead with calm
For if we miss the chance to speak up tonight
there won't be another one in our lifetime

The day after the new anthem was released, the blue ribbons hit back with their own musical number. "Hong Kong Life" was written by pro-Beijing loyalists to celebrate the bravery and sacrifices of the police force. The lead writer of the tribute was none other than the proverbial skunk at the garden party Leticia Lee. The clumsy production was taken by the public as a joke. In fact, the involvement of the likes of Lee – in sharp contrast to the dream team on the other side – did more damage than good to the police's flagging public image. More importantly, these court jesters raised serious questions about the vigor of the CCP's recruitment process for its ground troops in Hong Kong, despite its deep pockets and far-reaching tentacles.

Just because a singer wears a yellow ribbon on his chest, however, does not guarantee his entry into the Umbrella Hall of Fame. The line between a sympathizer and an opportunist is fine, and in the case of one busker named Bananaooyoo, razor-thin. Every evening, the one-man band could be spotted with his guitar and amplifier outside Admiralty Centre belting out the latest Cantopop hits. The lack of a real political message and a fondness for media attention put the busker under heavy scrutiny. Protesters complained that he was drowning out serious debate happening nearby with his loud, irrelevant music. The last straw came when Bananaooyoo launched a crowd-funding campaign to finance his début album months *after* the occupy movement had ended, which drew scathing responses from netizens who accused him of using the movement for commercial gains. The episode was a sobering reminder to aspiring singers that mixing political activism and show business could be a tricky proposition.

Green living

Living underneath dusty highways and sterile footbridges can get a little drab. To change that, protesters launched a village-wide forestation campaign that breathed life into the milieu. Potted plants began to appear at various supply and first aid booths. A section of the sidewalk in front of the Lennon Wall was dug up and converted into an organic farm for lettuce and tomatoes. Even the empty highway reflector slots on Harcourt Road became mini-flower beds for shrubs. Unwary pedestrians often kicked the plants right out of the slots. Like many others, I made a habit of checking on them and putting the displaced plants back in their homes each time I walked up or down the expressway.

With thousands of villagers eating, sleeping and living in close quarters, waste management had become a high priority. Residents were asked to dispose of their garbage outside the protest zones and use the commercial-sized tanks to refill reusable water bottles. Volunteers set up designated areas to sort paper, plastic, aluminum and cardboard. The neatly organized refuse would then be collected by trash pickers from outside the village and sold for money. To turn the disposable into collectibles, volunteers taught visitors how to make handicrafts out of water bottles and aluminum cans, which made for nifty souvenirs for foreigners and powerful teaching materials for young children. Visitors were equally impressed by the giant handloom that volunteers used to weave handmade scarves and table runners from recycled yarn.

In the early days, Renee volunteered at a recycling depot outside the Legco Building. She spent the evening sorting garbage, removing caps and labels from water bottles, and washing plastic cutlery to be reused. She also learned to make hand soap by composting fruit peelings she collected from the garbage. She had to wear a construction mask because the stench of rotting kitchen waste was unbearable. She also tried her best not to soil her squeaky white school uniform or else she would never hear the end of it from her mom.

The growing energy demand in Umbrellaville gave engineering students a chance to flex their brain muscles. They installed a wind turbine at the foot of the Harcourt Road expressway and a pair of exercise bikes at the Study Corner that doubled as power generators. These features were more symbolic than functional, since the main source of light was streetlamps and battery-operated LED lights, and enclosed areas like Station G1 and the Study Corner were powered by portable generators that ran on gasoline.

I asked Yoko about news reports that some protesters had been caught siphoning electricity from highway lampposts. The supply manager was unapologetic. "That's true. But those kids were breaking the law anyway by occupying a highway – I think they can handle one more felony charge." Sensing my skepticism, Yoko added, "In any event, they stopped doing it after the news story broke."

The Peak General Hospital

Humans have an amazing ability to adapt. It didn't take long for protesters to get used to the idea of eating, sleeping and studying on the streets. Likewise, commuters quickly found new ways to get to work around the occupied zones and would no longer bat an eyelid when they saw people shaving and brushing their teeth on an eight-lane highway.

Meanwhile, what used to feel like an outdoor rock concert now resembled a refugee camp. When thousands of young people congregated in a dense area, health issues began to surface. Villagers fell sick from the changing weather, spoiled food or general fatigue. The more accident-prone tripped over cables or slipped on a wet sidewalk. What's more, skirmishes with police and thugs, which happened sporadically in

Admiralty and Causeway Bay but on a daily basis in Mongkok, meant pepper spray burns, gashes and broken bones.

The responsibility of caring for the sick and the wounded fell on the medic units: villagers who congregated at the protest sites like everyone else but, on a moment's notice, threw on their yellow fluorescent vests, grabbed their walkie-talkies and turned into superheroes to save the world.

Medical teams

Dr. Au Yiu-kai was the convener of the **OCLP Medical Team**. A volunteer for Doctors Without Borders, the seasoned surgeon was no stranger to conflicts and violence. He had toured some of the most dangerous corners of the world: Palestine, Iran, Syria and Yemen. When Benny Tai announced his high stakes plan to occupy downtown Hong Kong, Dr. Au naturally put up his hand.

The original mission was well-defined and self-contained: the Occupy Trio and their sympathizers, estimated at a few thousands at best, would stage a two- to three-day demonstration in Chater Garden. Dr. Au and his recruits undertook to provide round-the-clock medical support to the demonstrators, among whom were veteran activists in their advanced years, such as 76-year-old Martin Lee and 82-year-old Cardinal **Joseph Zen**. The medical team put together meticulous shift assignments based on the volunteers' work schedules and family obligations. With some coordination and a bit of luck, seamless coverage was thought to be achievable.

The 9/28 Crackdown threw a monkey wrench into the clockworks. When Napoleon famously said that no plan survives the first contact with the enemy, he might have had Dr. Au's shift assignments in mind. The surgeon now had to follow a different script and respond to a much more formidable set of challenges. That night, the number of protesters on Harcourt Road reached six figures. Police responded with heavy arms like tear gas and possibly rubber bullets. Decades of working in remote war zones suddenly came in handy on Dr. Au's home turf.

Also handy was the doctor's longstanding relationship with the Hong Kong Red Cross, which was headquartered on Connaught Road and a stone's throw away from where the first tear gas grenade was fired. On September 28th, the Red Cross Building became the first asylum for injured protesters and frightened citizens fleeing from riot police. In the coming weeks, the OCLP Medical Team would continue to call upon the

Red Cross for medical supplies, basic equipment and telephone hotlines for psychological counseling.

By the second week, the number of medical stations in Admiralty had nearly tripled from the original five to 13. A medical tent was set up in each of Mongkok and Causeway Bay, but both were dismantled after the 10/3 Mob Attacks. Around 300 volunteers, including 30 doctors, over 100 registered nurses, and scores of medical students from HKU and CUHK – the only two medical schools in the city – took shifts responding to medical emergencies in Admiralty. To indicate their humanitarian roles (to avoid being arrested for unlawful assembly), they wore vests bearing a large red cross. When they ran out of vests, they made arm bands and buttons.

The largest medical booth, the Admiralty Centre Station, was located next to the G1 supply tent on Harcourt Road. It was the only place in Admiralty authorized to dispense medication. The station also had medical equipment such as automated external defibrillator (AED) pads, bag valve masks, asthma inhalers, blood glucose meters, stretchers and wheelchairs. Some of them were purchased with funding from OCLP, while others were on loan from the Red Cross.

Dr. Au's role in Admiralty was in part Surgeon General and in part diplomat. Given the distrust between students and law enforcement, a neutral third party was needed to resolve sticky situations. For instance, on September 29th, protesters guarding the borders – the **border control unit**, also known as the "local lords" – stopped a number of police trucks from entering the site. Police maintained that the vehicles contained lunch boxes for the officers on duty, but border control refused to let them in, convinced that it was a shipment of ammunition and riot gear for an imminent crackdown. To break the impasse, Dr. Au called in a team of Red Cross medics to board the trucks and verify their contents like U.N. inspectors at an Iranian nuclear facility. After that incident, the OCLP Medical Team worked with the local lords to open up a "humanitarian passage" through the protest zone to let emergency vehicles in and out of Admiralty to avoid a protracted negotiation each time.

The medical team also acted as an important liaison with the more neutral government offices like the Department of Health, and the Food and Environmental Hygiene Department. The personal friendship between Dr. Au and Health Secretary Dr. Ko Wing-man allowed the Grand Stage to receive important intelligence ahead of major police operations that might involve a large number of causalities. In mid-October, a 22-year-old student came down with a flu and was diagnosed with a rare strand of pneumonia. It was Dr. Au who negotiated with protesters for a low-profile visit by Dr. Ko and a team of medical experts to collect water samples from the village.

First aid teams

To support the medical teams, there were roughly eight first aid units in Admiralty, three in Mongkok and one in Causeway Bay. Their brightly-colored vests and bulky fanny packs made them hard to miss. Through Hinson, I got to know the team at Station A7, also known as the Peak General Hospital. A7 was an architectural marvel said to be designed and constructed by architecture and civil engineering students to withstand a signal 8 typhoon[62]. During the police clearance in December, frustrated removal crew tried but failed to take the booth apart. In the end, a crawler-excavator had to be called in to dismantle the stubborn thing – a story that Hinson likes to tell and retell with great pride.

Every first aid station followed the same pyramid structure. There was one medical doctor overseeing two to three registered nurses, who in turn worked with a larger team of certified first aid responders. At Station A7, for instance, there were 12 first aiders who took turns manning the booth. They were bankers, accountants, university lecturers and students with prior training in emergency care.

During the week, the medics showed up after work or after school, and left at various points in the evening depending on their availability. For instance, Hinson arrived every evening at 5:00pm and caught the last subway train home after midnight. That created a vacuum during the mornings and afternoons. In the event of an emergency, the supply units – some of which were on duty around the clock – would send out urgent WhatsApp messages to call the first aiders back. At A7, they were fortunate to have a student who had deferred his studies for a year and could take the day shift.

If the supply stations were like a convenience store, then the first aid booths could be likened to a health clinic. Each station had a stash of bandages, gauzes, cooling patches and saline water. There were also

---

62 – Hong Kong is susceptible to the threat of tropical storms during the summer months. There are four categories of typhoons depending on their strength and destructiveness: signals 1, 3, 8 and 10. In the event of a signal 8 or 10 typhoon, the entire city shuts down and citizens get a day off, much like a snow day in North America.

thermometers and blood glucose meters to monitor the health of hunger strikers on site. Because the procurement of medical supplies required specialized knowledge, it was more difficult for the first aid units to rely on civilian donations other than face masks and cold medication. Well-intended supporters sometimes dropped off rubbing alcohol not knowing that it posed a fire hazard. As a result, the medics had to purchase much of what they needed out of their own pockets. Meanwhile, Dr. Au made his rounds almost every night to ensure each booth was well-stocked and well-run.

The first aid teams worked closely with the supply crews and the border control units. The three support functions formed a symbiotic relationship: the supply stations provided food and drinks, the first aiders rendered emergency care, and the border controls kept intruders at bay. They operated under a flat organizational structure without reporting lines. The dynamics were somewhat different with the site marshals, the de facto policemen in Umbrellaville. Hinson, for one, found them a bit too eager to boss other volunteers around.

From headache to head trauma

For most of the evening, the medics hung around the campsites on standby. Every now and then, they received the odd call from the supply crew to treat a heat stroke, stomachache or fever, or to check up on hunger strikers and senior villagers.

Occasionally, they encountered non-combat injuries like bruises and cuts. The hilly Harcourt Road was a hotbed for accidents: one student fell off a skateboard and broke his fibula, while another dislocated his shoulder when his bicycle tripped over a highway pothole. Still, the single biggest safety hazard was the 3-foot-tall concrete highway divider that bisected the village. Pedestrians climbed over the hurdle thousands of times at all hours of the day. Even though stairs and handrails were later added to reduce fall risks, it nonetheless presented ongoing challenges for the elderly and teenagers known for their "texting while walking."

Major incidents of violence rarely happened in Admiralty – protesters could count them with one hand (see Table 10).

Date	Incident	Use of force by police	No. of arrests
Sep 28th	Police crack down on peaceful protests who have spilled onto Harcourt Road.	• Tear gas • Pepper spray • Batons • AR-15 rifles and rubber bullets (threatened but not actually used)	89
Oct 13th	Taxi drivers and organized thugs attempt to forcibly remove barricades on Harcourt Road.	• None (police officers accused of inaction)	0
Oct 14th	Protesters occupy the Lung Wo Road tunnel in response to the police clearance of Queensway.	• Pepper spray • Batons • "Dark Corner Beating" of Ken Tsang	45
Nov 30th	Protesters heed the HKFS's call to gather in Tamar Park to besiege the Government Headquarters.	• Water cannons • CS spray • Pepper spray • Batons	20

Table 10. Major clashes in Admiralty

The most common malady in a police confrontation was pepper spray burns, which could be treated by running distilled or saline water over the affected areas. The burn would go away within 30 to 45 minutes. Over time, protesters had gotten so used to being sprayed that they administered their own treatment without assistance.

Sensing a build-up of immunity against pepper spray, law enforcement switched to CS spray, the liquefied form of a highly potent riot control agent designed to create panic by causing nausea, watery eyes and shortness of breath. "It is 10 times more powerful than tear gas," Hinson observed. The spray took twice as long to wash off and was a trap for the unwary: many protesters used regular water to rinse their eyes, only to have the oil-based irritant run down their bodies burning every inch of skin in its path.

Almost all the major combat injuries happened in Mongkok, where street brawls between protesters on one side, and police and mobsters on the other side, were as violent as they were frequent. Clashes were so commonplace in Mongkok that the press became selective with their coverage and onlookers began to treat them like a street show. This increasingly blasé attitude had emboldened police officers to use even greater force.

My students participated in the Mongkok confrontations to different extents. Ken, for instance, stayed clear of all police clashes because of a pact he had made with his parents: they would let him go to the protest sites as long as he did not get himself injured or arrested. Kent, on the other hand, liked to put himself in the thick of things. He was once whacked by a police baton on his lower back and right hand. He sprained his ankle running away from pursuing officers and had to hop around like a cripple for a week. His index finger was severely bruised and it took more than two months to heal. The incident gave him pause because a serious physical injury or a criminal record would dash the aviation major's dream of becoming a commercial pilot.

Hinson's role as a first aider put him face-to-face with angry police officers on the frontlines. On the night of the 10/17 Mongkok Operation, his team received a call for reinforcement and they immediately hopped onto a subway train with medical supplies and protective gear. Once there, the medics' role changed from first aid to search and rescue. Because most of the injuries were too severe for volunteers to treat, their job was to pull the fallen from the frontlines and carry them to the ambulances parked nearby. The gruesome scene – a battlefield of bleeding faces and broken limbs caused by batons, crowbars and steel pipes – left an indelible mark on Hinson. He was shocked by the way some officers attacked protesters and medics alike purely out of spite, swinging their batons like mad men and tackling protesters who so much as talked back at them. It was a clear violation of law enforcement protocol. The experience angered the 17-year-old, but it also exhilarated him. Mongkok was the kind of grassroots revolt that he had read about in history books and epic novels. Compared to MK, Admiralty was like a summer camp.

As resentful as he was toward the police based on what he saw and heard, Hinson knew that not all cops were bad guys who followed orders like the Imperial Stormtroopers in *Star Wars*. The teenager remembered one particularly cold November night in Mongkok, when a young officer found him shivering under his first aid vest and brought him a warm blanket from the police car. From that, he figured the world was a lot more complicated and much less black-and-white than the one he read about in history books and epic novels.

Peace and safety

There were roughly 200 site marshals on duty in Admiralty, organized into teams covering different subdivided areas within the village. Each team had a leader, who in turn reported to one of the three unit chiefs with extensive experience managing big crowds at street rallies and other political campaigns. There were no marshal units in Mongkok and Causeway Bay, because the former was well-staffed by hard-boiled splinter groups and the latter was too small to warrant peacekeepers.

Site marshals were responsible for de-escalating conflicts between protesters and blue ribbon troublemakers. They would break up the

A first aider treats a student protester

fight, and if things got out of hand, call in the police. They were also in charge of safety issues like spotting fire hazards and ensuring that supply and first aid stations were set up securely and at an appropriate location. In addition, various surveillance points were installed to identify suspicious visitors who might be Triad members, undercover policemen or Communist spies.

Peacekeeping can be a thankless, if not altogether unpopular, job. Every position in the village, from the respected medical unit to the lowly janitorial staff, was self-appointed. No one had to take orders from anyone else, and yet everybody wanted to be consulted on decisions that directly or indirectly affected them. A series of incidents in early October involving site marshals moving steel barriers around without the border control units' blessing had damaged the already tenuous relationship between the two functions. The stories were picked up by social media, and were sensationalized and blown out of proportion. Since then, many site marshals stopped wearing their uniforms and badges for fear of being heckled and harassed.

On November 12th, Day 46, media mogul Jimmy Lai was attacked by a trio of assailants with animal offal – a bizarre weapon choice – outside his tent in Admiralty. Site marshals Alex Kwok and Ricky Or tackled the organ-throwers to the ground, before all of them – assailants and peacekeepers alike – were arrested by police for "fighting in a public place." The incident caused an outrage and thrust Kwok into the media spotlight as a local hero. Kwok's 15 minutes of fame, however, came with a price. His suddenly recognizable face had made him an easy target for splinter groups who were hell-bent on dismantling the marshal unit and the Grand Stage, especially after the 11/19 Wreck-and-run.

Hygiene and sanitation

Between dispensing medical care and peacekeeping, there were more mundane issues to look after. Every day, garbage had to be collected, rain water had to be drained, and giant cockroaches had to be squashed. Volunteers at the outset agreed among themselves that these janitorial duties would be performed by the supply units. Lucky for Yoko.

Among the half-dozen bathrooms in the area, the two that were most heavily patronized were the public toilets next to the Lennon Wall and the mall restrooms on the second floor of Admiralty Centre. They offered villagers relative privacy to brush their teeth, put on makeup, take off contact lenses, shave, change, wash clothes, and wipe their bodies with wet hand towels in lieu of showering.

The high traffic at those two bathrooms made them ideal galleries for arts students and media majors to début their latest creations. Men urinated on pictures of C.Y. Leung placed in the urinals while chuckling at satirical cartoons posted at eye level. Women, according to Renee, swooned over pictures of Team Alexter plastered across tiled walls and mirrors.

If you think that having thousands of sweaty, smelly protesters share a handful of communal bathrooms would be a recipe for a public health crisis, you would be wrong and way off base. Several times a day, cleaning crews from the supply units fanned out across the village with rags, brushes and buckets. They scrubbed toilets, wiped countertops and replenished toilet paper. Anyone would have been impressed by the impossible selection of facial cleansers, toners, moisturizers, shaving cream and body lotion arranged impeccably next to the sink with the labels always facing outwards. Visitors were encouraged to use the products free of charge, or add to the collection if so inclined.

According to Renee, the ladies' rooms were packed with whitening creams, rinse-free shampoo and high-end beauty products. There were signs reminding the ladies that "even suffragettes need to look pretty." Near the entrance sat a huge cardboard box of sanitary napkins with a dire warning: "Take more than you need, and you won't stop the bleed." It was an unnecessary threat, because by Renee's estimate there was enough stock to last every ovulating female in the village for a year. Her only gripe was the long queues at the bathroom because some women would take a long time washing and even dyeing their hair at the sink.

Over time, there were pest problems: mosquitoes, fleas, cockroaches, and – brace yourself – giant rats. Villagers dumped sauces, soups and other liquids into the highway gutters designed to drain only rainwater. The accumulation of food attracted rodents from nearby Hong Kong Park where there was dense vegetation and lots of ground holes. In mid-October, the medical teams launched a village-wide street cleaning campaign and asked the Health Department for mousetraps (instead of rat poison for safety reasons).

Being a germophobe, I tried to minimize my visits to the public toilets despite their cleanliness and rich collection of skincare products and street art. I adhered to a strict no-fluids-after-8:00pm policy on my sleepover night every Friday and Saturday. I brushed my teeth standing outside the bathroom and went in just to spit and rinse. If I had to do Number Two, I would take the seven-minute walk to the Mandarin Oriental and pretend to be a valued guest at the hotel. The friendly staff would leave you alone – and even open the door for you – if you walked in with a confident swagger.

The biggest personal hygiene complaint was the lack of proper showering facilities. Many protesters were too lazy to take the 15-minute walk up Cotton Tree Drive to shower at the Hong Kong Park Sports Centre, and relegated to wiping themselves down with a wet towel. During the second week, someone – perhaps a first year engineer student – decided to build a shower station. It was the size of a telephone booth covered by tarps. Inside, a 2-gallon family-sized water bottle hung overhead, with a short rubber tube mounted over its mouth to act like a shower head. Ingenious as it was, the station was abandoned after the first few uses, when villagers found out in horror that flimsy tarps and strong winds do not mix well. The defunct shower station was then converted into a makeshift barbershop that operated three hours a day. Kent told me one of his friends had a buzz cut and the styling wasn't half bad.

佔中法律事務所

OCLP Law Offices

Umbrellaville was many things: campus, residence, food bank, cultural center and hospital. In the eyes of law enforcement, however, it was nothing but a crime scene. Beneath the halcyon village life, there were rip currents that could pull protesters deep into the abyss of the criminal justice system.

Nothing sobered up the mood in the village faster than a call to arms to the frontlines. That was especially the case in Mongkok, where borders were many and violent scuffles were frequent. When the blue ribbons showed up to pick a fight, police often intervened not to disperse the crowd but to secretly remove steel barriers left behind by distracted protesters. Someone would catch the officers in the act, and the street brawl would turn into a three-way Mexican standoff. Amidst the chaos, an unsuspecting protester might suddenly find himself in the back of a police car and on the wrong side of the law.

The fearless frontliners

I was always clear about my role as a fly-on-the-wall reporter and a pro bono tutor. As much as I wanted to help, I had neither the skills nor the stomach for combat. Each time there was a standoff with police, protesters would rush to the frontlines with their helmets, goggles, and sometimes a Guy Fawkes mask (from the *V for Vendetta* movie). I would follow them with my reporter's notebook and camera. I did so at the risk of being called a "peanut eater" – a bystander who watches from a comfortable distance while others fight.

For better or for worse, my students were far less risk-averse than I was. They charged without a plan and operated on the assumption that they would somehow escape injury and arrest. Deep down, they knew that the assumption was based on a combination of chivalry and blind faith. One of Kent's favorite tactics was to create a diversion during a police confrontation by faking a fight elsewhere – banging objects and shouting about – with the goal to spread out the officers. That's probably how he got whacked in the lower back by a baton.

Protesters learned that not all police officers were the same, and that some were trickier and brasher than others. The Organized Crime and Triad Bureau (OCTB), who wore black vests over plain clothes, were the least disciplined and most gangster-like. They were known to beat protesters out of anger, release blue ribbon instigators captured by citizens, and tell dark-complexioned demonstrators to "go back to India." Several officers involved in the Dark Corner Beating belonged to the OCTB. By contrast, the Police Tactical Unit (PTU), who wore sage green uniforms and carried their signature round carbon-fiber shields, were better trained and more professional. They focused on crowd dispersion rather than getting even with protesters.

There was little I could say or do to dissuade my students from taking up arms. I did my best to at least urge the girls to stay behind in the Study Corner, even though most of them were just as fearless as the boys. Renee and her girlfriends never hesitated to follow Hinson and Kent to Mongkok, often still wearing their school uniform: a white blouse and a short skirt. I would tell Kent, who was one of the oldest in the group, to look after his "little sisters" and make their safety – and not his own bravado – his top priority.

On the night of the 10/17 Mongkok Operation, many of my students gallantly headed to Nathan Road as reinforcement. Before leaving Admiralty, they took turns dictating to me their personal details: full name (in both English and Chinese), HKID card number, age, and emergency contact. If any of them got arrested or ended up in the hospital, he would send me a WhatsApp so I could notify his parents and call a lawyer. We also agreed that the sender would then immediately quit the WhatsApp group and erase all chat history – or initiate the "restore phone to factory settings" procedure – to avoid implicating the rest of the group. If asked, the Water Blowers' Society would disavow any knowledge of his action, just like the IMF would to a captured agent in the *Mission Impossible* movies.

Legal defense team

I practice securities law. Criminal law is not my area and I refrained from dispensing legal advice to protesters. Those disclaimers had not stopped villagers from asking me what they should do in the event of an arrest. Most of the time I ended up recycling second-hand advice I overheard from defense lawyers and savvy protesters.

The dos and don'ts after an arrest, based on conventional wisdom in the village, are summarized in Table 11 opposite.

Questions about arrest and bail were precautionary most of the time, but occasionally they arose out of an actual, pressing need. Case in point: at 1:00am on an October night, I received a missed call from Yoko. Already in bed, I sent her a WhatsApp to find out what she needed. She replied saying that she and several of her kids had been arrested for theft over a dozen wooden pallets they were carrying into the village. Details of the events have been omitted here as criminal charges are still pending, but suffices to say that Yoko and her station-mates were in a fair bit of trouble and urgently needed legal help. I asked her if she had the legal defense hotlines with her and she said she did. I told her the same thing I would tell everyone else: keep calm, say as little as possible, and wait for the lawyer to arrive.

There were a few dozen – as many as 50 at the peak of the occupy movement – lawyers on the **OCLP Legal Defense Team**. Many of the members were affiliated with the pan-dem parties, including barrister and long-time Civic Party member Alvin Yeung who acted as the team's spokesman. Like the OCLP Medical Team, volunteer lawyers followed shift assignments and were organized into sub-teams to take calls from arrestees. Like Dr. Au, Yeung did not expect the protests to last more than three days.

Do:	Do not:
• Draft a text message with your full name, phone number and HKID number, and save it on your phone. • Leave the same information with someone you trust. • Upon arrest, send the draft text message to one of the legal aid hotlines. • If there is a high chance of getting arrested, leave your smart phone at home to avoid police gaining access to private information. • If you don't have a phone to send text messages, shout out your full name and HKID number, or write the information on your lower arm with a marker so that friends and volunteers can get you help. • Exit all protest-related WhatsApp, LINE, Kakao Talk and other chat groups, and erase all chat history before arriving at the police station. • Carry a pen and paper to record the time, place and other details of every event between the time of arrest and release. • While in police custody, ask for water and bathroom breaks if needed. • Inform your lawyer and/or report to the station's duty officer about any abuse or irregularity.	• Resist an arrest. • Taunt, insult or argue with police officers. • Engage in small talk with other protesters or police officers while in custody. • Assume friendly people are your friends. • Over-estimate your memory and expect to remember details of the arrest without writing them down. • Give in to excessive body searches or seizure of personal items such as handwritten notes. • Make a statement before your lawyer arrives. • Sign any document you have not carefully read or do not fully understand.

Table 11. Dos and Don'ts after an arrest

The OCLP Legal Defense Team got busy as early as September 26th, when Alex Chow, Lester Shum and Joshua Wong were arrested for obstruction and unlawful assembly during their demonstration on Civic Square. After the 9/28 Crackdown, arrests of protesters continued intermittently. There was typically a two-hour lead time between a major police operation and the arrival of the first SOS call, which allowed the legal team to monitor the latest developments on television and mobilize resources to handle the deluge of new cases that followed.

Right to remain silent

Protesters who guarded the barricades in the first row were most at risk. They were most likely to get snatched by police, usually by their shirts or backpacks. If the people around them failed to pull them back in time, they would be tackled, handcuffed and taken to a nearby police van. Somewhere during that process, the officer in charge would recite their so-called "Miranda rights" – the familiar script about the right to remain silent – and name the charges for which the arrest was being made. Common charges included general assault, assaulting a police officer, unlawful assembly, inciting others to commit a crime, and the catch-all offense of "obstructing the police."

A protester under arrest

Once the arrestees were taken to the police station, they would be divided into groups and told to wait for an officer to be assigned to have their statements taken. Being a suspect meant that many civil rights would be restricted. Each arrestee would be given a Ziploc bag to keep his valuables including mobile phone and wallet. The bag would then be sealed and he would be cut off from the outside world until his release. He would be permitted to use the land line at the police station to call a lawyer and inform his family of the arrest. If he appeared agitated, he would be asked to surrender sharp objects like pens and keys for safety reasons as well loose items such as belts and shoelaces to prevent a suicide.

While in police custody, most protesters knew to keep their mouths shut and not engage in any form of chitchat with anyone, including officers who appeared friendly and sympathetic. This was no joking matter: once the Miranda rights are read to the accused, anything he says can and will be used against him in a court of law.

After some time, the defense lawyer would arrive to assist not one, but a group of, protesters arrested at the same time. The lawyer would first check to see if anyone had been injured during the arrest and needed medical attention. He would address the arrestees en masse, informing them of their legal rights and walking them through the statement and bail procedures. Given the limited resources and time, the lawyer would not be able to personally review each statement before it was signed. So while having legal representation was helpful in terms of answering inquiries and offering peace of mind, protesters needed to rely on their own vigilance and clear-headedness in getting through much of the process themselves.

The police statement was supposed to be not more than a few sentences long and contain only basic facts about the time and place of the arrest and the alleged crimes. To solicit more information, the police officer assigned to the case would typically conduct a Q&A with the suspect. The best approach was to answer "I have nothing more to add" to every question asked, and keep the statement as brief as possible.

Lawyers familiar with the process told me that sometimes – not often, but on occasion – the police would intentionally ask incendiary questions to elicit an inadvertent confession. For instance, the officer might invent a fact such as: "My colleague said he saw you stab a man with your umbrella. Did you?" Feeling defensive, the arrestee might blurt out self-incriminating information like "No such thing! The man tried to grab me and I pushed him away!"

Once the written statement was agreed and signed, the suspect would be asked to have his palm prints and fingerprints taken. Next came the bail negotiation, which put the arrestee in a catch-22 situation. One option was to pay the bond, which would range from few hundred to a few thousand dollars, or whatever amount of cash he happened to have in his wallet at the time. Accepting bail would allow the arrestee to sign himself out and be released from police custody. The downside of this option was the burden of having to report back to the police station every month until the charges were either dropped or pressed. Option two was to refuse bail, which many protesters chose to do, and risk being held for up to 48 hours in a cold and unpleasant detention center. Because of the large number of arrests during the occupy movement, in most cases police would just let everyone go home.

Apart from the Dark Corner Beating, there were several incidents of less egregious – but no less troubling – post-arrest physical and sexual assault by police officers reported in the local press. A number of student protesters alleged that they were dragged by officers on the sidewalk or roughed up inside interrogation rooms. Joshua Wong claimed he was groped in the groin by a number of male officers while he was in custody after the September 26th arrest.

Civil rights watchdogs had expressed concerns over the low charge rate of arrested protesters. One estimate put the rate at just below 10%[63], which meant for every 10 arrests, only one resulted in actual charges being filed against the accused. There were also incidents where prosecutors were chastised by trial court judges for sloppy case management and citing erroneous facts, which raised the specter of malicious prosecution and exposed the Justice Department to potential civil suits.

My friend Yoko and her kids were among the 90% of arrestees who never got charged. After making a statement and refusing bail on that October night, they were told to go home and not cause any more trouble on the streets. Yoko and company have not heard back from the police since then. All that drama was believed to be part of a systematic effort by the authorities to intimidate citizens and scare them from returning to the protest sites.

---

63 – According to InMedia, a Hong Kong-based independent news site, 1,726 people were arrested during public events in 2014, of which 955 were during the occupy movement and 48 in subsequent *gouwu* and other demonstrations (see *Part IV - Last Days*). Of the 1,726 arrests, only 163 arrestees or 9.4% were formally charged, compared to the charge rate of 50% in 2013.

踏出傘村、走進世界

Out of the Village, Into the World

It is not every day that Hong Kong makes it to the front page of *The Wall Street Journal* or *The Guardian*. In fact, the world knows pitifully little about our city, other than some vague notion of a shopping paradise in the Far East or, to the movie buff, home to Jackie Chan, Chow Yun-fat and the dramatic skyline in *Batman: Dark Knight* and *Transformers: Age of Extinction*.

The last time Hong Kong was put under the foreign media's glare was summer 2014, when former CIA employee-turned-NSA whistleblower Edward Snowden checked into a Kowloon hotel under a pseudonym, and spent a month in Tsim Sha Tsui before seeking asylum in Russia.

It was remarkable that the world would pay attention to a southern Chinese city over some local political issues. Before September 28th, 2014, few people could even locate us on the map or name a single

Hong Kong politician. After September 28th, 2014, the Umbrella Man[64] and Joshua Wong graced the covers of two consecutive issues of *Time* magazine's Asian edition. Little known terminology such as "Basic Law," "chief executive" and "special administrative region" were tossed around on CNN and Bloomberg News like they were part of the mainstream lexicon. When we heard Brian Williams and Anderson Cooper struggle to enunciate street names in Cantonese, we knew the city had finally stepped onto the world stage.

Bringing the world to Umbrellaville

Beijing tried to make the occupy movement a national security issue. Mainland officials spoke ominously but without specificity about the invisible hand of "foreign forces," and accused suffragists of being used by the West to destabilize Hong Kong with the ultimate goal to topple the Chinese government. None of the allegations had traction or basis, or resulted in charges or arrests.

Most of the Western faces at the protest sites were expatriates who live and work in Hong Kong. Some passed through the area on their daily commute, while others genuinely wanted to contribute by donating supplies or just being there. Not a night went by that I didn't run into a colleague or a friend, and proceed to have an hour-long discussion over the movement's direction. Some of them confessed that they had hesitated about visiting Admiralty for fear that it would add to the impression that "foreigners" were behind the movement. I would tell them that back when I was living in New York, I would attend rallies for gun control and marriage equality as a concerned resident, even though I am not American. Likewise, anyone who lives in Hong Kong has a stake in its political future, whether or not they were born here.

Other than the expats, the only international presence in Umbrellaville was the foreign news media and academia. Scholars in East Asian studies, political science and international law flew in from across the world and made their way to Admiralty and Mongkok to interview protesters and take notes for their research papers. During my "office hours" sitting on Harcourt Road, I spent many an evening exchanging views on political theories and constitutional law issues with them, including a law professor from the University of California, Los Angeles (UCLA), a political science

---

64 – Not to be confused with the wooden sculpture in Admiralty, the Umbrella Man here refers to the masked protester who was seen holding up two black umbrellas and engulfed in tear gas during the 9/28 Crackdown. The name originates from the famous Tank Man who stood in front of a column of tanks on June 5th, 1989 in Beijing.

lecturer from the Hebrew University of Jerusalem, and a Ph.D. candidate from a mainland university that he did not wish to name.

There was the occasional celebrity sighting too. Actor and filmmaker James Franco was spotted in the village wearing a beanie and leather jacket on November 21st, Day 55. About a month prior to Franco's low-key visit, saxophonist Kenny G too made an appearance, albeit with much less finesse. Within hours after G tweeted a picture next to pro-democracy banners on Harcourt Road, the Communist machine hit back with a back-handed threat. A Chinese Foreign Ministry spokesperson said at a press conference: "I understand that Mr. G's music is rather popular on the mainland. He should watch what he says and does." The comment prompted the soft jazz artist to promptly delete his Twitter post and recast his visit to Admiralty as "an innocent walk around Hong Kong." As if begging for forgiveness, he tweeted: "I love China... I feel close to and care about China very much!" Kenny G might have averted a diplomatic crisis with Beijing, but he also became the butt of the joke on social media in Hong Kong.

No all foreigners were granted safe passage in and out of the protest zones. On October 18th, renowned American photojournalist Paula Bronstein was arrested for vandalism in Mongkok after she got on top of a parked car to avoid a street fight. Working for the Getty photo agency and wearing a press pass, Bronstein was taken into police custody and later released without being charged. On November 28th, Day 62, a delegation of British lawmakers, including Richard Ottaway who headed the House of Commons Foreign Affairs Committee at the time, was denied entry to Hong Kong altogether. They had planned to travel to the former crown colony to check up on the implementation of the Joint Declaration. China's deputy ambassador to Britain put it in plain English for Ottaway, telling him that his visit would "send the wrong signals to the figures of Occupy Central... and [show] encouragement for illegal actions."

Bringing Umbrellaville to the world

I visit my family in Toronto and New York every fall, usually around the last week of October to coincide with an annual law conference in Manhattan. It is not a trip I can skip or postpone. That meant I had to tear myself from Umbrellaville for two weeks and would potentially miss out on major events. On October 22nd, Day 25, I stowed away my personal belongings with Fat Girl and gave everyone I knew a bear hug. I told my friends and students that it wasn't goodbye, it was just a leave of absence. My heart was as heavy as it was the day I left my family for boarding school in my teens.

On the 15-hour flight, while going through the village pictures on my iPhone, I had a sudden epiphany. Instead of brooding over the life I left behind in Admiralty, why not make the best of my absence instead? Why not take the village to the places I was visiting?

Yes and yes.

As soon as I arrived at my parents' house, I started sending emails to various universities in Toronto and New York offering free lectures on the Umbrella Movement. All of them responded positively. Despite the short notice, I was able to arrange talks at four schools: Columbia University's School of International and Public Affairs, New York University's (NYU) Department of Politics, York University's Osgoode Hall Law School, and my alma mater, University of Toronto's Faculty of Law.

It took me two days to put together a 30-slide PowerPoint presentation that stepped through the genesis and development of the protests. The abundance of powerful images on my camera had made the preparation work rather effortless.

I did not expect college students half a world away would care much about a city of so little political importance and personal relevance to their own lives. Their reactions during the lecture and the Q&A session that followed, however, revealed a level of interest that was far beyond mere curiosity. There were gasps when I showed the picture of the sea of lights in Admiralty on September 29th, and there were chuckles when I talked about the Study Corner, the Alexter bromance and the iPhone charging stations. More importantly, I sensed a deep appreciation among the audience for protesters their own age fighting for basic civil rights that every North American took for granted.

For faculty and students who came from more troubled parts of the world, it was the universal themes in our story that resonated with them. My NYU talk was moderated by political science professor Shinasi Rama, an Albanian native who understands well the romance and peril of a popular uprising. During the 90-minute session, professor Rama chimed in frequently with his own observations about a leaderless movement, drawing many comparisons with the Albanian Rebellion of 1997 and the 2012 Orange Revolution in Ukraine.

While most members of the audience were sympathetic, there was invariably a group of foreign students from mainland China who were there to heckle the speaker. According to the professors I spoke to afterwards, some were citizen spies sent by the CCP to monitor campus activities deemed sensitive or strategic. Chinese students are known to systematically record lectures and report back anything and any person of interest, such as a seminar sympathetic to Tibet's independence or a class on advanced weapon technology. They also spy on each other as a way to deter potentially subversive behavior while studying abroad.

The author (left) and his brother Dan on Times Square in New York City

Enough credible people I know have corroborated the spy theory, that I now take it more seriously than I used to. *The New York Times* and BBC News have made repeated assertions that the Chinese government has spread its tentacles all over the world to conduct economic and military espionage. In typical Chinese fashion, the Communists intend to overrun their enemies with sheer numbers – there are far too many student spies for the CIA and MI6 to perform counterintelligence or simply to keep track of. These claims add to the rich irony of Beijing's incessant allegations that foreign intervention was behind the occupy movement.

Thankfully, the hecklers at my talks were innocuous enough. Their challenge revolved around the same few points: that the Umbrella Movement was motivated by jealousy toward China's economic growth, that Hong Kong people were ungrateful toward Beijing's generosity, and that the 8/31 Framework was in compliance with the Basic Law. None of these arguments was new, nor was it difficult to rebut (see the list of FAQs in the next section).

Frequently asked questions

While in New York, I invited my brother Dan (who lives there with his family) and some friends to take pictures with the yellow umbrella. It had become something of a global campaign to photograph the movement's symbol at famous landmarks around the world – the Eiffel Tower, the London Eye and the Golden Gate Bridge – and post them on social media as a show of solidarity. I had just added Times Square, Central Park, the Flatiron and Rockefeller Center to that list.

One of the friends I took an umbrella selfie with was Matthew Torne, the British director who made a 2014 documentary based on Joshua Wong's story called *Lessons in Dissent*. Matthew and I knew each other in Hong Kong but he happened to be in New York that week to promote *Lessons*. He asked me to join him at a screening in Greenwich Village and I did. The event ended with a Q&A session with a panel of American journalists who used to be based in Hong Kong and Beijing. The Q&A was a bit of a disappointment. The panelists perpetuated many of the myths about the occupy movement (which Matthew was quick to debunk on stage) and misread the political situation in Hong Kong (which caused Matthew to furrow his eyebrows at me a few times). It goes to show that even the well-informed in the Western media do not always grasp the nuance and complexities of our pro-democracy struggle.

That experience, combined with the questions I was asked during my own university talks, gave me the impetus to compile a list of FAQs to defend and demystify the movement. Below are the top 10 questions that came up time and again and my responses to them. I hasten to caveat that there is more than one way to tackle these questions and whether someone is persuaded by my answers depends on his personal politics and peer influence.

1. Hong Kong didn't have universal suffrage during British rule. Why are you suddenly demanding it from China now?

It feels almost funny to have to defend our desire for democracy – something that the rest of the civilized world takes for granted. If we go by the question's logic, then women and African Americans would never have won the right to vote. I am sure someone probably said this to Emmeline Pankhurst in the 1900s: "Lady folk haven't been able to vote for the past 100 years, why do you suddenly want to vote now?"

Besides, Hong Kongers have been asking for a free vote since the 1980s – so we aren't "suddenly" making these demands. The democratization of the city is written into the Basic Law and Beijing made a commitment in 2007 to implement these constitutionally guaranteed rights by 2017 and 2020. We are merely asking for what was promised to us, nothing more.

I find it ironic that our motherland is hiding behind the notion of European imperialists and telling us that "Look, if your colonizer didn't give you the right, then you shouldn't expect it from us either!"

2. Isn't it possible that China has already kept its word, just that its definition of universal suffrage is different from yours?

The Basic Law provides that the Chief Executive be selected "by universal suffrage" and "in accordance with democratic procedures." Both "universal suffrage" and "democratic procedures" are in lower case, which means they are not defined within the constitution. In law, undefined terms are interpreted in their broadest possible sense, and scholars and judges will look to context and precedents for reference. That's why the pan-dems are always talking about an "international standard," because that is the most objective and least disputable benchmark.

But I don't even think we need to go there. All the chatter about an international standard and the United Nations Charter has only given Beijing an excuse to wag its fingers and tell us that "Western democracy" doesn't apply in China. I think we should stop playing the semantics game and just use our common sense. Having two to three pre-selected Communist-loving candidates to choose from is *not* a free election. End of discussion. If your parents tell you can marry whomever you want but only let you pick from their list of Girl A and Girl B, then they are lying to your face. If a waiter says you can order anything you want on the menu except you can only have fried rice with chicken or fried noodles with chicken, then he is lying to your face too. Beijing needs to stop taking us for fools.

3. The Basic Law says there needs to be a nominating committee. So what's the problem?

Yes, the Basic Law does require a Nominating Committee, but it is silent on its size and composition. The purpose of the public consultations by the Electoral Reform Taskforce was to discuss the make-up of the committee and work out a solution that satisfies all sides. What's the point of even having a public consultation if the Standing Committee calls all the shots by unilaterally issuing the 8/31 Framework?

Beijing has essentially told everyone to shut up and accept its words as gospel. None of the new restrictions in the 8/31 Framework is in the Basic Law – they are invented by the Communists with the sole purpose of controlling the outcome of the election.

4. Is street occupation the best way to fight for universal suffrage?

The short answer is "no." No one wants to break the law and sleep on the streets night after night. Who doesn't want to sit in a meeting room and talk to each other like civilized adults? But Beijing has shut the door on meaningful talks by making it clear that the 8/31 Framework is its first and final offer.

To be fair, we have tried everything – public debate, street rallies, open letters to the Communist leadership – but nothing has worked. Student leaders sat down and talked to top government officials on October 21st and that didn't work either. We have exhausted our options. If you can name it, we've tried it.

So we got creative. We believe if we can't outgun the Communists, we will have to outsmart them. Occupy Central and now the Umbrella Movement have achieved just that. The whole world is now talking about Hong Kong because of a bit of outside-the-box thinking.

5. Isn't it selfish of the students to hold the city hostage for their own political ideals? Aren't they doing so at the expense of Hong Kong's global image as a politically stable financial capital?

In 1989, no one accused the Beijing University students of being selfish for occupying Tiananmen Square. In the 1960s, no one accused Martin Luther King, Jr. of inconveniencing other African Americans for his own political agenda. No one ever questioned the activists' integrity or motive.

But Hong Kong is different, isn't it? Hong Kongers love their convenience. People raise their fists in the air if their commutes take 10 minutes longer than usual, or if they have to take the subway instead of a bus. We aren't asking them to take part in the protests; we are only asking them to show a little understanding. After all, these so-called "political ideals" affect them too. If there is more accountability and less cronyism in the system, perhaps they wouldn't have to work so hard and worry so much about their commutes, only to turn their paychecks over to greedy property developers.

Government officials like to remind protesters that there are only a few thousand of them in Admiralty, that means the other 7 million citizens are satisfied with the Beijing-backed proposal. It is a bogus argument, of course. Imagine a restaurant has served unclean food and sickened hundreds, and imagine the manager responds, "No fair! What about the thousands of other customers who didn't complain?"

The global image argument is even more laughable. What's tarnishing Hong Kong's reputation is not the protesters but Beijing's heavy-handed political interference and endangerment of the "one country, two systems" framework. What's happening in Hong Kong is a textbook case of domestic violence. The aggressor wants his victim to keep her mouth shut to preserve the "stability" and "harmony" of the household. If she so much as cries for help, she is destroying the family's image and that makes her the bad person. Where's the logic in that?

6. Is the occupy movement really about democracy, or is it more about young people feeling insecure about their future and Hong Kong being threatened by Chinese cities like Shanghai and Shenzhen?

Young people in Hong Kong are frustrated. They are angry about rising property prices and a lack of social mobility. More importantly, they fear that the Hong Kong they know is vanishing in front of their eyes. They are seeing the city's core values – freedom of speech, freedom of the press, and the rule of law – under threat. They see electoral reform as the only solution to all of these problems.

None of that has anything *whatsoever* to do with China's wealth. If Shanghai or Shenzhen – or Singapore, for that matter – wants to dethrone Hong Kong as Asia's financial capital, they should go right ahead. Only a very small number of very wealthy people care about whether Hong Kong is No. 1 or No. 2 in some *Forbes* ranking. These bragging rights mean nothing to the average citizen – they don't help him put food on the table or put a roof over his head. That's why Hong Kong people love Taiwan. The country is not the wealthiest or the most economically competitive (Hong Kong is ranked fourth in the world and Taiwan 13th), but at least there is democracy and people there have a say in how the country is run.

7. Why bother protesting if you already know that Beijing won't back down?

Consider this hypothetical: if a group of gangsters break into your house and threaten to take your children away, will you fight back even though you are outnumbered and resistance is futile? I hope the answer is "yes."

Sometimes we do things out of principle and out of instinct. Sometimes we do things because they are the right things to do, whether or not it makes a difference in the actual outcome. And sometimes we just have to try even if the odds are stacked against us, because not trying at all makes us irresponsible, even pathetic.

Rosa Parks never thought she would change the course of history by refusing to give up her seat on the bus. Thomas Edison never thought he would light up the world when he fiddled with carbon strips on an old train. Neither Parks nor Edison would have been in the history books if they had constantly calculated their costs and benefits or weighed the pros against the cons.

Another thing about futile resistance is that it sends a strong message to the oppressors that you won't roll over and play dead. If you don't put up a fight *this* time, you can bet they will come for even more *next* time.

8. *Where is this all going? How long will the protesters be on the streets?*

They are prepared to stick around for as long as it takes, or until public opinion turns overwhelmingly against them.

Protesters don't have a timetable or calendar. They are taking it one day at a time. They know that once a political movement begins, it takes on a life of its own. Nothing in politics moves in a straight line and so they are going with the flow and playing it by ear.

9. *What if the movement ends badly?*

There is always that risk and the question is how great the risk is. We hope that Beijing learned its lesson in 1989. The Chinese government paid a hefty price for the bloody crackdown on Tiananmen Square and it is not about to make the same mistake.

It also doesn't make sense from a tactical standpoint. A crackdown will discredit and weaken President Xi Jinping's leadership. The best strategy for Beijing is to wait it out.

10. Is Hong Kong ready for democracy?

This question always gives me a chuckle. I consider democracy a basic human right and not a privilege or a Western import. It is as fundamental as food and water. You don't need to get ready for food and water.

I also like to compare democracy to swimming. You don't learn how to swim in the classroom – you just jump into the water. Likewise, democracy has nothing to "get ready" for – you just implement it and let people make their own decisions. If voters make the wrong choice this time, they will vote for someone else next time. Live and learn – that's how you get ready for democracy.

But to answer your question: of course we are ready for democracy. We are sleeping-on-the-streets ready.

Part 4

Wilting

"Turning and turning in the widening gyre
   The falcon cannot hear the falconer;
Things fall apart; the center cannot hold;
   Mere anarchy is loosed upon the world,
The blood-dimmed tide is loosed, and everywhere
   The ceremony of innocence is drowned;
The best lack all conviction, while the worst
   Are full of passionate intensity."

– William Butler Yeats
The Second Coming

Last Days

So far, nothing in the Chinese stew of carrots and sticks had done much to dampen the core group's determination to fight on. Every plan of attack devised by the bosses up north had either failed or backfired.

Equally stumped, C.Y. Leung's administration had been flip-flopping between tactics, sending in riot police with high-powered crowd control weaponry, then pulling them all back; promising another round of talks with the student leaders, then canceling it last minute; condemning the protests as an illegal act, then allowing them to go on for weeks.

Indeed, law enforcement had ample resources to perform an all-out clearance – especially during the early hours between 4:00 and 7:00am when the occupied zones were virtually deserted – but they chose not to act. Perhaps they were waiting for Beijing's green light that never came. Perhaps Beijing didn't want to make a sudden move until the APEC Summit was over in mid-November.

Or perhaps the cat-and-mouse game was trickier than met the eyes. For instance, if an officer tried so much as remove a single steel barrier, a protester would scream for help and a squad of poncho-clad student warriors would come to the rescue. Their swift response was made possible by walkie-talkies, WhatsApp chat groups and the city's efficient subway system that could whisk passengers between protest zones in minutes. One failed police operation and tens of thousands could return to the streets – everything would be back to square one.

Tell it to the judge

A tie-breaker in the stalemate between authorities and protesters emerged in late October, when somewhere, somehow, someone within C.Y. Leung's camp had a eureka moment: *what about the courts? Why don't we get the judges to do something?*

Legal action has always been a last resort for the government because of the uncertainty of outcome. In the not-so-perfect separation of powers in Hong Kong – where a legislature stacked with Beijing loyalists marches in lockstep with the Beijing-appointed Chief Executive – the judicial branch has stayed by-and-large independent. Even though lower court judges are becoming more government-friendly in the post-Handover era, appeal and final court justices[65] are mostly colonial appointees who do not always play ball with the ruling elite. If the government rolled the dice in the courtroom and lost, a judgment in favor of the protesters would put them on *both* the moral and the legal high ground to remain on the streets indefinitely.

Then, somewhere, somehow, someone within the Leung camp had another eureka moment: *why don't we ask (or pay) private citizens to file for court injunctions to ban the protests?*

Brilliant idea. While liberal judges might view the government as the oppressor trying to silence dissent, private citizens were on an equal footing with the protesters and therefore made better claimants. Small business owners could trump up stories of personal hardship to appeal to the judge's sympathy. They would argue that the students' political ideals, however lofty and respectable, could not be sought at the expense of the rights of fellow citizens, in particular those who were disproportionately affected by snarled traffic.

Instead of seeking monetary compensation for business losses (which would have a low chance of success[66]), plaintiffs would file for cease-and-desist orders against the street occupation. Sure enough, beginning in

---

65 – The Court of Final Appeal is the highest court in Hong Kong. That said, the SAR government may override its decisions by seeking an "interpretation" from the Standing Committee pursuant to Article 158 of the Basic Law. Although they happen very rarely (less than five times since the Handover), these interpretations are viewed with great suspicion by the legal community as they undermine the city's judicial independence. The most famous case was the right of abode controversy in 1999, when the Standing Committee overturned the Court of Final Appeal's ruling that granted residency to hundreds of thousands of Chinese-born children of new immigrant parents.

66 – Case law has shown that, as a matter of public policy, monetary damages are rarely awarded to lost business activities as a result of public demonstrations, workers' strikes or other collective actions.

late October, tour bus operators, unions representing taxi drivers, and an owner of a commercial building in Admiralty filed for injunctions in the civil courts, claiming that their business operations had been disrupted as a result of the street blockades. The lower courts sided with the plaintiffs and authorized bailiffs to clear parts of the protest zones. Appeals to the higher courts were dismissed, which encouraged other plaintiffs to come forward and apply for similar injunctions.

The fall of Mongkok

On November 24th, Day 58, bailiffs and lawyers representing taxi unions descended on Mongkok with court papers in their hands, and started posting notices in the area telling protesters to vacate within 24 hours. They chose a Monday because most people would have returned to work or class after the weekend and the crowds would remain thin until Friday.

The next morning, on November 25th, bailiffs returned with professional removal crews to carry out the injunctions. They read out the court orders through megaphones and began dismantling a fort of steel barriers on Argyle Street with chainsaws and sledgehammers. The crowds grew quickly after protesters called in reinforcements to block the clearance. 3,000 police officers arrived on the scene to "assist" the bailiffs in their operation, which was highly unusual considering it was a civil dispute between two private parties. Argyle Street was reopened at around 4:00pm, but the number of protesters continued to swell.

By 6:00pm, riot police were mobilized – the first time since the 9/28 Crackdown – to push back defiant protesters. Long-range CS spray was fired from mobile watchtowers (a new piece of police equipment), and over 80 protesters were arrested. Among them was a NOW TV engineer who was charged with assault after his step ladder (used by the cameraman to get a better vantage point) accidentally brushed an officer's leg.

The same exercise repeated on Wednesday, November 26th, except that even more people joined in this time. As bailiffs were about to clear Nathan Road, a large team of unidentified men wearing red baseball caps and white "I Heart Hong Kong" T-shirts showed up with pliers and handsaws. Alex Chow, Lester Shum and Joshua Wong arrived soon thereafter to challenge the operation, claiming that it had exceeded the scope of the injunctions. All three student leaders were arrested for obstruction and contempt of court, along with another 70 or so protesters. During the pandemonium, the *Guan Gong* shrine was destroyed and discarded, as was every tent, supply station and roadblock in the area. By 3:30pm,

Nathan Road was reopened and was once again teeming with traffic and pedestrians.

That was how the 60-day Mongkok occupation met its end. Over the course of two months, the tough middle child had seen the good, the bad and the ugly. It survived the worst of the mob attacks and the most brazen of police brutality. In doing so, it won the hearts and minds of protesters and earned the title of the "true battlefield." Its demise dealt a serious blow to the occupy movement, for everyone remembered the villagers' prophecy: *when one site falls, so will the others.*

Taking the protesters to court was a gamble that paid off handsomely for the government. In the end, the wooden gavel proved to be mightier than any police weaponry or gang members. The strategy worked because an independent judiciary has long been the pride of Hong Kong and the bedrock of its economic prosperity. Like press freedom, it is one of the few things that distinguishes the SAR from the rest of China and is therefore held in very high regard by citizens. The Umbrella Movement was an act of civil disobedience, but to go from challenging an unjust electoral reform proposal to taking on the entire judicial system would significantly expand the scope of attack and stretch the message far too thin.

Timing was also a key factor: the injunctions were issued at a time when public support for the protests was already dwindling. By then, the initial anger toward the tear gas crackdown had long subsided and given way to annoyance with the daily disruptions. The court decisions were the checkmate in a drawn-out political chess game that many felt should have concluded a long time ago.

The aftershocks

The fall of Mongkok spawned a new sideshow. Beginning in December, there were flurries of spontaneous demonstrations by splinter groups in Mongkok and Tsim Sha Tsui. *Gouwu*[67] was a rallying cry for protesters to visit busy shopping streets in large numbers to overrun the area. The aim was twofold: first, to get even with the police for aiding and abetting the clearance operation in Mongkok the week before; and second, to mock C.Y. Leung who had called on citizens to do more shopping to "revive" the economy.

---

67 – The word is a double entendre of sorts: it means shopping in Mandarin and pointless wailing in Cantonese. The term originates from an anecdote in August 2014 when a participant of an anti-OCLP rally was asked by a news reporter what had motivated her to take to the streets. Clearly part of the rent-a-crowd, the woman answered in heavily accented Cantonese, "I'm here to *gouwu*!" It became one of the top 10 buzzwords in 2014.

Based loosely on Bruce Lee's combat philosophy to "be formless and shapeless like water," the new form of protest – known as flash mobs in North America – gave police the runaround. Because the line between shoppers and protesters was blurry, it also made it harder for participants to be arrested for unlawful assembly. *Gouwu* shoppers found unlikely allies in the United States, where citizens had been staging "die-ins" at shopping malls and train stations by playing dead on the floor in protest of the fatal police shooting of an unarmed teenager in Ferguson, Missouri.

Once in a while, the pretend shoppers would raise their right hands and give the three-finger salute in defiance. To taunt police, some recited passages from the Bible while others chanted unintelligible verses from the *Nilakantha Dharani*, an ancient Buddhist script. When their path was blocked by police barricades, they would fall into a tactical formation like a Roman battalion and use umbrellas and homemade shields to breach police lines. From time to time, shoppers would lead officers on a wild goose chase through the dizzying warren of backstreets between Mongkok and Tsim Sha Tsui in an all-night game of human Pac-Man.

Sporadic outbreaks of *gouwu* protests continued after the movement ended and well into Christmas and the new year.

II

Yoko's complaint was getting louder by the day.

"I miss my soft bed at home," she pouted like a 4-year-old without her favorite stuffed animal. She had been sleeping at Station G1 for so long that she had forgotten the security code to her apartment building. Still, she couldn't abandon her kids to go back to her bed and her middle class life – not as long as Umbrellaville was still standing.

I reminded her what she used to say to me: every day could be our last. "But I've been saying that every day for the past two months!" Yoko protested in mock anger.

"What if the police never clear the site and those HKFS kids keep twiddling their thumbs?" As manager of the largest supply station in Admiralty, she had been invited to attend strategy meetings by members of the Five-party Platform. She had seen Alex Chow and Lester Shum in action, although she had not been impressed with their wishy-washy responses and disinclination to take a stance on almost any issue.

"I don't want to spend Christmas here!" Yoko protested. "I want to go shopping and buy presents for my nieces!"

Escalation now

Yoko wasn't the only one who felt compelled to stay but eager to leave. With Mongkok gone, it was only a matter of time before bailiffs and lawyers would make their way to Harcourt Road. If someone wanted to do something to turn things around, now would be the time. Everyone was looking to the HKFS for an Umbrella 2.0, but 2.0 never came.

My students were among the grumbling villagers. They had come to Admiralty to fight for universal suffrage, not to eat McDonald's every night at an outdoor summer camp. Hinson, who used to idolize the HKFS leadership, now took every chance to berate it. "What are those guys waiting for?" he would ask testily. "What do they do all day? Interviews and more interviews."

Some of Hinson's frustration was stoked by angry splinter groups who wanted the HKFS to get down from the stage and out of the way. Members of Civic Passion and other localist groups had been showing up at the village on a nightly basis. From the Lion Rock Villas, I could hear muffled shouts coming from the melee down the hill. On my way to the bathroom by the Lennon Wall, I would pass by the challengers and get an up-close look at them. They were men and women in their 20s and 30s, some of whom I recognized from watching the evening news. They would chant "Take down the Grand Stage!" and "Disband the marshal units!" Sometimes the verbal altercations would turn physical and the marshals would be called in to break them up – which incited the other side even more.

The infighting was tearing the occupy movement asunder, and the HKFS needed to make up their mind on the way forward. Alex Chow showed great bravado in the early days of the protests when he told reporters that he would order suffragists to occupy various government buildings unless their demands were met. He talked a big game back then, and protesters now wanted him to put his money where his mouth was.

Final nail in the coffin

On November 30th, Day 64, my students finally got what they wanted. The HKFS announced Operation Tamar Siege, a make-or-break effort to revive the occupy movement – their own version of the Boston Tea Party or the Storming of the Bastille. Text messages were sent around asking protesters to gather near Tamar Park and await further instructions. The vague mission was to besiege the Government Headquarters and, as many hoped, occupy it. Everyone was on high alert: Yoko had her piles of protective gear at the ready at Station G1; Hinson put on his yellow vest and fully-loaded fanny pack; Kent, Renee and the others had their lab goggles and construction masks around their necks. As usual, I followed them with my notebook and camera to document it all.

The standoffs started shortly after dinner. Protesters continued to pour in – the crowd inside the Lung Wo Road tunnel was more than 20 people deep. There were site marshals everywhere directing pedestrian traffic. Every few minutes, people would be asked to move aside to make room for heavy steel barriers to be carried to the frontlines.

In Tamar Park, makeshift triage units had been set up to treat the injured. Every five minutes or so, another student would be escorted by medics to the lawn, before he frantically took off his T-shirt and sometimes even his pants to reveal a body burned to a pinkish red by pepper spray. One of the volunteers would pour distilled water down his shoulders, torso and legs, while another one would fan him with a magazine.

I knew my students would go headfirst to the frontlines and fight tooth and nail that night. The operation was made out to be a do-or-die offensive that would make the last 63 days of their lives all worth it. I took out my phone and messaged Kent to remind him to look after the girls. It took me a while to get through to him because the reception would get jammed every time there were this many people in a small area. Or did the authorities make service providers switch off the signals in Admiralty again, as they allegedly did on September 28th? Further afield, I ran into Hinson who was in the middle of treating a protester. His walkie-talkie was broadcasting the locations of the latest cases of head injuries caused by police baton. Despite the mayhem around us, the La Salle kid had a big grin on his face. "Tonight's the night," Hinson said, brimming with an excitement I hadn't seen in him for weeks.

Somewhere in the crowd, I spotted a brunette news reporter and her tall, blond cameraman setting up a tripod for a live broadcast. It was rare to find foreign news media this late in the occupy movement – by November, most of the international press had moved on to more exciting news stories. I walked up to the couple and introduced myself. Luiza was a Hong Kong-based correspondent for RedeTV!, a Brazilian television network. She and her partner had come to cover what had been touted as a "major escalation operation" by the student leaders. Luiza asked me if I wanted to be interviewed but I declined, explaining that I was there as a reporter myself. I suggested that she speak to Renee instead, which would have the added benefit of keeping her out of harm's way for at least half an hour.

I found Renee by the Lung Wo Road tunnel and brought her back to the lawn. With her safe in Luiza's care, I went back to the tunnel where I was reunited with Kent and my other students. Tension was high but there was hardly any action as far as I could see. Protesters forming long human chains would advance toward a phalanx of police officers, and the police officers would push back with their shields, batons and CS spray. One side would chant, and the other side would blast scripted warnings from megaphones. The same routine played out repeatedly throughout the night. Everyone was just gesturing – there was no major offense or arrest. Nor was there a plan. *How are we supposed to besiege the Government Headquarters? Which entrance should we target? Is there enough manpower? Is backup on the way?* No one had a clue.

I left at 2:00am, when both sides seemed to have reached an unspoken agreement to pull back and take a break. All my students in the WhatsApp group were accounted for. In fact, most of them had already gone home. Looking at my watch, it dawned on me that two hours ago the movement had just entered another month. It was December 1st. Final exams were around the corner. Christmas was only three weeks away.

The next morning, a Monday, I checked the news in the office and found out what had transpired in Tamar since I left. The answer was "not much." The tug-of-war between protesters and police went on until 6:00am, and then it was over. Without any direction or game plan, the crowds continued to fizzle out until they were eventually outnumbered and overcome by police. I checked my students' WhatsApp group and saw there were over 100 unread messages. Everyone was fuming over the complete fiasco that was the overnight operation. Later that day, my students' anger turned into outrage, after they heard Alex Chow's callous remark about using the siege to make a point to the escalation-prone protesters. It turned out that all those head injuries and pepper spray burns were just so the HKFS could check the "escalation" box and say to the radicals that their way didn't work any better either.

III

On December 5th, the Hong Kong Observation Wheel began spinning on the Central waterfront. The 200-foot-tall, 42-gondola Ferris wheel was the city's answer to the London Eye and the Singapore Flyer. Dozens of eager tourists, most of them from mainland China, lined up at the ticket counter for a 20-minute visual feast of the glorious Victoria Harbour.

Next to it, construction workers were busily setting up huge marquees for the upcoming Great European Carnival sponsored by insurance giant AIA. The fair, replete with a carousel and other theme park rides, would open for business just in time for Christmas.

To the protesters camping out 500 yards away, December 5th was simply Day 69. The latest tourist attraction was just another searing reminder that the scars of the tear gas crackdown had healed and that the city had moved on. Nathan Village was already history – the entire area was cleared within 48 hours nine days earlier. The Occupy Trio had left Admiralty and turned themselves in to police. Urging everyone to go home, Benny Tai wrote an op-ed in *The New York Times* and described the lingering occupy movement as a "high-risk, low-return business."

Meanwhile, Chinese tourists were coming back with a vengeance. According to the Travel Industry Council, the number of mainland visitors for the month of October actually went up compared to the same period in 2013, despite a temporary ban on mainland tour groups. The engine of capitalism, symbolized by the giant wheel of fortune that now towered over the protesters, was once again running at full speed. The resilience of Hong Kong people is a double-edged sword – it gets them through adversities like pandemics and financial downturns, but it also trains them to seek normalcy even under the most abnormal of circumstances. The heart of the city would continue to beat, with or without the blood clot in its biggest artery.

A farewell to arms

The 11/30 Tamar Siege was a public relations disaster. The incident was all the evidence citizens needed to conclude that prolonging the occupation any further would bring no political concession from the authorities, only more public grievances. That conclusion, together with the fall of Mongkok and a new round of court orders issued against the Admiralty encampment, had given the police the moral high ground to close in on Umbrellaville. They even set a date: December 11th.

On December 10th, Day 74 and the eve of the scheduled police clearance, I did my final lunch box run at the City Hall Maxim's restaurant. I said goodbye to the staff and thanked them for putting up with me and my coworkers in the past 10 weeks. None of them said anything to me; they just nodded and smiled. Their muted response had to do with the restaurant manager being present that day and watching them like a hawk. Perhaps management didn't want to openly endorse what the government had repeatedly called a criminal act. Before I left, the chef who was always chopping things behind the roast meat counter[68] suddenly came out to shake my hand, before he swaggered back to his corner without paying any attention to the manager.

That evening, I went tent by tent to say goodbye to my friends. There was a huge turnout on Harcourt Road, the biggest crowd I had seen since the one-month anniversary on October 28th. Citizens had returned to the sacred ground to pay their final respects – and to do one last Facebook check-in. At the Far East Supply Station, Fat Girl hollered my name and said she had something for me. It was the blue and white tarp I no longer needed after moving into the Lion Rock Villas. She had folded the sheet nicely and put it in a linen bag, as if it was a prized oil painting. On the front side of the bag were two rows of Chinese characters in big, bold handwriting: "Do not remove. This belongs to Jason Gor!" I gave her my thanks, and took pictures with her holding up a chalkboard that read "We'll be back."

I proceeded to Station G1, where I found a visibly upbeat Yoko. 74 days of protest fatigue had been wiped off her face by the prospect of spending Christmas at home. "It's finally over!" she beamed, sounding like an Allied soldier returning from Normandy. Her post-war glee was in stark contrast to the valedictory sadness all around us. "Help yourself to whatever you want from these piles. Take as much as you can carry," she said, while stuffing a bunch of bananas into my hands. She told me that most of the supplies would be donated to old people's homes, but other things, like fruits and drinks, had to be consumed that night. In less than 12 hours, anything left behind would become part of the rubble.

I finally arrived at the Study Corner, where my students – at full complement for the first time ever – were already snapping selfies. After taking about 100 group photos in every possible pose and with every combination of people, we sat down for a heart-to-heart. I wished Ken and his two classmates all the best with their media project. I told Hinson and Renee to study hard for their upcoming DSE exams[69]. As for Kent, I said something about mending fences with his mom but his mind seemed to be someplace else. We all promised each other to keep in touch and made plans for reunion dinners and beach barbecues. The more sentimental ones began reminiscing about the highs and lows and the ups and downs in the past two months. As expected, Kent brought up my ridiculous air mattress that took up two-thirds of our shared tent. I

---

68 – Most local fast food chains in Hong Kong have a separate roast meat kitchen that serves barbequed pork and roast duck.

69 – The Diploma of Secondary Education (DSE) Examination is a series of university entrance exams held between March and June every year. The DSE is taken very seriously because of the tremendous impact it has on a student's future, and hence the multi-billion-dollar cram school industry in Hong Kong.

teased him back, reminding everyone that he was never there because he was always out with some girl.

On that subject, Kent finally mustered enough courage that evening to confess his feelings to the object of his affection – which explained why he looked so restless all night. A true procrastinator, the self-proclaimed apartment male waited until the very last night to do something he should have done a long time ago. Knowing that he would never get another chance to spend this much time with the girl, the aviation major bit the bullet and swallowed his pride – he took her by her hand and whisked her away for a romantic night walk by the harbor front. Call it beginner's luck, but it worked. For the rest of the night, the two lovebirds held hands and gazed at each other like a pair of turtledoves.

That was just the distraction I needed to lighten the mood. Given everything that we had been through – and the city had been through – it was impossible not to get a little emotional about the end. I had to leave before the sweet sorrow got to me. Just before midnight, I gave everyone a hug and walked out of Umbrellaville for the last time.

The fall of Admiralty

On December 11th, Day 75, the clearance operation began at 10:00am. By then, social media was already covered wall-to-wall with gut-wrenching pictures of mass arrest and wholesale destruction. I was in the office resisting the temptation to check the news. For the rest of the day, I placed myself in a media blackout, like a soccer fan who doesn't want to be told the World Cup results until he watches the game at his own time.

It wasn't until much later that day that I felt ready for the grim reality. I turned on the evening news at 11:00pm and braced myself for heartbreak. As expected, bailiffs and removal crews had made their way to Harcourt Road with their court papers, all the while being escorted and assisted by the police, who had no business meddling in a private affair.

Unlike the clearance in Mongkok, the 13-hour Admiralty operation went ahead without incident. There was no need for riot police, pepper spray or batons. Protesters sat on the ground arm-in-arm and waited for an arrest. In all, 247 people were taken away, among them were the famous Uncle Wong Trio. The three elderly men, aged 70, 82 and 90, shared the same family name (but were not related) and had been sighted frequently at the three encampments offering moral support to the students. The Admiralty clearance was momentous enough to finally bring the three uncles together in one place. Less welcome were members of the pan-dem parties, many of whom had not been seen in Admiralty for weeks.

Much to the annoyance of the core group, they decided to turn up on the last day to take part in a photo op.

A team of police officers take apart an umbrella sculpture in Admiralty

After the arrest, police officers and removal crews began to dismantle dome tents, supply stations, first aid booths, the Study Corner, and all the artworks that weren't rescued in time. I switched off the television before the camera cut to the bulldozers and excavators.

On December 12th, the day after the clearance, I walked to Admiralty at lunch time to survey the damage. In classic Hong Kong fashion, the government acted with frightening efficiency. Every street, footbridge and sidewalk had been restored to the way it was on September 27th. Cars and double-decker buses hurtled through Harcourt Road at 50 miles per hour like they always had.

Near the spiral staircase where the Lennon Wall once stood, the sanitation department was busy scrubbing away every last yellow sticky note. One of the workers unrolled a heavy garden hose and started to spray down the entire area. Two Caucasian women, each carrying a yellow umbrella, stood in front of the hose to intercept the clean-up. The worker didn't want any trouble and went splashing somewhere else.

Other than a few stubborn stickers that refused to come off, there was no trace of a mass sit-in that comprised thousands of tents and 10 times more people. That was precisely the point. The authorities were determined to erase a seminal moment in our history and quickly turn the page as if it never happened at all. The scene recalled the morning of June 5th, 1989, when the PLA mobilized sanitation trucks to wash off the blood on Tiananmen Square and hired masons to cover up bullet holes in nearby buildings. C.Y. Leung may or may not be a CCP member, but he certainly acted like one.

A few nights later, I had dinner with a friend in Causeway Bay. It was my first proper sit-down meal since I took my parents out in Toronto the month before. After we finished, I offered my friend a ride home. It was my first time driving on the Harcourt Road expressway since the clearance. I struggled not to be distracted (and endanger my passenger) by all the memories rushing through my head. As we drove past Admiralty Centre, I couldn't help but say to my friend, "I used to teach here." Then I pointed at the slope in front of us and sighed, "We're about to drive through my bedroom." My friend could probably hear the lump in my throat. It would be another two weeks before I could post anything on social media that did not relate to the protests: restaurant check-ins and other frivolous things. It felt strange to be business-as-usual when it was not.

On December 15th, four days after Admiralty fell, Hennessy Road and Yee Wo Street in Causeway Bay were cleared by the police. The villagers' prophecy was finally fulfilled, and the Umbrella Movement was officially brought to a close. Over the course of 79 days, 955 individuals were arrested, 75 protesters turned themselves in, 1.2 million citizens participated in one way or another, but not a single soul was killed or seriously hurt. A few dozen tents remained on the pedestrian sidewalk in front of the Legco Building on Tim Mei Avenue. Dubbed "New Tim Mei Village," the small encampment would remain until June 2015, probably because it did not impede traffic or slow down the engine of the city.

Success or Failure

Did it succeed or did it fail? That is the $500,000 question.

Protesters had been debating that subject long before the last dump truck drove out of Causeway Bay on December 15th, and long before political pundits began cranking out obituaries and post mortems on the 79-day struggle.

In fact, I was asked that very question as soon as the protests began. A reporter from *Maclean's*, a Canadian newsmagazine, approached me the day after the 9/28 Crackdown with the conjecture: "If the students don't end up getting what they ask for, if China refuses to cave in, will they consider this whole thing a failure?"

I told the reporter that the answer depends on two things: how he defines success and whom he asks.

What it didn't achieve

There was no dispute what the protesters' goal was. OCLP, the 9/22 Class Boycott and ultimately the Umbrella Movement were all motivated by one unifying demand: a free vote. To make sure no one would forget that, there were "We demand real universal suffrage" and "Forget not why you are here" stickers on every surface in the village: lampposts, doors, stairwells, and sometimes even people's foreheads for dramatic effect.

If we are to frame the Canadian reporter's question in binary terms, then the answer is "yes, the occupy movement failed." The facts are undeniable: every political demand made by the protesters was rejected outright. Beijing's position on electoral reform was every bit as unyielding on December 15th as it was 79 days earlier. Despite everything that had happened, not a word in the 8/31 Framework was revised, retracted or reinterpreted. Even secondary demands, such as the resignation of C.Y. Leung, were summarily ignored. So yes, the movement failed.

Admitting defeat is not easy; it is heartbreaking stuff. But is the result really that surprising? Taking the city hostage as leverage to haggle with Beijing was at best a long shot. Every commentator and political analyst had told us that the Communists wouldn't back down for fear of appearing weak and encouraging similar behavior on the mainland. If you had asked any protester anywhere at any time during the occupy movement, he would have told you that a policy reversal by Beijing was wishful thinking. A protester's response to *The New York Times* summed up that collective sentiment: "Belief is the only reason to be here, even if it's not a realistic belief. Changes will always take time." We did what we did despite – and because of – the slim chance of victory.

So when the movement didn't ultimately deliver the result that everyone wanted but no one thought they would get, the proper response should have been "Alright, we expected that. Now what do we do next?" rather than reducing a hard-fought battle to a single-word verdict of "success" or "failure." The situation is similar to that of a political newcomer who runs an honest, respectable election campaign but ultimately loses to a powerful establishment candidate. Would you call the dark horse a loser for trying, or would you pat him on the back and say "better luck next time"?

The Umbrella Movement began as a spontaneous reaction to an excessive use of police force and blossomed into a full-on political movement, before it became a war of attrition that wore everyone down. Whichever way you look at it, it was meant to be an evolution, not a revolution. It was but a small step on the long road to full democracy.

What it did achieve

Hong Kong has one of the lowest voter registration and turnout rates in Asia. Civic participation is scant in part because the core middle class does not have much to ask for in terms of social welfare provided by the government, and in part because of the tacit acceptance of the plutocracy passed down from the colonial days. Citizens operate in a state of willing submission where "oh well" is the response to many government policies and decisions. On occasions when the ruling elite go too far, citizens vent their frustration through the annual July 1st rally and ad hoc mass demonstrations, like the two in 2012 in response to the Express Rail-link and the Patriotic Education Plan.

But the Umbrella Movement was different, both in scope and in depth. Overnight, our first lesson on civil disobedience transformed the collective consciousness and awakened citizens, in particular those in their 20s and 30s, from their existential slumber. Politics was suddenly on everyone's minds and lips, and social justice was placed at the top of their priority list. Government officials could no longer get away with pulling the wool over citizens' heads, for every policy and decision would be scrutinized, debated, and scrutinized some more. The occupy movement has succeeded in planting a seed in our youth, a generation that Beijing has tried so hard to win over since reclaiming the territory. Social awakening is *not* a consolation prize – in a grassroots fight for justice and democracy, it is all the ammunition we need.

A shrub planted in a highway reflector slot

More importantly, ordinary citizens now realize the enormous power they have if they act together. The movement provided an important data point on how to wage a leaderless uprising, and a common vocabulary for the next round of fighting in whatever form it may take. This self-actualization, combined with the use of social media to engage the international community, has brought a new force of highly informed and highly motivated stakeholders into the fold, demanding the political map to be redrawn. Not only did the protesters expose Beijing's lies and broken promises to the watching world, they also sent an unequivocal message to the CCP that Hong Kongers will not take its political abuse lying down – as so many thought we would. Before party seniors push through their next political agenda item, whether it is another attempt to enact an anti-subversion law or electoral reform for the 2020 Legco election, they will have to think a little harder about how this new Umbrella Generation will react.

On a personal level, the greatest achievement of the movement was beyond social awakening or keeping Beijing on its toes. The movement has opened my eyes to the untapped goodness in all of us. I have seen firsthand the courage, generosity and tenacity demonstrated by my fellow citizens in the most hopeless of circumstances. From here on out, if I hear someone accuse Hong Kong people of being materialistic and shallow, or call them selfish or cold, I will say he never spent a day in the village. Like my fellow villagers, I have emerged from there a higher being, if only by an inch or two.

The backlash

The Umbrella Movement, as one observer put it, was "political in purpose but social in practice." Like Zuccotti Park during Occupy Wall Street, Admiralty was more campground than battleground. Tens of thousands of protesters lived in a self-sustaining community, supported by a network of supply managers, first aid responders, doctors, marshals, teachers, artists, musicians, and many more volunteers who fed each other and cleaned after themselves. The summer camp atmosphere drew equal parts praise and criticism during the movement, but the criticism has grown louder *after* the protests ended.

Surprisingly, the most vociferous critics are not the government or the blue ribbons, but the protesters who once took part and took pride in it. Many former villagers, including some of my students, look back on what they did during those 79 days, and are suddenly disapproving of, even embarrassed by, their own behavior. They liken their old selves to the Smurfs who live merrily in their mushroom houses deep in the forest, oblivious to the happenings in the outside world. The occupy movement is compared to a poorly staffed basketball team with 100 cheerleaders but only two to three players. In other words, there were far too many volunteers building a real life SimCity, but not nearly enough of them doing the actual fighting.

The dramatic change of heart is caused primarily by a deep sense of failure. When protesters packed it in in December, they went back to their parents and friends to face their judging eyes. They had nothing to show for their efforts other than the yellow ribbons they wore on their chests. They failed to get any political concessions from either the SAR government or Beijing. The empty-handedness turned into shame, and shame gave way to anger and contempt.

The bitterness is being fanned even more by splinter groups who never saw eye to eye with the student leaders and have jumped on the opportunity to vilify the movement. Their aggressive rhetoric – some see it as far-right demagoguery – on social media resonates with many former protesters who are struggling with post-traumatic remorse. They start to label everyone a self-deluding leftard, which includes the pandems, the Occupy Trio, the HKFS, and pro-democracy activists who do not buy in to their combative tactics.

At a reunion dinner, my student Kent even turned on the congee lady who once brought him breakfast. "She and the rest of the leftards spent all day in Admiralty doing chores," he hissed, "just so they could feel good about themselves. But this is a war and wars require soldiers, not tea ladies and janitors!" Knowing my penchant for metaphors, he continued, "When someone burns down your house, you go after the bastard who did it. You don't sing songs with your neighbors."

According to Kent and his new localist friends, the leftards are in denial of the fact that the Umbrella Movement has failed miserably. The so-called "social awakening" that everyone talks about is classic leftards' kumbaya self-congratulation. The losers confuse participation with victory, and are far too willing to celebrate a failure and call it a job well done.

The localists do have a point. Their criticism recalls the ones leveled against the *Kony 2012* YouTube video and the "Bring Back Our Girls" online campaign after nearly 300 Nigerian schoolgirls were kidnapped by the Islamic extremist group Boko Haram in the spring of 2014. Millions of keyboard warriors around the world changed their Facebook profile pictures and wore different color bracelets in the name of raising awareness, when none of that "slacktivism" actually achieved any results. How is that any different from taking selfies with yellow umbrellas or doing homework at the Study Corner?

In the weeks and months following the December clearance, I had frequent debates over the merits of the occupy movement with my students in our WhatsApp chat group and sometimes in face-to-face gatherings – like the reunion dinner I had with Kent. I would try my best to explain that participants of every political movement contribute in their own ways based on their ability, belief and circumstances. Take the American Civil Rights Movement as an example. Rosa Parks refused to give up her seat on the bus, John Lewis led the march on the Edmund Pettus Bridge, and most people just held hands and sang "We Shall Overcome." The fact that neither Parks nor Lewis nor the singers threw a single rock at state troopers did not make any of them a leftard. Likewise, there might be a dozen reasons why a protester in Admiralty preferred to stay back and perform a support function instead of facing off with the police. He might have a family to feed and couldn't afford to get arrested or physically injured. He might have a personal philosophy against violence that precluded him from crossing the line. Neither case deserves attack or ridicule.

I also tried to make the case that political changes do not happen overnight, especially when we are up against the Communist machine. It took Nelson Mandela 27 years to end apartheid in South Africa, and Mahatma Gandhi 29 years to succeed in his fight for India's independence. African Americans fought nearly two decades for racial equality before Lyndon Johnson signed the Civil Rights Act in 1964. We cannot expect a single act of defiance to get us everything we wanted. If it were that easy, the world would have been a much happier, less complicated place.

The backlash makes my heart bleed. Without the Umbrella Movement (or OCLP that paved the way for it), most of these young people would still be playing video games and talking about Cantopop hits. They wouldn't be able to spell the word "suffragist" with a dictionary in their hands. It is all the more ironic that the same people who were enlightened by the occupy movement and who were taught everything they knew about politics have now turned their back on it and call it a waste of their time. I now understand why Shakespeare compared a thankless child to a serpent's tooth. Perhaps the students have outgrown their teacher, and perhaps the occupy movement has become a victim of its own success. Perhaps a bleeding heart, too, is a small step on the long road to full democracy.

Nowadays, most of the conversations with my students will end with an agreement to disagree. After all, dissent is a good thing and it is what separates Hong Kong from the rest of China. We remain cordial and respectful of each other's political views, and we still laugh about some of the silly things we did together. Kent and Hinson still tease me about that air mattress, although they will quickly catch themselves reminiscing about the past and change the subject. I can tell that deep down they are torn between their old memories and new ideologies. The same young men who once took great pride in wearing a first aid vest, who once wrote "*wir sind das volks*" on the Lennon Wall, who once teared up when a stranger handed them taxi money must now reconcile those sweet moments with the thirst for change and results. Their hearts are feeling one thing but their heads are thinking another. In time, they will understand that past and future, empathy and ambition are not mutually exclusive, and that there is enough room for them to co-exist.

What's next

Now, the $1,000,000 question: *where do we go from here?*

The short answer is "we don't know" and that's a perfectly acceptable answer. The Umbrella Movement managed to catch Beijing off guard precisely because no one knew it would or could happen. The surprise element gave it strength and longevity. As long as "what's next" remains an unknown, it will keep the authorities up at night and think twice before they attempt another political stunt.

When foreign news media like the *Los Angeles Times* and the Associated Press interviewed me to talk about life after the occupy movement, I would compare Hong Kong to a house with a gas leak: all it takes for it to blow up is a single spark. In our case, that spark can be anything from the Occupy Trio and prominent student leaders like Joshua Wong being convicted for their roles in the occupy movement[70] and becoming prisoners of conscience, to C.Y. Leung winning the re-election in 2017[71]. With confidence, I told the reporters that our government may not be good for much, but we can always count on it to do something spectacularly stupid. When that happens, citizens will once again put down their differences and come together, no matter how fractured and polarized they seem at the moment.

The occupy movement is alternately praised and criticized for the lack of a leadership. The way the protests went on for weeks without a central command has its pros and cons (see Table 12). Going forward, this trend is expected to not only continue but become more pronounced. The question becomes: *what will we do differently next time around?*

Perhaps no one is in a better position to answer that question than Benny Tai. The law professor was not only the commander-in-chief of OCLP, he also worked tirelessly behind the scenes throughout the occupy

---

70 – For the prosecution and conviction of the protest leaders, see *Part IV — Afterword*.

71 – In December 2016, C.Y. Leung announced that he would not seek a second term to avoid putting "'unbearable pressure" on his family. In the 2017 Chief Executive election, Carrie Lam defeated John Tsang and retired judge Woo Kwok-hing with 777 votes (out of 1,200) and became the city's first female Chief Executive.

movement to keep a close eye on every development and play shuttle diplomacy among various political parties and support groups.

Pros	Cons
• No one person or one group of people to be taken down or bought off by the authorities.	• Lack of coordination among various stakeholders and support functions.
• No one person or one group of people to dominate the debate or make unilateral decisions.	• Lack of a decision-making body with a clear mandate to direct the movement, or to take timely action in response to a fast-changing situation.
• A more transparent, participatory and inclusive decision-making process, taking into account the demands and views of different stakeholders.	• Lack of a point of contact to receive or disseminate information, to negotiate effectively with the authorities, or to communicate with the press.
• Decisions more principle-driven than agenda-driven.	• No one person or one group of people to take responsibilities or be held accountable for missteps or failures.
	• Tendency to lose control if mob mentality takes over.

Table 12. Pros and cons of a leaderless movement

I sat down with Tai nine months after the movement and he shared with me some of his key takeaways from the experience:

• ***Be prepared for radicalization***: Every social uprising is a continuous self-selecting process. As time passes, the doves will leave or get driven out, and the hawks will take over. It happened to the Tiananmen Square Protests and again to the Umbrella Movement. Organizers of future campaigns should anticipate this pattern and come up with a mechanism to better manage the dynamics.

• ***Decentralize decision-making***: The most effective mechanism to ensure legitimacy and prevent more zealous forces from dominating the debate is a referendum-based system. It is the only way to run an amorphous, leaderless campaign where every decision can and will be challenged by fringe groups. Tai has been working with his HKU colleagues to develop a mobile phone app to allow registered participants to instantly vote on key decisions concerning major operations and overall direction. The idea is to replace leaders with facilitators, and replace decision-makers with a decision-making platform.

• ***Trust your allies***: Once leaders and decision-makers are dispensed with, participants can feel more at ease toward offers of assistance from outside support groups and not worry so much about someone "hijacking" the campaign – as many did during the occupy movement. Taiwan's Sunflower Movement succeeded in large part because of the enormous support provided by seasoned politicians, strategists and academics, all of whom operated in the background. The future depends on our ability to work together and not against one other, regardless of our political leaning and personal agenda.

According to Tai, that really is all we need to know before the next wave of social uprising hits. He of all people would know about over-planning and over-thinking a political campaign. If there is one thing he has learned from the protests of 2014, it is that once the first shot of a revolution is fired, the beast will take on a life on its own and no amount of planning will prepare anyone for what is to come. The lesson underscores the importance of having an equitable and transparent platform to drive the campaign forward and respond to the unexpected. In the meantime, we just sit and wait for that spark to set the house on fire again.

Winners and Losers

Reasonable people may disagree on the merits of the Umbrella Movement. They may argue whether it was a success or a failure, a breakthrough or a setback, a service or disservice to the 7 million residents of Hong Kong.

Far less contentious is how the movement has fundamentally changed the city's political dynamics, and who has come out on top and who has gone down in flames. The victors take home the spoils – they have the last word on this debate and the first dibs in leading the next battle. The losers, however, find themselves on the wrong side of history and stand to live in infamy for an eternity.

C.Y. Leung

Hong Kong's unpopular Chief Executive has been called many names: 689, vampire, werewolf, Teflon politician. The last one refers to his ability to weather any political firestorm, including the UGL Scandal that dominated the headlines less than two weeks after the movement began.

Then came the unfortunate gaffe to a *New York Times* reporter about how he believed a free vote would skew social policies toward the poor. None of those incidents managed to gain traction or cost him his job. It proved that only two things can survive a nuclear holocaust: a cockroach and C.Y. Leung.

Villain-in-chief C.Y. Leung has a lot to sweat about

Removing Leung from office would have been a simple and elegant solution for Beijing to appease suffragists without making major concessions on electoral reform, but appeasement was not the CCP's style. On the contrary, when James Tien, leader of the pro-Beijing Liberal Party, broke ranks and called for Leung to resign, the Chinese government once again rallied behind Leung and fired Tien from the **CPPCC**, a political advisory body in China and an exclusive club for the wealthy elite in Hong Kong. Leung seemed to know all the right buttons to push to curry favor with his Communist bosses. Some say it is his unflinching loyalty to the CCP and

Machiavellian ruthlessness toward his own kind that appeal to President Xi Jinping.

But are those qualities enough? The plain fact that the biggest affront to the party's authority since 1989 blew up under Leung's watch, and that it happened because of his poor judgment in ordering a tear gas crackdown have not won him many friends within the Communist leadership. Xi may tolerate, even applaud, some of Leung's decisions, but the Paramount Leader is not prepared to expend his own political capital to keep bailing him out if he continues to make a bumbling villain of himself. There are far more important things on Xi's mind, such as trying to pull off an anti-corruption campaign without setting himself on fire. Observers generally expect Beijing to tell Leung to stand down in 2017 and let someone else run. There are plenty of hopefuls vying for the job, such as Chief Secretary Carrie Lam, Finance Secretary John Tsang and Legco Chairman Jasper Tsang[72].

The same fate may befall the Liaison Office, the apparatus set up in Hong Kong to ensure things like the Umbrella Movement does not happen. While Beijing will not engineer a high-profile personnel change immediately following the protests, heads are expected to roll at the local outpost, starting with Director Zhang Xiaoming right about the time C.Y. Leung loses his job in 2017. After the CCP cleans house, the Liaison Office itself will likely see many of its powers and privileges stripped away and transferred to the Beijing-based Hong Kong and Macau Affairs Office[73].

The Hong Kong police

If C.Y. Leung goes down, he will take everybody with him, including his 30,000-strong army. Two weeks after the 9/28 Crackdown, the Chief Executive went on television to throw the police under the bus. He denied any personal involvement in the unpopular decision to use tear gas, and blamed it on field commanders on duty that night. Pitting his own army against his people is a tried and tested strategy – it worked well for Mao Zedong during the Cultural Revolution, and it worked again half a century later.

Ever since the 9/22 Class Boycott, Leung had intended to turn a political problem into a police problem. Saddled with the blue uniform and weighed down by their badges, frontline officers were sandwiched

---

72 – See Footnote 70.

73 – In September 2017, Zhang Xiaoming left Hong Kong for Beijing to take up the post as Director of Hong Kong and Macau Affairs Office. Zhang's promotion surprised many, giving proof that factional dynamics within the Beijing leadership remain opaque and unpredictable.

between bureaucrats and protesters, wedged between a rock and a hard place. They worked 16-hour shifts with hardly any rest, taking all the heat while government officials sat in their air-conditioned offices and refused to engage the students. By assisting bailiffs to carry out court injunctions issued for civil claims, law enforcement overstepped their boundaries and became the government's political tool, or worse, a cog in the Communist apparatus.

79 days of bruising battles between police and citizens took its toll. Despite repeated claims that they exercised "maximum restraint[74]" and used "minimum force," the Hong Kong Police Force will forever be associated with selective arrests, unreasonable search and seizure, random acts of violence against protesters and bystanders, and the infamous Dark Corner Beating. An HKU poll conducted in December 2014 showed that the police were the least popular among the city's disciplined services[75]. Once revered in the region for their professionalism and positive image, they now rank even lower than the PLA in terms of public trust.

Beijing

Recognizing that anyone born in Hong Kong before the 1980s – who grew up with the haunting memory of the Tiananmen Square Massacre – is probably a lost cause, China has been focusing its charm offensive on the new generations. The Chinese government spends hundreds of millions every year to buy their love. It bankrolls local schools to institute Mandarin classroom instruction and send students on free field trips to the mainland, while quietly tweaking textbooks to portray the CCP in a positive light. The infamous Patriotic Education Plan in 2012 was another example of Beijing's social engineering initiatives. Alas, years of hard work was undone in a couple of months by the Umbrella Movement. China might have preserved political control, but it has lost an entire generation of Hong Kong youth – the Umbrella Generation.

What's more, Beijing's response to the occupy movement exposed the many fault lines in the senior leadership. The sheer length of the protests and the many conflicting whispers over C.Y. Leung's political

---

74 – In a television interview, Police Commissioner Andy Tsang tried to deflect complaints about law enforcement with his personal anecdotes. He said he had witnessed female officers in Mongkok acting like "loving mothers" by shielding protesters with their own bodies and taking them to safety. "Loving mothers" quickly became another popular catch phrase on social media.

75 – There are eight disciplined services in Hong Kong, including the police force, the fire department, correctional services, customs, immigration, the air force (with a fleet of five helicopters), a search and rescue team, and an auxiliary medical unit.

fate (including the carefully timed leak of the UGL Scandal to the press) revealed the Chinese government's indecision and internal power struggles. The leadership also seems poorly advised on Hong Kong matters. 17 years after the Handover, Beijing continues to underestimate and misjudge Hong Kong citizens, and continues to hire the wrong hands – from Tung Chee-hwa to Robert Chow and Leticia Lee – to be opinion influencers.

Considering contemporary China is bubbling with spontaneous regional insurgencies, especially in hot zones like Tibet and Xinjiang, Beijing appears shockingly ill-prepared for Internet-organized uprisings. As if it had learned nothing from Egypt and Turkey, the Chinese government continues to use old tricks to fight new enemies. The Umbrella Movement was a wake-up call for the party seniors that their decades-long model of unbridled economic development without corresponding political reform is unsustainable. Unless and until the leadership unclenches its fists, they will always be one trigger away from the next occupy movement or color revolution. They will be up at night up wondering when that proverbial 3:00am phone call will come. They join other autocratic regimes from Myanmar to Singapore and North Korea as members of an insomniacs' club that operate a franchise of aging dystopias in Asia.

The pan-dems

Before the occupy movement, they were the city's best hope for democracy. The annual July 1st rally they organized was the largest political event and the only public forum for citizens to voice their grievances against social injustices and bad government policies. Inside the Legco, their lawmakers held the critical bloc needed to veto dangerous bills such as regressive electoral reform proposals. They did what they could on a playing field that was heavily tilted toward the establishment.

Because they play by the rules, they will always be bound by the rules. They aren't trained to challenge, let alone break, the law, which means civil disobedience and urban guerilla warfare are way out of their comfort zone. Being career politicians, they can never take their eyes off or look beyond the next election. They also seem more interested in holding on to their waning political power than nurturing new blood – indeed, the senior leadership within the Democratic Party has not changed much in the past 30 years. That's why they were sidelined and kept at a safe distance by protesters during much of the movement.

At the same time, their moderate voices are increasingly drowned out by more zealous groups that are louder and more seductive. In the eyes of the radicalized youth, these old-timers are redundant and irrelevant. The only reason for their political existence is the 25 or so seats they hold in the Legco, which they may or may not be able to keep in the next general election.

The HKFS

Joining the pan-dems in the doghouse is the HKFS. The federation's initial popularity – epitomized by the Alexter phenomenon – evaporated with their stubborn indecision. The bungled 11/30 Tamar Siege to escalate the protests was at best clumsy and at worst a premeditated scheme to abandon a sinking ship. Part of the problem was systemic: according to seasoned commentator Johnny Lau, every course of action taken by the HKFS required a unanimous vote among all eight member universities, which gave each member an effective veto and paralyzed the organization.

The last weeks of the protests did a lot of damage to the HKFS's credibility and gave splinter groups ammunition to launch an all-out public relations assault. The fact that none of the senior positions in the federation was democratically elected also spawned accusations of nepotism and hypocrisy, considering their leadership role in a pro-democracy movement.

All that culminated in a coup d'état orchestrated by the localist forces a few months after the occupy movement ended. In March 2015, a series of referenda were held at university campuses across the city to decide whether member universities should withdraw from the HKFS as a result of its failed leadership during the protests. In the end, four of the eight members, including HKU, voted to leave. Lingnan University's Nathan Law succeeded Alex Chow as the new secretary general. If more members are to cut their ties in the future, the 57-year-old institution will be forced to disband, and the next battle will be over the multi-million-dollar trust fund it has amassed over the years.

Joshua Wong

The 18-year-old college freshman not only came out of the occupy movement unscathed, he emerged a local hero and an international icon.

Wong is Hong Kong's answer to Wael Ghonim, the Egyptian Google executive who became the face of the Jasmine Revolution in 2011. The only difference is that Wong is younger, more recognizable and has more staying power. He appeared on the cover of *Time*'s Asia edition and was nominated for the magazine's 2014 Person of the Year – he received more votes than even Barack Obama and India's Prime Minister Narendra Modi. In early 2015, he was named one of *Fortune* magazine's top 10 world leaders alongside Pope Francis and Apple CEO Tim Cook. There were even whispers that he should be nominated for a Nobel Peace Prize[76].

If C.Y. Leung is the Teflon politician, then G-phone is the non-stick activist. Whereas so many others have fallen off the greasy pole of politics, the teenager has hung on and stayed above the fray. Wong is so focused on his single-minded pursuit of universal suffrage that he has rendered himself virtually incorruptible and indefatigable. He unequivocally declared to *The New York Times* that "electoral reform is a generational war." Even in the final days of the occupy movement when over 75% of the public was against it, he and his Scholarism cadre still had the resolve and stamina to stage a hunger strike[77] in an attempt to revive the campaign.

After the occupation was over, Wong channeled his energy into taking the fight from the streets to the legislature. In March 2016, he disbanded Scholarism and a month later, with the help of Nathan Law and a number of former Scholarism members, launched a new political party called Demosistō. Outside Hong Kong, Wong continued to use his star power to tell our story at human rights symposiums and leadership conferences around the world. In March 2017, a documentary about Wong, titled *Joshua: Teenager vs. Superpower*, was released worldwide, which went on to win the World Cinema Audience Award in the documentary category at the Sundance Film Festival. Eighteen months later, Wong received the prestigious Lantos Human Rights Prize for his role in Hong Kong's pro-democracy struggle. Nevertheless, his exposure has come at great personal cost, including a complete loss of privacy and the frequent harassment which he and his loved ones must endure.

Localist groups

Newton's third law of motion applies as much in politics as it does in physics: action and reaction. The appointment of C.Y. Leung in 2012 sped up Beijing's political agenda for Hong Kong – including the Four Great

---

76 – Wong's achievements notwithstanding, most commentators agreed that it is *Hong Kongers* as a whole, who have spent over three decades fighting for democracy patiently, peacefully and creatively, who deserved a Nobel Prize.

77 – The tactic echoed the mass hunger strike by Beijing University students during the Tiananmen Square Protests. It is worth pointing out that Joshua Wong's decision to initiate a hunger strike was a unilateral one. Alex Chow confessed during a radio interview that Wong did not confer with him ahead of the campaign, which suggested a growing rift within the student leadership.

Tasks – but it also radicalized the opposition. It wasn't that long ago when Long Hair and his LSD party (the creative bunch behind the 2010 De Facto Referendum) were the firebrand rebels operating on the fringes of the political spectrum. These days, the same politicians are regarded as moderates and targeted by splinter groups such as Civic Passion and the HK Indigenous. The Umbrella Movement has given the localist forces a chance to flex their muscles, and the post-movement emotional void experienced by former protesters has left the field wide open for the likes of Wong Yeung-tat to preach their right-wing gospel.

Numbering only a few thousand, this small group of radicals has successfully exploited its social media following to take control of the public narrative. Their take-no-prisoner rhetoric resonates with the youth who are devastated by the disappointing outcome of the occupy movement and want to do more to make up for lost time and lost opportunity. New converts are recruited to fight the "War on China" by indiscriminately going after mainland visitors and local businesses that cater to their shopping needs. Some of the groups go a step further and advocate for Hong Kong independence by any means possible[78]. The growing localist influence has torn the fabric of society and pushed the city further into an us-versus-them standoff.

After the occupy movement, the splinter groups turned their attention to border towns in the New Territories, the epicenter of parallel trades. Vowing to help local residents take back their way of life, angry demonstrators descended on neighborhoods with banners and bullhorns to drive out the *persona non grata*. Some mainlanders were heckled and mobbed, while others had their possessions searched or thrown about. The counter-parallel trade protests ended with the SAR government finally giving in to the bullies and reaching an agreement with their Shenzhen counterpart to put new restrictions on travel permits issued to Chinese nationals. As much as citizens found the splinter groups objectionable, their tactics appeared to have yielded some results.

It is too early for the localists to celebrate their new political standing. Politics is a blood sport after all, and it is only a matter of time before someone more willing to bleed will come along and claim the title of the city's most radical. The day will come when pelting water bottles at police and harassing Chinese visitors are considered pointless and leftarded.

---

78 – Several pro-independence political parties sprang up shortly after the occupy movement, including Hong Kong National Party, Hong Kong Indigenous and Youngspiration. The last two groups won seats in the 2016 Legco election, only to lose them in the infamous Oathgate saga (see *Part IV — Afterword*). In September 2018, Hong Kong National Party was officially banned by the Hong Kong government on national security grounds, the first time in the city's history for a political party to be outlawed.

What the splinter groups are doing to the HKFS is a carbon copy of what the HKFS did to the Occupy Trio when they ignored OCLP and launched their own 9/22 Class Boycott, or what the LSD and People Power have been doing to the moderate pan-dems for years. When the hunter becomes the hunted, the splinter groups will feel just as redundant and irrelevant as their political opponents are made to feel today.

Worse, the radical wing may be playing into the hands of the Communists and, in doing so, become their biggest ally. The localist groups have not only fractured and weakened the pan-dems (which in turn creates a huge advantage for the pro-Beijing camp in future elections), but they are also alienating the public who find the opposition increasingly off-putting and disruptive to society.

For now, whether you like it or not, the localist groups and the more moderate Joshua Wong appear poised to take center stage in future anti-government protests. The two emerged from the Umbrella Movement as the clear winners, at least in terms of their ability to control the narrative and dominate the debate, relative to the rest of the pro-democracy camp. Whether they can hold on to the lead and whether inheriting this massive responsibility is a blessing or a curse remains to be seen[79]. Just ask Alex Chow.

Hong Kong

The Umbrella Movement was both a win and a loss, which made us – the people of Hong Kong – winners and losers at the same time.

We have gained a number of things: social awakening and battle wounds that didn't kill us but made us stronger. We have also managed to capture the world's attention by exposing China's hypocrisy and expressing our collective want for self-determination.

These gains have come with a heavy price tag. Society is more bitter and divided than ever. Public trust in the government and law enforcement has hit rock bottom. The "one country, two systems" model appears to

---

79 – In the evening of February 8th, 2016, riots broke out in Mongkok in response to the government's crackdown on unlicensed street vendors. Known as the "Fishball Revolution" (fishballs were a popular street food sold by the vendors), the clash with police was led by Hong Kong Indigenous, a localist group that advocates Hong Kong independence. The group's charismatic leader, Edward Leung, was among the dozens of protesters who were arrested and charged with rioting, and eventually sentenced to harsh prison terms. The imprisonment of Leung and other members of the radical wing dealt a mortal blow to the localist movement.

exist only in name but not in substance. Our relationship with Beijing has soured, and the CCP is all but certain to tighten its grip on Hong Kong to prevent future insurgencies. We may have inadvertently set the city back years or even decades on the journey to full democracy, just as the Tiananmen Square protesters did to China's own political reform.

The short-term and long-term impact of the Umbrella Movement on the city is summarized in Table 13 below.

Area	Short-term impact	Long-term impact
Economy	• During the occupy movement, a sharp drop in sales experienced by high-end retailers in the affected areas and by tour bus operators and other ground transport. • No impact after the protests ended.	• No long-term impact, other than the wake-up call that Hong Kong needs to diversify its tourist base – mainlanders currently account for nearly 80% of all visitors to the city.
Society	• Polarization of society into blue versus yellow, radical versus leftard, liberties versus stability. • A surge in number of expatriates and Hong Kongers with dual citizenship leaving the city; more parents sending their children abroad. • Shutting down of magazines and newspapers operated by pro-democracy activists, such as *House News* and *Sudden Weekly* (owned by Jimmy Lai's Next Media)	• Social awakening and civic participation of the Umbrella Generation. • A stronger and more distinct "Hong Kong identity" – citizens increasingly identifying themselves as "Hong Kongers" instead of "Chinese."

Governance	• Complete paralysis of government due to non-cooperation campaigns such as filibusters by the pan-dem lawmakers. • Decimation of police image after being used by the government as a political tool.	• Government's increased focus on social policies (e.g. housing and education) instead of electoral reform. • The SAR's reversion to a bureautocracy, with the Chief Executive acting as a caretaker instead of a leader and deferring to Beijing on major decisions. • Increased police violence with the use of more powerful crowd control weaponry. • Strained relationship between police and citizens due to mutual distrust and animosity; "self-selecting" police recruitment as the applicant pool skews toward pro-Beijing or pro-government candidates.
Cross-border relations	• Increased tensions between mainlanders and Hong Kongers. • More coordinated efforts by Beijing to inculcate patriotism through youth programs such as government-funded field trips to the mainland and the Hong Kong Army Cadet program. • Increased rhetoric against foreign forces and separatism to discredit the opposition. • Renewed push to pass an anti-subversion law to prevent future insurgencies.	• Tightened control by Beijing on all fronts, including press freedom, academic freedom and freedom of assembly; closer monitoring of political activities by surveillance and infiltration. • Less emphasis on "two systems" and "autonomy" and more on "one country" and "national security." • A weakened Liaison Office and a more active and intrusive Hong Kong and Macau Affairs Office.

Politics	• Likely defeat of the 2015 Reform Bill (see *Part IV – Afterword*) by the pan-dem lawmakers and end of the road for one-person-one-vote in 2017. • Weakening of traditional pan-dem parties for supporting OCLP and the occupy movement. • Greater prominence and press coverage of localist groups; more combative campaigns by splinter groups against the SAR government, mainland visitors and the pan-dems. • Increased voter registration and voter turnout among the Umbrella Generation. • Emergence of a new crop of bipartisan "middle men" (such as former Civic Party lawmaker Ronny Tong) who are more reconciliatory toward Beijing and willing to engage Chinese officials.	• Fracture within the pan-dem camp will split the pro-democracy votes and hand Legco seats to the pro-Beijing camp. • Potential loss of the critical veto vote at the Legco if the opposition fails to keep at least 23 seats. • Future pro-democracy or anti-government political movements will likely be led by new political forces. • Markedly lower turnouts at July 1st rallies and other street protests. Future political movements will likely take forms other than mass demonstrations and street occupations due to general protest fatigue and a collective "been there, done that" sentiment.

Table 13. Impact of the Umbrella Movement

In the end was it all worth it? Is there light at the end of the tunnel? Is our broken system beyond repair? Will we live to see the arc of history bend toward justice? I am afraid I have no better answer than the one I gave the Canadian reporter: it depends on how you define these questions and whom you ask.

Afterword

Now, an update.

Electoral reform

On June 17th, 2015, six months after the curtains came down on the Umbrella Movement, the controversial proposal for the 2017 Chief Executive election was finally submitted to the Legco for a vote. The 2015 Reform Bill followed the Standing Committee's 8/31 Framework to a tee, from the size and composition of the Nominating Committee right down to the cap on the number of candidates permitted to run.

The vote was preceded by a second round of public consultation (running from January to March 2015) and a government-funded media blitz featuring Chief Secretary Carrie Lam as peddler-in-chief. Contrary to what the HKFS had promised after the Admiralty clearance, a "new wave of occupation" did not happen during the second stage of consultation. It was clear that protest-fatigued citizens had no appetite for a sequel at least for the time being.

Not surprisingly, the 2015 Reform Bill was vetoed by the pan-dems, who carried enough seats to prevent the government from securing a super majority needed to pass it. What was surprising was that only eight out of the 43 pro-Beijing legislators ended up casting a "yes" vote. The rest of them had staged a walkout hoping to delay the proceeding, unaware that the voting bell had already rung and that there were enough lawmakers inside the room to constitute a quorum. By the time they realized their mistake, it was already too late. In the end, the reform proposal that was practically drafted by the Communists themselves and that had sparked the city's largest political crisis received only eight meager votes.

The comedy of errors was a sigh of relief for the pan-dems, who had feared that voters might punish them at future elections for their participation in the occupy movement and for vetoing a reform package that would have given citizens a chance to choose their Chief Executive come 2017 (however restricted the vote may have been). Luckily for the pan-dems, the Legco blunder by their political rivals shifted the public's focus, and the pro-Beijing camp could no longer accuse the likes of Emily Lau and Alan Leong of depriving citizens of the right for one-person-one-vote, for the accusers themselves did not vote for the bill.

In the end, what was already a sore subject became an international joke. The day after the Legco fiasco, C.Y. Leung – who by then had already failed two of the Four Great Tasks (patriotic education and electoral reform) – announced at a hastily called press conference that he would spend his remaining term focusing on the economy rather than politics. That's communist speak for "forget about electoral reform." Even Liaison Office Director Zhang Xiaoming promised that he would now "shut his mouth" and never bring up the topic.

And so the Chinese government managed to keep at least one promise: that universal suffrage in Hong Kong would be a take-it-or-leave-it, my-way-or-the-highway proposition. With the Beijing-backed 2015 Reform Bill defeated, Hong Kongers can kiss goodbye their right to freely elect their leader for as long as President Xi Jinping stays in power. Article 45 – the Basic Law provision that guarantees that right – is now expected to be indefinitely shelved and erased from the government's agenda. In the meantime, citizens brace themselves for the other shoe to drop: electoral reform to implement Article 68 of the Basic Law for a free vote to elect all members of Legco by 2020 – the second promise under the 2007 Decision – is also dead in the water .

A week after the Legco vote, residents of New Tim Mei Village – the dozens of tents set up in front of the Legco Building – voluntarily moved out and allowed government workers to clear the area. Among the last men standing was one of the Uncle Wong Trio and his wife of 50 years, both of whom had vowed to continue the sit-in "until the government's undemocratic proposal is blocked." Their promise fulfilled, the old couple could finally return to their retirement.

Hong Kong

The city has caught a virus and it's neither SARS nor the avian flu. Ever since the occupy movement ended, it has been suffering from a bad case of "ridiculitis" – a term I coined to describe the political absurdity that is fast becoming the new normal. Each morning, citizens wake up to another bizarre headline in local politics that makes them wonder whether they have been reading the April Fool's Day edition of *The Onion*.

In December 2014, a 14-year-old girl was caught drawing a yellow flower on the former Lennon Wall with chalk and was charged with vandalism. Police filed for a child protection order and threatened to take the kid from her parents. Then in July 2015, a lower court judge sentenced a woman protester at an anti-parallel trade protest to three and a half months in prison for assaulting a male police inspector with, of all things, her breasts. Within the same month, a police superintendent who was caught on video beating innocent onlookers with his baton during a *gouwu* protest defended himself in an investigative hearing by calling the baton an "extension of [his] arm" with which he had "patted" passersby to speed up pedestrian traffic.

In September 2015, Liaison Office Director Zhang Xiaoming dropped a bombshell at an event celebrating the 25th anniversary of the Basic Law. With a straight face, Zhang told an audience of Beijing loyalists that a separation of powers did not exist in Hong Kong, because the Chief Executive, with his dual accountability to both Hong Kong and Beijing, was in a special legal position that was "above the legislative and judicial branches." A few days later, C.Y. Leung weighed in and told reporters that he was not exactly above the other branches of government, but that he "transcended" them. These remarks sent commentators and the pan-dems into a tizzy, and gave Leung still another nickname: the "Transcender."

In the 2016 Legco election, Demosistō – the grown-up version of Scholarism – succeeded in sending 23-year-old Nathan Law into the legislature, making him the youngest person ever to become a legislator in Hong Kong. His victory was a testament to the surge in civil engagement, especially among the youth, fomented by the occupy movement[80]. Nevertheless, Law's political career proved to be short-lived. 10 months after his history-making Legco win, Law, along with the five other newly and democratically elected opposition lawmakers, lost their seats for straying from the prescribed oath during the swearing-in ceremony. Known as "Oathgate," the purge was engineered by the SAR government

---

80 – In the first post-occupy district council election held in November 2015, so called "Umbrella soldiers" (occupy movement activists-turned-politicians) ran in 50 out of the 431 constituencies in the city's 18 districts. Eight of them defeated their pro-establishment opponents, including several heavyweight incumbents. The turnout at the election was the highest on record, at 47% compared to 41% in the previous district council election in 2011. The same encouraging trends continued in the 2016 Legoc election, which saw a high voter turnout and sent a dozen progressive candidates into the legislature (before some of them were disqualified).

and aided and abetted by the Standing Committee[81], with the aim to assume complete control over Legco. As if that wasn't absurd enough, several candidates (including some of the ousted legislators themselves) were barred by the government from running in the subsequent by-elections to fill the six vacated seats. Their nominations were denied on the grounds that they did not "uphold the Basic Law", having previously advocated some form of self-determination.

These post-occupy developments have left citizens slack-jawed and thinking only one thought: *are these people for real?* It is a sign that, in the aftermath of an epic political upheaval, both the SAR government and the Communist machine have cranked up their attack on free expression and other civil liberties – the so-called "white terror" – in an effort to regain control and stomp out dissent. During the occupy movement, the authorities put all their energy into figuring out how to end the protests rather than addressing the fundamental issues that engendered them. After the movement, the same energy has been plowed back into ways to snuff out the next uprising – an Umbrella Movement 2.0 of sorts – instead of coming up with long term policies that would get at the underlying causes. Some people will never learn.

As the SAR government and Beijing become more brazen, citizens turn more cynical and numb. They roll their eyes at each new case of ridiculitis and turn the page with a dry laugh. The troubling new dynamics are symptomatic of the post-traumatic stress disorder in the wake of the Umbrella Movement. After all, citizens had taken the drastic step of staging a massive protest that paralyzed large swaths of the city for 11 weeks. If doing *that* didn't work, what chance did they have with anything else? Their kicking and screaming is like throwing eggs at a stone wall: all that's left is a mess of broken shells and sticky yolks, but not a scratch on the wall.

It is said that revenge is a dish best served cold. The Department of Justice appears to have taken that saying to heart when going after the faces of the occupy movement. In July 2016, Joshua Wong, Alex Chow and Nathan Law were convicted of various unlawful assembly charges over the storming of Civic Square on September 26th, 2014 — a pivotal event that kickstarted the mass protests. The three were each sentenced

---

81 – In November 2016, the Standing Committee issued an interpretation of Article 104 of the Basic Law, which requires lawmakers to swear allegiance to the SAR as part of China when they take office. According to the interpretation, elected legislators who fail to recite their oath "sincerely" or "solemnly" will be barred from taking office, which was how Nathan Law and five others lost their seats.

to several months in prison[82]. In October 2017, Wong and Lester Shum were among 20 protesters found in contempt of court for violating an injunction to stay clear of the Mongkok protest site on November 26th, 2014.

Then in November 2018, four long years after the occupy movement had ended, the Occupy Trio, along with other six other protest leaders, were tried in court for their roles in the movement. The Department of Justice scoured the law books for possible crimes to convict non-violent demonstrators and eventually charged the so-called "Occupy Nine" with three archaic crimes that few knew existed: public nuisance, incitement of others to commit public nuisance, and most unfathomably, incitement of others to incite public nuisance. Five months later, Benny Tai and Chan Kin-man were convicted and each sentenced to 16 months in prison, while Chu Yiu-ming received a suspended sentence. Tai and Chan joined Joshua Wong, Alex Chow and Nathan Law, among others, to become the city's first prisoners of conscience. They went to prison so the rest of us didn't have to.

Even though these convictions bore the hallmarks of political prosecution and drew widespread criticisms both in Hong Kong and overseas, they were not enough to provide the "spark" to set off another round of political uprising. By the time they were put behind bars, nearly half a decade had passed and the occupy movement had become a distant memory for many. Time, as it turns out, is yet the most powerful weapon wielded by the authorities. As for those who are waiting for Umbrella Movement 2.0 to break the political impasse, they will have to wait some more.

China

Since the occupy movement, President Xi's anti-corruption campaign has shown no sign of slowing down. After taking down former security czar Zhou Yongkang in December 2014, the Paramount Leader promptly moved on to old presidential aids, ex-army generals, children of retired party chiefs, and senior management of red chip state-owned enterprises.

Xi's political house-cleaning is matched by his diplomatic muscle-flexing in the region. His ambition to redraw geopolitical boundaries in the South China Sea, including turning reefs into artificial islands for military use, has rattled the Philippines, Vietnam, Malaysia and Taiwan, and touched

---

82 – Wong and Law were originally sentenced to community service while Chow received a suspended sentence. The Department of Justice appealed their sentences and in August 2017, the Court of Appeal sided with the prosecution and sentenced the three student activists to six to eight months in prison.

a nerve with Japan and the United States. All the swaggering culminated in Beijing's lavish celebration of the 70th anniversary of the end of World War II. In September 2015, China staged a huge military parade showing off the latest missiles and fighter jets, with three generations of leadership standing side-by-side to paint a harmonious political picture. One of the world's most secretive ruling regimes was making no secret of its military might.

Meanwhile, China's economy has taken a serious beating. GDP growth for the full year 2014 was 7.4%, the worst in 24 years. The growth slowed further to 6.9% in 2015. The reality is likely much worse considering that Chinese economic data are heavily doctored. In the summer of 2015, the country's two largest stock exchanges in Shanghai and Shenzhen experienced a series of market routs. Nearly US$5 trillion in market value – more than the entire economic output of Japan – was wiped out within a few weeks. Regulators halted initial public offerings, arrested short-sellers, and forced mutual funds and brokerages to buy stock to prop up prices. In August, the PBOC (China's central bank) suddenly lowered the *renminbi*-U.S. dollar exchange rate by 2%, the sharpest devaluation since the country's modern exchange rate system was introduced in 1994. It was meant to support exports and stimulate growth. Such heavy-handed market intervention is a sign that the CCP is in panic mode. Xi's leadership is pulling out all the stops to resuscitate the economy – the only thing that is keeping rival factions at bay and the general population from challenging its legitimacy.

That is why Beijing is also stepping up its crackdown on dissenters. In July 2015, the **National People's Congress** voted unanimously to pass a sweeping national security bill that aims to bolster the state's supreme power, covering a range of issues from cyber-security to religion (a state spokesperson said the new law would not apply to Hong Kong). Two weeks later, the Chinese authorities arrested over 100 human rights lawyers and activists – all allegedly part of a "major criminal gang" – for inciting disorder and subverting the state.

The crackdown on dissent in mainland China has even spread to Hong Kong. In the fall of 2015, five members of Causeway Bay Books and Mighty Current Media, a Hong Kong-based publishing house known for printing "tell all" books about mainland officialdom, went missing. They were believed to have been abducted and detained by mainland Chinese agents operating in Hong Kong and overseas – one of the five was kidnapped in Hong Kong, another one in Thailand, and the remaining three on the mainland. Months later, the booksellers reappeared on Chinese state television making scripted confessions to various crimes. The abductions were believed to be part of a larger state-sponsored initiative to clamp down on Hong Kong's freewheeling publishing industry. It is an industry already in distress as the Liaison Office holds a firm grip on the city's book distribution, having acquired the city's major local bookstore chains since the Handover.

Xi is at a crossroad. One one hand, he has managed to consolidate power not least by enshrining his own political thought in the CCP's constitution and abolishing limits on presidential terms, effectively crowning himself Emperor for Life. On the other hand, he may be overreaching and painting himself to the corner, by crafting a Mao-like cult of personality and waging an ever-escalating enemy purge under the thinly veiled pretext of combating corruption.

All that has called into question how much longer the juggler can keep all the balls in the air before he starts dropping them one by one. More importantly, it makes us wonder whether the house of cards will fall before July 1st, 2047 – the date that no one in Hong Kong wants to talk about – when the "one country, two systems" policy expires and the city's semi-autonomy comes to an end. If we can't outgun or outsmart the Communists, at least we will try to outlive them – just as the East Germans did the GDR in 1989 and the Russians did the USSR two years later.

Water Blowers' Society

After the last tent in Admiralty was taken down, Kent shifted his focus back to his studies at City University. The aviation major needed to work doubly hard to pull his grades back up after a disastrous fall term because of the protests. Still, his GPA wasn't high enough to get him admitted into Cathay Pacific's pilot cadet program, and he has given up on his ambition to become a commercial pilot altogether. Meanwhile, he has broken up with his girlfriend of two months, citing irreconcilable differences (although he puts it in less delicate terms: "That girl is a leftard!"). His Umbrella romance might have been short-lived, but it was enough to upgrade his relationship status from "A0" to "A1." Kent now works at Greenpeace Hong Kong and plans to emigrate to Europe one day.

Hinson took the DSE exams in March 2015, which lasted until mid-May. While waiting for his results, the high school graduate became a core member of an online student group and took part in a number of localist demonstrations. He organized regular reunion gatherings with former first aid teammates, even though they rarely talked about the protests any more. In August 2015, he accepted an offer from the University of New South Wales in Sydney, Australia, to study accounting. Hinson is now a certified public accountant and works at one of the Big Four audit firms.

Renee also took the DSE and was accepted to the radiography program at Polytechnic University. She was disappointed that she didn't get into biomedical science but was glad that high school was finally over. After the occupy movement, her woes have shifted from social to romantic in nature. The 18-year-old began dating a man almost twice her age – the techno DJ/musician with whom she had been performing in underground shows for years. The relationship didn't last and she has been dating casually ever since. Renee suffers from a general lack of direction in life and doesn't feel she has much to look forward to. These days, she finds everything around her, including the city she lives in, rather depressing. She travels outside Hong Kong every chance she gets.

Six months after the movement, I ran into Ken at an exhibition in Sai Wan featuring protest-inspired art. The first thing he told me was that he and his two classmates got an A-minus on their media assignment titled "Journalists in the Umbrella Movement." He thanked me again for doing the interview at the Study Corner and for giving him the Foreign Correspondents' Club notebook, which remained unwrapped because it was "too precious" to be used. The journalism sophomore landed a part-time job as an editor at *Headline Daily,* a free newspaper operated by the Sing Tao Media Group. He and a childhood friend also founded an online platform for residents in the Sai Wan area to donate and exchange furniture, home appliances and clothing. Their effort was featured in an article by media network Coconuts. Even though Ken was not the most popular boy at the Study Corner, he has certainly done well for himself.

The day after Admiralty was cleared, Yoko returned to her desk job at the local bank and resumed her nine-to-five routine. She has gone back to getting her weekly manicures, binge-shopping beauty products, and collecting colorful cast-iron cookware by Le Creuset. Her eye bags are gone and her hands no longer feel like 80-grit sandpaper. Yoko has kept in touch with her kids and they meet up every now and then for outdoor barbecues and hotpot dinners. More than anything else, Yoko is happy to finally be sleeping in her soft bed at home.

*   *   *

As for me, I continue to talk about the Umbrella Movement on the lecture and literary circuits both in Hong Kong and abroad. In March 2015, I traveled to Beijing to attend one of the leading writers' festivals in China. My moderator was Julie Makinen, an American journalist from the *Los Angeles Times* Beijing bureau, who peppered me with questions about the protests and the political future of Hong Kong. It was my first time speaking about the occupy movement in mainland China, and my first time speaking about anything under police surveillance. Thankfully, the *gong'an* present at the event did not give me any trouble, perhaps because the panel discussion was conducted in English and most of the attendants were Western expatriates.

A year later, I returned to the same literary festival in Beijing to launch this book. The event comprised two panel discussions about post-occupy Hong Kong, in which I was once again joined by Julie, together with Didi Tatlow of *The New York Times* and Tom Phillips of *The Guardian*. Evident that Beijing has stepped up its surveillance over the years, there was a palpable increase in *gong'an* presence at the festival, some of whom video-recorded our talks using their smartphones, while others followed me back to my hotel after the event, ostensibly to make sure that I did not cause trouble by reaching out to human rights lawyers and dissidents in Beijing. That was the last time I set foot on the mainland.

A lot has changed in Hong Kong since I relocated from New York in 2005, some for the better, but most for the worse. The booksellers' abductions in 2015, for instance, shocked the city to its core and prompted me and a few like-minded friends to co-found PEN Hong Kong, a organization that aims to defend the city's freedom of expression. Our work is challenging and often depressing, but it also gives us a renewed sense of purpose and hope.

Still, in all my years in Hong Kong, the happiest memories were spent with my students in Umbrellaville. These days whenever I am about to lose my cool, be it to a rude taxi driver or someone who talks too loudly on his cell phone, I will ask myself, "What would a villager do?" (or WWVD, with no disrespect to Jesus), and calm will be restored.

Once in a while, I will dust off the box of mementos tucked in the deep corner of my closet. I will take out my cardboard signs, the blue-and-white tarp, sundry umbrella-themed pendants and bracelets, and the two yellow umbrellas that have logged some serious air miles with me. I will hold them in my hands and let my mind drift. Then I will smile.

Appendices

I. Timeline of Key Events

Date		Events
1984	Dec 19th	British Prime Minister Margaret Thatcher and Chinese Premier Zhao Ziyang sign the Joint Declaration over the handover of Hong Kong.
1989	Jun 4th	The CCP sends in the PLA to clear the student encampment on Tiananmen Square in Beijing, killing and injuring thousands of protesters.
1997	Jul 1st	Hong Kong reverts to Chinese rule as a special administrative region and the Basic Law comes into effect. Shipping tycoon Tung Chee-hwa assumes office as the SAR's first Chief Executive.
	Oct 23rd	The Hang Seng Index falls over 23% after a week-long market rout, marking the beginning of the two-year Asian Financial Crisis.
1999	Dec 20th	Macau, a Portuguese colony, reverts to Chinese rule as a special administrative region.
2002	Feb 28th	Tung Chee-hwa wins a second term unopposed in the 2002 Chief Executive election.
2003	Feb 22nd	A mainland Chinese doctor visiting Hong Kong is diagnosed with SARS, marking the beginning of a five-month outbreak.
	Jul 1st	Half a million citizens take to the streets to protest against Tung Chee-hwa's administration for its ineffective disease control, a decimated economy and an unpopular anti-subversion bill.
	Jul 28th	China launches the Individual Visit Scheme to relax travel restrictions on mainlanders visiting Hong Kong in an attempt to revive the local economy and quell public anger over Tung Chee-hwa's failed administration.

2005	Mar 12th	Tung Chee-hwa resigns as Chief Executive. Then Chief Secretary Donald Tsang takes over as acting Chief Executive.
	Jun 25th	Donald Tsang wins the 2005 Chief Executive by-election unopposed and becomes the SAR's second Chief Executive.
	Aug 18th	Pan-dem legislators vote to defeat the 2005 Reform Bill.
2007	Mar 25th	Donald Tsang wins a second term after defeating pan-dem lawmaker Alan Leong in the 2007 Chief Executive election.
	Jul 1st	Donald Tsang begins his second term as Chief Executive.
	Dec 29th	The Standing Committee issues the 2007 Decision to implement Articles 45 and 68 of the Basic Law by 2017 and 2020, respectively.
2008	Sep 15th	Lehman Brothers files for bankruptcy in New York, triggering a sub-prime mortgage crisis and a global financial tsunami.
2010	Jan 15th	Demonstrators begin a two-day siege of the Legco Building in protest of the HK$70 billion Express Rail-link project.
	Jan 21st	Five pan-dem legislators resign from their Legco seats to trigger a citywide by-election to allow the public to take a stand on the 2010 Reform Bill.
	Jun 25th	Democratic Party and ADPL lawmakers side with the pro-Beijing camp and vote in favor of the 2010 Reform Bill.
2011	May 29th	14-year-old Joshua Wong founds student activist group Scholarism.
2012	Mar 25th	Land surveyor C.Y. Leung defeats textile tycoon Henry Tang and pan-dem lawmaker Albert Ho in the 2012 Chief Executive election.
	Jul 1st	C.Y. Leung begins his first term as the SAR's third Chief Executive.
	Oct 8th	C.Y. Leung announces the withdrawal of the Patriotic Education Plan after a series of mass rallies organized by Scholarism.

	Nov 15ᵗʰ	Xi Jinping succeeds Hu Jintao as the Paramount Leader of the People's Republic of China.
2013	Jan 16ᵗʰ	HKU professor Benny Tai publishes an article in a local newspaper proposing a civil disobedience campaign to pressure Beijing to deliver its promises of universal suffrage pursuant to the 2007 Decision.
	Mar 24ᵗʰ	Qiao Xiaoyang, Chairman of the Standing Committee's Legal Subcommittee, says that any Chief Executive candidate must be someone who loves China and loves Hong Kong.
	Mar 27ᵗʰ	The Occupy Trio hold a press conference announcing OCLP.
	Oct 15ᵗʰ	The SAR government denies the application of Ricky Wong's HKTV for a free-to-air television broadcasting license.
	Oct 17ᵗʰ	C.Y. Leung announces the creation of the Electoral Reform Taskforce to be led by Chief Secretary Carrie Lam.
	Dec 4ᵗʰ	The first phase of electoral reform public consultation begins.
2014	Feb 26ᵗʰ	Assailants stab Kevin Lau, former editor-in-chief of *Ming Pao*, six times outside a restaurant.
	Mar 18ᵗʰ	University students in Taipei, capital city of Taiwan, storm the legislature and occupy the parliamentary chamber in protest of a trade agreement with mainland China, marking the beginning of the three-week Sunflower Movement.
	Jun 10ᵗʰ	The State Council of China publishes the 6/10 White Paper asserting China's complete jurisdiction over Hong Kong.
	Jun 22ⁿᵈ	OCLP organizes the eight-day 6/22 Referendum to collect views from the public on three alternate electoral reform proposals.
	Jul 15ᵗʰ	C.Y. Leung submits a report to Beijing summarizing the results of the first phase of electoral reform public consultation.
	Aug 31ˢᵗ	The Standing Committee issues the 8/31 Framework.
	Sep 13ᵗʰ	Scholarism stages the 9/13 Tamar Demonstration outside the Government Headquarters to oppose the 8/31 Framework.

	Sep 22nd	The HKFS announces the week-long citywide 9/22 Class Boycott and stages a mass protest on University Mall at CUHK.
	Sep 23rd	The HKFS moves its protest to the Tamar Government Headquarters, where it joins forces with Scholarism.
	Sep 26th	Scholarism expands the 9/22 Class Boycott to secondary schools.
		Joshua Wong and supporters storm Civic Square outside the Legco Building. Police arrest more than 78 protesters, including Wong and the HKFS's Alex Chow and Lester Shum.
	Sep 28th	Riot police fire the first shot of tear gas at 5:57pm, marking the beginning of the Umbrella Movement.

See Appendix II *for the intervening events
during the 79-day occupy movement
between September 28th and December 15th*

	Dec 15th	Police dismantle the last tent in Causeway Bay, marking the end of the Umbrella Movement.
2015	Jan 7th	The second phase of electoral reform public consultation begins.
	Apr 22nd	The Electoral Reform Taskforce announces the 2015 Reform Bill based entirely on the 8/31 Framework.
	Jun 18th	Legco defeats the 2015 Reform Bill by a vote of 28 to 8. The remaining 34 legislators fail to cast a vote.
	Oct 14th	Lee Bo, one of the owner-managers of Mighty Current Media, disappears from Shenzhen. Four other members of the publishing house also go missing in the weeks that follow.
2016	Feb 8th	A street riot breaks out on Chinese New Year's Day as localist protesters clash with police over the government's crackdown on unlicensed street vendors. Protesters throw bricks at police and set objects on fire, prompting a police officer to fire two warning shots into the air. The riot continues to the following morning, resulting in numerous injuries and arrests. Known as the "Fishball Revolution," it is the worst outbreak of violence in Hong Kong since the 1967 Leftist Riots.

	Apr 10th	Joshua Wong, Nathan Law and several former members of Scholarism form a new political party called Demosistō.
	Jul 21st	Joshua Wong, Nathan Law and Alex Chow are found guilty of various unlawful assembly and incitement charges over the storming of Civic Square two days before the occupy movement began.
	Sep 4th	Nathan Law wins a seat in the Hong Kong Island geographical constituency in the 2016 Legco election, becoming the youngest lawmaker in the city's history.
	Dec 9th	C.Y. Leung announces that he will not seek a second term in the 2017 Chief Executive election.
2017	Mar 26th	Carrie Lam wins the 2017 Chief Executive Election and becomes the first female to lead Hong Kong.
	Jul 1st	Carrie Lam begins her first term as the SAR's fourth Chief Executive.
	Jul 14th	The High Court rules that Nathan Law is to lose his Legco seat for failing to properly take his oath during the swearing-in ceremony. Five other opposition lawmakers also lose their seats for the same reason.
	Sep 22nd	Liaison Office Director Zhang Xiaoming leaves Hong Kong for Beijing to head the Hong Kong and Macau Affairs Office.
	Oct 13th	Joshua Wong, Lester Shum and several other protesters are found in contempt of court for violating an injunction to stay clear of the Mongkok protest site during the occupy movement.
2018	Nov 18th	Trials of the Occupy Trio and six other protest leaders begin.
2019	Apr 9th	The Occupy Trio and six other protest leaders are found guilty of various public nuisance and incitement charges for their roles in the occupy movement.

II. Umbrella Movement Day by Day

Date		Events
Day 1	Sep 28th (Sun)	At 1:40am, outside the Tamar Government Headquarters, HKU professor Benny Tai announces the start of OCLP.
		Crowds gather at the Admiralty subway station after dawn. By noon, protesters have spilled onto Harcourt Road, taking over the expressway. At 5:57pm, riot police fire the first shot of tear gas to disperse peaceful protesters.
		Tens of thousands of citizens descend on Admiralty as a show of support. Peaceful occupation spreads to Mongkok and Causeway Bay.
		At 8:00pm, police release Scholarism's Joshua Wong from custody after a judge granted a *habeas corpus* petition. Wong was arrested two days earlier for inciting others to storm Civic Square.
Day 2	Sep 29th (Mon)	Protesters continue to occupy Admiralty, Mongkok and Causeway Bay. Water, food and medical supplies begin to trickle into the protest sites.
		Banks and shops in the affected areas remain closed. Public bus operators announce the suspension and diversion of more than 300 bus routes. Police negotiators are mobilized to no avail. Chief Secretary Carrie Lam announces the suspension of the second phase of electoral reform public consultation.

Day 3   Sep 30th (Tue)

Volunteers set up supply stations at all three protest sites. Admiralty protesters advance to Arsenal Road in Wanchai and Pedder Street in Central.

The SAR government declares all kindergartens, primary and secondary schools in the affected areas closed. Steve Hui of the police's Public Relations Bureau begins his daily press conference at 4:00pm.

The HKFS issues an ultimatum for the SAR government to hold direct talks with the student leadership by midnight on October 2nd, failing which they will escalate the protests by occupying key government buildings.

A car plows through a crowd of protesters on Argyle Street in Mongkok but injures no one. Police later arrest the driver for reckless driving.

Day 4   Oct 1st (Wed)

Official National Day celebrations go ahead. Joshua Wong and other Scholarism members are refused entry to the flag-raising ceremony at Golden Bauhinia Square on the Wanchai waterfront. District councilman Paul Zimmerman holds up a yellow umbrella outside the cocktail reception as a show of defiance.

An estimated 200,000 citizens turn up in Admiralty on the National Day public holiday. Protesters occupy a section of Canton Road in Tsim Sha Tsui.

Leung Chai-yan, daughter of Chief Executive C.Y. Leung, posts a picture on her Facebook page showing off a diamond necklace and thanking citizens for funding her expensive wardrobe. The story is picked up by, among others, the Jon Stewart Show.

Day 5	Oct 2ⁿᵈ (Thu)	Chung Yeung Festival – a back-to-back public holiday – draws new crowds to the protest sites.

Pro-Beijing protesters launch a "Blue Ribbon Campaign," led by Robert Chow and Leticia Lee, to support swift police action to end the protests.

Police officers are seen moving a large amount of ammunition and riot control equipment, including chests labeled "CS grenades" and "rubber bullets" into the Chief Executive's Office in Admiralty.

Professors Peter Mathieson and Joseph Sung, respective presidents of HKU and CUHK, make a night visit to Admiralty and urge students to put safety first.

20 minutes before the HKFS's ultimatum expires, C.Y. Leung announces that Carrie Lam will hold talks with student leaders on an unspecified date.

Day 6	Oct 3ʳᵈ (Fri)	Counter-protesters, many of them masked and believed to be Triad members, attack protesters and journalists in Mongkok and Causeway Bay. In response to police inaction during the thug attacks, the HKFS suspends plans to hold future talks with Carrie Lam.

Police clear the Tsim Sha Tsui protest site and reopen Canton Road.

Day 7	Oct 4ᵗʰ (Sat)	Pan-dem lawmakers condemn the police's inaction during the 10/3 Mob Attacks and accuse the government of using the Triads to clear the protest zones. Security Secretary Lai Tung-kwok denies any claim of collusion.

Around 200 blue ribbon protesters descend on Admiralty to stage a pro-government rally. Yellow ribbon protesters encircle the intruders at Admiralty Centre and stop them from entering the protest site.

A group of musicians, including Cantopop stars Anthony Wong and Denise Ho, release the anthem "Raise Your Umbrellas" on YouTube.

Day 8	Oct 5th (Sun)	The Umbrella Man wooden statue, created by local artist Milk, appears in Admiralty.
		The HKFS dispels rumors that protesters have agreed to withdraw from Mongkok. Former Chief Secretary Anson Chan, Cardinal Joseph Zen and university presidents urge students to end the protests.
		Under the guise of a concerned citizen, a professional stuntman stages a mock suicide by threatening to jump off a footbridge in Admiralty if protesters do not end the occupation.
Day 9	Oct 6th (Mon)	The occupy movement enters its first full work week. Protesters clear a 10-foot-wide path in Tamar to allow government employees to go to work.
Day 10	Oct 7th (Tue)	Government officials and the HKFS agree on holding the first round of talks on October 10th.
		Primary and secondary schools in the affected areas resume classes.
Day 11	Oct 8th (Wed)	C.Y. Leung's involvement in the UGL Scandal is leaked to the Australian press.
Day 12	Oct 9th (Thu)	The HKFS announces a non-cooperation campaign against the SAR government. Joshua Wong calls on protesters to bring tents and camping equipment to Admiralty to prepare for a protracted occupation. The actions prompt Carrie Lam to put the October 10th talks on hold.
		The Study Corner first appears in Admiralty. Mongkok protesters set up a *Guan Gong* shrine at the intersection of Nathan Road and Mongkok Road.
		Nurseries and kindergartens in the affected areas resume classes.
Day 13	Oct 10th (Fri)	The Five-party Platform organizes a mass gathering on Harcourt Road in response to the government's refusal to hold talks. The event draws an estimated 100,000 people. At the urging of Joshua Wong, a tent city emerges in Admiralty.
		German Chancellor Angela Merkel receives Chinese Premier Li Keqiang on his first state visit to Germany.

| Day 14 | Oct 11th (Sat) | The HKFS issues an open letter to Chinese President Xi Jinping urging him to disregard the report submitted by C.Y. Leung on July 15th and to withdraw the 8/31 Framework. |

Day 14   Oct 11th (Sat)

The HKFS issues an open letter to Chinese President Xi Jinping urging him to disregard the report submitted by C.Y. Leung on July 15th and to withdraw the 8/31 Framework.

Day 15   Oct 12th (Sun)

Lingnan University professor Chin Wan, spiritual leader of the local separatist movement, calls on splinter groups to heckle and encircle pro-democracy protesters in Mongkok whom he considers an impediment to the localist agenda.

Day 16   Oct 13th (Mon)

Taxi union representatives and masked men carrying crowbars and cutting tools attempt to forcibly remove barricades in Admiralty. They clash with protesters and are later dispersed by police. To reinforce the borders, volunteer construction workers erect three-story high bamboo scaffolding and use cement to anchor steel barriers in Admiralty.

Blue ribbon protesters besiege the headquarters of Jimmy Lai's Next Media and hijack several delivery trucks of *Apple Daily*.

Day 17   Oct 14th (Tue)

In a pre-dawn operation, police reopen the westbound lane of Yee Wo Street in Causeway Bay. Later that morning, law enforcement sends in heavy equipment to remove bamboo scaffolding and reinforced steel barriers on Queensway and reopen the thoroughfare. In response, protesters attempt to occupy the Lung Wo Road tunnel around midnight. A police standoff ensues and continues to the following morning.

For the second night, blue ribbon protesters arriving by the busload surround the headquarters of Next Media and attempt to block its newspaper delivery.

Day 18   Oct 15th (Wed)

At 3:00am, Civic Party member and registered social worker Ken Tsang is handcuffed and carried to a dark alley off Lung Wo Road where he is assaulted by a group of seven plainclothes police officers. The incident is caught on video by a TVB cameraman.

In the afternoon, 500 social workers march to the Police Headquarters on Arsenal Road in protest of the Dark Corner Beating.

British Prime Minister David Cameron addresses parliament and calls on Britain to stand up for Hong Kong people's rights guaranteed in the Joint Declaration.

| Day 19 | Oct 16th (Thu) | To quell public outrage over the Dark Corner Beating, C.Y. Leung announces that government officials will hold talks with the student leadership. |

Day 19 | Oct 16th (Thu) | To quell public outrage over the Dark Corner Beating, C.Y. Leung announces that government officials will hold talks with the student leadership.

Day 20 | Oct 17th (Fri) | Police initiate a pre-dawn clearance operation to reopen Nathan Road, Argyle Street and Shantung Street. Nearly 10,000 protesters show up to reoccupy the area and a three-day violent standoff ensues. Police arrest American photojournalist Paula Bronstein for vandalism in Mongkok after she got on top of a parked car.

Blue Ribbon Campaign convener Leticia Lee leads a group of 30 protesters to HKU and CUHK to protest against Benny Tai and Chan Kin-man for inciting students to partake in the occupy movement.

Day 21 | Oct 18th (Sat) | The violent police standoff in Mongkok continues into the weekend. Hundreds of protesters and a number of reporters are injured, many of them are treated at the nearby Kwong Wah Hospital. Police maintain that they have used "minimal force" to disperse protesters.

Carrie Lam reaches an agreement with the HKFS to hold talks on October 21st, to be moderated by Lingnan University president Leonard Cheng.

Day 22 | Oct 19th (Sun) | Violent clashes in Mongkok continue. Protesters reoccupy Nathan Road and Argyle Street.

Day 23 | Oct 20th (Mon) | A taxi driver union and tour bus operator obtain court injunctions banning the occupation of certain sections of Nathan Road. The owner of CITIC Tower in Admiralty obtains a similar injunction for the area outside the building's parking garage entrance.

C.Y. Leung tells a *New York Times* reporter that a freely elected Chief Executive will skew government policies to favor the poor.

Day 24	Oct 21st (Tue)	Bailiffs and removal crews arrive at CITIC Tower to clear a small area outside the building, removing some but not all steel barriers. A similar clearance action in Mongkok fails due to vehement resistance from protesters.

Senior government officials led by Carrie Lam hold televised talks with HKFS student leaders. The talks end without any resolutions, other than Lam's promise to submit a supplemental report to Beijing reflecting the students' demands.

Day 25	Oct 22nd (Wed)	More tour bus operators, including Kwoon Chung Bus, file for court injunctions banning the occupation of Harcourt Road.

Bailiffs and removal crews try for a second time to enforce their court injunctions in Mongkok, resulting in a series of violent clashes between protesters on one side, and removal crews and counter-protesters on the other side. During the confrontations, unidentified individuals throw paint and animal feces from nearby buildings. The clearance action is eventually halted.

American saxophonist Kenny G visits Admiralty and tweets pictures with pro-democracy banners.

Day 26	Oct 23rd (Thu)	A group of 14 self-proclaimed "Spider-kids" scale Lion Rock and drape a giant "We demand real universal suffrage" banner on the south face.

The Five-party Platform announces plans to hold a two-day electronic referendum at all three protest sites beginning on October 26th to determine the direction of the occupy movement.

Kenny G denies support for the occupy movement after his visit to Admiralty was criticized by the Chinese Foreign Ministry.

UN Human Rights Committee rapporteur Konstantine Vardzelashvili calls the election guidelines in the 8/31 Framework "unreasonable."

Day 27	Oct 24th (Fri)	A government helicopter is dispatched to remove the Lion Rock banner for "public safety" reasons.
		Former Chief Executive Tung Chee-hwa holds a press conference to urge students to end the protests. Pro-Beijing Liberal Party chairman James Tien calls for C.Y. Leung to take responsibility for the political crisis and step down.
		Counter-protesters show up in Mongkok to attempt to remove barricades, which leads to minor scuffles and a few arrests. Police take advantage of the mayhem to reopen Shantung Street to traffic.
Day 28	Oct 25th (Sat)	Robert Chow, convener of the Anti-Occupy Central Alliance, organizes a nine-day citywide campaign to collect signatures from citizens in support of the police. He claims to have received over 320,000 signatures in a single day.
		Participants at a Blue Ribbon Campaign gathering in Tsim Sha Tsui attack several TVB and RTHK reporters.
Day 29	Oct 26th (Sun)	The Five-party Platform cancels plans to hold an electronic referendum, citing insufficient preparation.
		Hong Kong Stock Exchange CEO Charles Li announces that the launch of the highly anticipated Shanghai-Hong Kong Stock Connect platform will be delayed.
Day 30	Oct 27th (Mon)	Giant "We demand real universal suffrage" banners appear on the campuses of the city's eight universities.
Day 31	Oct 28th (Tue)	Protesters observe 87 seconds of silence on the one-month anniversary of the 9/28 Crackdown.
		Benny Tai and Chan Kin-man announce that they will leave the Admiralty encampment and resume teaching at HKU and CUHK.
Day 32	Oct 29th (Wed)	The CPPCC votes 267-to-2 to remove James Tien from the Chinese advisory body for his October 24th statement calling for C.Y. Leung to step down.
Day 33	Oct 30th (Thu)	A half-dozen counter-protesters pelt eggs at pan-dem lawmaker Long Hair in Admiralty.

Day 34	Oct 31st (Fri)	Swaths of construction site safety nets are spread across Nathan Road to protect protesters from fallen objects from nearby buildings. Another group of climbers drape a giant "We demand real universal suffrage" banner on Fei Ngo Shan (also known as Kowloon Peak), the highest mountain in Kowloon.
		The functional constituencies veto motions at the Legco to investigate the police's handling of the 9/28 Crackdown and the 10/3 Mob Attacks.
Day 35	Nov 1st (Sat)	The Five-party Platform meets to discuss a proposal for lawmaker Albert Ho to resign his Legco super seat to trigger a citywide by-election, which will be used as a de facto referendum to gauge the city's position on electoral reform. Participants at the meeting fail to reach any conclusion.
		Climbers drape a giant banner on Tai Mo Shan, the highest mountain in Hong Kong.
Day 36	Nov 2nd (Sun)	Climbers drape a banner on Lantau Island's Sunset Peak.
Day 37	Nov 3rd (Mon)	Volunteers install a wind turbine on Harcourt Road.
		The Anti-Occupy Central Alliance submits to Carrie Lam 1,830,000 signatures it claims to have been collected from citizens who oppose the occupy movement.
Day 38	Nov 4th (Tue)	"Macau demands real universal suffrage too" banners appear on the Hengqin campus of the University of Macau.
Day 39	Nov 5th (Wed)	Protesters sporting Guy Fawkes masks gather in Mongkok and Lung Wo Road to confront the police. They stage flash mob protests by walking in slow motion to clog sidewalks and pretending to drop and pick up loose change to stop traffic.
Day 40	Nov 6th (Thu)	Flash-mob protests continue.
Day 41	Nov 7th (Fri)	A Scholarism member is denied entry to mainland China at the Shenzhen border.
		The HKFS visits Tung Chee-hwa's office and requests that the former Chief Executive broker talks between students and Beijing officials.

Day 42	Nov 8th (Sat)	The police end the daily press conference hosted by Steve Hui.
		The Hong Kong Pride Parade begins in Victoria Park and ends at the Admiralty protest site. It draws the largest crowd in the event's history.
Day 43	Nov 9th (Sun)	C.Y. Leung arrives in Beijing to attend the three-day APEC Summit and is received by Xi Jinping at the Great Hall of the People.
		Pan-dem activists organize a mass rally from Chater Garden to the Liaison Office asking C.Y. Leung to discuss their pro-democracy demands with the Communist leadership during his Beijing visit.
Day 44	Nov 10th (Mon)	The APEC Summit begins in Beijing, attended by world leaders including U.S. President Barack Obama and Russian President Vladimir Putin.
		Chinese securities regulators announce that the Shanghai-Hong Kong Stock Connect will be launched within a week.
		The courts extend various injunctions banning the occupation of Nathan Road, Harcourt Road and the area outside CITIC Tower.
Day 45	Nov 11th (Tue)	The APEC Summit enters its second day. In C.Y. Leung's absence, acting Chief Executive Carrie Lam indicates that there is little room for further talks as the schism between both sides is too wide.
		Chin Wan visits Mongkok to teach protesters how to make shields out of old suitcases.
Day 46	Nov 12th (Wed)	The APEC Summit in Beijing ends.
		Assailants throw animal offal at media mogul Jimmy Lai outside his tent in Admiralty. Police arrest both the assailants and the site marshals who have tried to subdue them.
Day 47	Nov 13th (Thu)	A coalition of ground transport operators march to Admiralty demanding talks with the student leaders.
Day 48	Nov 14th (Fri)	Alex Chow, Nathan Law and two other HKFS members prepare for a trip to Beijing. They issue an open letter to Li Keqiang voicing their demands for universal suffrage.

Day 49	Nov 15th (Sat)	The Beijing-bound HKFS members are prevented from boarding their flight at the Hong Kong International Airport. Cathay Pacific says the passengers' home return permits have been revoked by the mainland authorities.
		The Court of Appeal rejects the protesters' challenge of the injunctions granted to taxi unions and tour bus operators.
Day 50	Nov 16th (Sun)	A dozen people claiming to be truck drivers show up in Admiralty demanding that protesters end the occupation.
Day 51	Nov 17th (Mon)	The Shanghai-Hong Kong Stock Connect goes live. Trading volumes on the first day are disappointing.
Day 52	Nov 18th (Tue)	Bailiffs armed with a court injunction clear the entire area outside CITIC Tower.
Day 53	Nov 19th (Wed)	Angered by a copyright amendment bill, a group of masked men break two glass doors of the Legco Building. They call on student protesters to enter the building but are stopped by site marshals. They flee the scene when the police arrive.
Day 54	Nov 20th (Thu)	Pan-dems and OCLP condemn the 11/19 Wreck-and-run. The HKFS and Scholarism disapprove of the action but stop short of condemning it. The pro-Beijing camp criticizes the Occupy Trio for losing control of the occupy movement and breaking their promise of "love and peace."
Day 55	Nov 21st (Fri)	Dozens of protesters gather outside the British Consulate in Admiralty accusing Britain of not doing enough to enforce the Joint Declaration.
		American actor/filmmaker James Franco visits Admiralty.
		Over 100 splinter group members show up in Admiralty at night to demand the Grand Stage be dismantled and the marshal teams be disbanded for sabotaging the 11/19 Wreck-and-run.
Day 56	Nov 22nd (Sat)	More student activists are denied entry to mainland China and Macau.

Day 57	Nov 23rd (Sun)	The pan-dems, the HKFS and Scholarism organize a community outreach day across the city to explain their political demands and defend their act of civil disobedience. Some participants are harassed and attacked by counter-protesters.
Day 58	Nov 24th (Mon)	Bailiffs and lawyers representing taxi unions post notices in Mongkok warning occupiers to vacate the area within 24 hours.

Police remove the barricades outside the British Consulate. |
| Day 59 | Nov 25th (Tue) | With the police's assistance, bailiffs and removal crews begin clearing Argyle and Portland Streets in Mongkok. Argyle Street is reopened by 4:00pm.

Violent clashes in Mongkok continue and dozens of protesters are arrested. In the evening, riot police are deployed for the first time since the 9/28 Crackdown. |
| Day 60 | Nov 26th (Wed) | Bailiffs and removal crews return to clear Nathan Road. They are aided by a team of unidentified men wearing "I Heart Hong Kong" T-shirts. Many more protesters are arrested, including Alex Chow, Lester Shum and Joshua Wong. The *Guan Gong* shrine is destroyed.

Nathan Road is reopened by 3:30pm, ending the occupation of Mongkok. |
Day 61	Nov 27th (Thu)	Protesters organize *gouwu* demonstrations in Mongkok and Tsim Sha Tsui in response to the Mongkok clearance in the past two days.
Day 62	Nov 28th (Fri)	The Chinese Embassy in London warns a delegation of British lawmakers, including Richard Ottaway of the House of Commons Foreign Affairs Committee, that they will be denied entry on their proposed trip to Hong Kong.
Day 63	Nov 29th (Sat)	The KMT suffers a resounding loss in the 9-in-1 elections in Taiwan, widely viewed as a referendum on President Ma Ying-jeou's Beijing-friendly policies.
Day 64	Nov 30th (Sun)	Nathan Law announces an escalation plan, calling on protesters to lay siege to the Tamar Government Headquarters. Thousands of protesters gather near Tamar Park. 4,500 police officers are mobilized in response to the escalation operation.

Day 65	Dec 1st (Mon)	The 11/30 Tamar Siege continues overnight until 6:00am. Police deploy water cannons and CS spray. The siege ultimately fails and Alex Chow apologizes for the bungled operation. Security Secretary Lai Tung-kwok calls protesters "rioters." Sporadic scuffles between police and protesters in Admiralty continue throughout the day.
		The High Court grants Kwoon Chung Bus an injunction against the occupation of a large section of Harcourt Road. Bailiffs begin coordinating with the police to set a date for an Admiralty clearance.
		Joshua Wong and four other Scholarism members begin a hunger strike.
Day 66	Dec 2nd (Tue)	Student leaders arrested during the Mongkok clearance are issued restraining orders banning them from the area.
Day 67	Dec 3rd (Wed)	The Occupy Trio, Jimmy Lai, Cardinal Joseph Zen and 60 other pro-democracy activists turn themselves in to police.
Day 68	Dec 4th (Thu)	Police arrest a 31-year-old man for the "use of a computer with criminal intent" after he created a Facebook event calling on volunteers to partake in a Christmas Eve *gouwu* protest.
Day 69	Dec 5th (Fri)	The Chinese authorities arrest former security czar Zhou Yongkang for corruption and revoke his CCP membership.
		Dozens of protesters dressed up as Christmas carolers march down Nathan Road from Tsim Sha Tsui to Mongkok singing Christmas songs with anti-government lyrics.
Day 70	Dec 6th (Sat)	Joshua Wong ends his 100-hour hunger strike.
Day 71	Dec 7th (Sun)	Around 2,000 "Umbrella parents" march in Wanchai in protest of the use of excessive force by the police.
Day 72	Dec 8th (Mon)	Other Scholarism members end their hunger strike.
		Chan Kin-man tells reporters that OCLP will be his last political campaign and that going forward he will focus on his writing.

Day 73	Dec 9th (Tue)	Bailiffs and lawyers representing Kwoon Chung Bus post notices on Connaught and Harcourt Roads warning occupiers to vacate the area within 24 hours.
		Police announce plans to clear the Admiralty encampment on December 11th.
Day 74	Dec 10th (Wed)	Tens of thousands of citizens gather in Admiralty on the eve of the clearance to pay their final respects.
Day 75	Dec 11th (Thu)	Bailiffs send in dump trucks and excavators to clear the Admiralty site. Protesters stage a peaceful sit-in, and 247 are arrested by the police.
		Connaught and Harcourt Roads are reopened by 11:00pm, ending the occupation of Admiralty.
Day 76	Dec 12th (Fri)	Christmas carolers and *gouwu* shoppers assemble in Mongkok and Causeway Bay. They are met with heavy police presence.
Day 77	Dec 13th (Sat)	Police announce plans to clear the Causeway Bay encampment on December 15th.
		Climbers drape a giant "C.Y. Leung Step Down!" banner on Lion Rock.
Day 78	Dec 14th (Sun)	Zhang Rongshun, Vice-chairman of the Standing Committee's Legislative Affairs Commission, says at a conference in Shenzhen that Hong Kongers need to be "re-enlightened" about the "one country, two systems" policy.
		Gouwu shoppers stage more protests in Mongkok. Police arrest two dozen protesters.
Day 79	Dec 15th (Mon)	Police clear the Causeway Bay encampment without incident. Hennessy Road and Yee Wo Street are reopened by 1:00pm. The 79-day Umbrella Movement comes to a close.
		Dozens of tents remain on the sidewalk of Tim Mei Avenue.

III. Who's Who in Local Politics

Name	Description*
Chan, Albert 陳偉業	Senior member of People Power, co-founder of the LSD, and pan-dem legislator. Chan was one of the five Legco members who participated in the De Facto Referendum in response to the 2010 Reform Bill.
Chan, Anson 陳方安生	Chief Secretary under Governor Chris Patten and founder of political think tank Hong Kong 2020.
Chan Kin-man 陳健民	Yale University graduate, associate professor of sociology at CUHK, and co-founder of OCLP.
Chin Wan 陳雲	Assistant professor of Chinese at Lingnan University and spiritual leader of the local separatist movement. In 2011, Chin authored the bestselling *On the Hong Kong City-state* advocating for the city's independence from mainland China.
Chow, Alex 周永康	HKU arts student, former vice president of the HKU student union, and secretary general of the HKFS. He, Lester Shum and Joshua Wong were the movement's three most prominent student leaders.
Chow, Robert 周融	Former radio host and journalist, co-founder of the pro-Beijing Silent Majority for Hong Kong, and convener of the Anti-Occupy Central Alliance. Chow, Leticia Lee and Patrick Ko were the most prominent figures of the counter-opposition political force.

* As of the time of the occupy movement.

Chu Yiu-ming 朱耀明	Human rights activist, Baptist Church minister, chairman of the Hong Kong Democracy Development Network, and co-founder of OCLP. Chu was one of the key organizers of Operation Yellowbird to smuggle hundreds of wanted protesters (including student leader Wu'er Kaixi) out of China after the Tiananmen Square Massacre.
Chung, Eason 鍾耀華	CUHK politics student, former president of the CUHK student union, and one of the five HKFS leaders at the 10/21 Talks.
Eu, Audrey 余若薇	Founding member and chairlady of the Civic Party and former pan-dem legislator. Eu gave a stellar performance in a one-on-one televised debate against Donald Tsang over the 2010 Reform Bill.
Four O'clock Hui Sir 四點鐘許Sir	Real name Steve Hui, head of the Hong Kong Police Force's Public Relations Bureau who hosted a daily press conference at 4:00pm during the occupy movement from September 30th to November 8th.
Ho, Albert 何俊仁	Senior member and former chairman of the Democratic Party and pan-dem legislator. Ho ran unsuccessfully against C.Y. Leung in the 2012 Chief Executive election. He and fellow Democratic Party member Emily Lau came under heavy criticism after conducting a closed door meeting with the Liaison Office and voting in favor of the 2010 Reform Bill.
Ho, Denise 何韻詩	Canto-pop singer and civil rights activist. Nicknamed HOCC, Ho came out of the closet in 2012. She was one of the few local entertainers who openly supported the occupy movement to the detriment of her career.
Ip, Regina 葉劉淑儀	Co-founder and chairlady of the New People's Party, cabinet member of C.Y. Leung's administration, and pro-Beijing legislator. Ip stepped down as Security Secretary in 2003 after failing to get an anti-subversion bill passed.
Ko, Patrick 高達斌	Former Democratic Party member, founder of the pro-Beijing Voice of Loving Hong Kong, and member of Regina Ip's New People's Party. Ko, Leticia Lee and Robert Chow were the most prominent figures of the counter-opposition political force.

Lai, Jimmy
黎智英

Longtime pro-democracy activist and founder of Next Media, which publishes the anti-Beijing tabloid *Apple Daily* and popular *Next* magazine. Lai made his fortune from clothing retail chain Giordano, which inspired Japanese businessman Tadashi Yanai to copy its business model and create Uniqlo in the 1980s.

Lam, Carrie
林鄭月娥

Chief Secretary under C.Y. Leung and leader of the Electoral Reform Taskforce in charge of promoting the Beijing-backed 2015 Reform Bill.

Lau, Emily
劉慧卿

Former journalist, chairlady of the Democratic Party, and pan-dem legislator. Lau and fellow Democratic Party member Albert Ho came under heavy criticism after conducting a closed door meeting with the Liaison Office and voting in favor of the 2010 Reform Bill.

Law, Nathan
羅冠聰

Cultural studies student and former president of the Lingnan University student union. Law was one of the five HKFS leaders at the 10/21 Talks.

Lee, Leticia
李偲嫣

Convener of the Blue Ribbon Campaign, president of the Federation of Parent-Teacher Associations of Hong Kong, and spokeswoman of the anti-gay Anti-reverse Discrimination League. Lee, Robert Chow and Patrick Ko were the most prominent figures of the counter-opposition political force.

Lee, Martin
李柱銘

Founding member of the Democratic Party, former pan-dem legislator, and a prominent human rights activist. Known as the "Father of Democracy" in Hong Kong, Lee was a member of the Basic Law Drafting Committee until he resigned after the Tiananmen Square Massacre. A senior barrister, he regularly provides pro bono criminal defense services to other pro-democracy activists.

Lee Shau-kee
李兆基

Property tycoon, founder and chairman of Henderson Land, and the second richest man in Hong Kong with an estimated net worth of US$24 billion. Lee's nicknames includes "Hong Kong's Warren Buffett," "Asia's God of the Stock Market" and "Uncle Four" (Lee being a fourth child).

Leong, Alan
梁家傑

Senior member of the Civic Party, former chairman of the Hong Kong Bar Association, and pan-dem legislator. Leong ran unsuccessfully against Donald Tsang in the 2007 Chief Executive election. He was one of the five Legco members who participated in the 2010 De Facto Referendum.

Leung, C.Y. 梁振英	The third Chief Executive of the SAR. Prior to public office, Leung was vice chairman of the Hong Kong branch of U.S. property management company Jones Lang LaSalle, and president of the Hong Kong Institute of Surveyors. Rumored to be an underground CCP member, he was appointed secretary general of the Basic Law Consultative Committee at the age of 34. Leung was elected Chief Executive by the Election Committee in 2012.
Leung, Yvonne 梁麗幗	HKU law student, former president of the HKU student union, and the only female HKFS leader at the 10/21 Talks.
Li Ka-shing 李嘉誠	Property tycoon, founder and chairman of Cheung Kong Holdings and Hutchison Whampoa, and the second richest man in Asia (after Alibaba's Jack Ma) with an estimated net worth of US$32 billion. Nicknamed "Superman" for his Midas touch, his two sons Victor and Richard are also successful businessmen running his vast empire.
Li Keqiang 李克強	The second-in-command in Beijing since the 2012 leadership change, as Premier of China and the second most senior member of the Central Politburo Standing Committee.
Long Hair 長毛	Left-wing civil rights activist, founding member of the LSD, and pan-dem legislator known for his grassroots image and theatrics. Real name Leung Kwok-hung, Long Hair was one of the five Legco members who participated in the 2010 De Facto Referendum.
Ma Ying-jeou 馬英九	President of Taiwan and former chairman of the KMT. A Harvard-trained lawyer, Ma won the presidential election in 2008 and was re-elected in 2012. His approval rating in the second term hovered at below 10%, the lowest among leaders in the developed world.
Patten, Chris 彭定康	The last Governor of Hong Kong, former European Commissioner for Britain, and Chancellor of Oxford University. Nicknamed "Fat Pat," Patten was a popular governor who oversaw the Handover. Since leaving office in 1997, he continues to advocate for the rights of Hong Kong citizens through newspaper columns and public speeches.
Shum, Lester 岑敖暉	CUHK engineering student, former vice president of the CUHK student union, and deputy secretary general of the HKFS. He, Alex Chow and Joshua Wong were the movement's three most prominent student leaders.

Tai, Benny 戴耀廷	Associate law professor at HKU, chief architect and co-founder of OCLP.
Tsang, Donald 曾蔭權	The second Chief Executive of the SAR. A career bureaucrat, Tsang served as Finance Secretary under Governor Chris Patten, and as Finance Secretary and Chief Secretary under Tung Chee-hwa. He succeeded Tung as acting Chief Executive after the latter stepped down in 2005. Tsang was elected Chief Executive by the Election Committee later that year and was re-elected in 2007. After leaving office in 2012, he was investigated by the ICAC for failing to disclose a rental arrangement with a mainland businessman and was subsequently convicted of misconduct.
Tung Chee-hwa 董建華	The first Chief Executive of the SAR. Prior to public office, Tung was chairman of Orient Overseas Container Line, a shipping empire he inherited from his father Tung Chao-yung. Tung was elected Chief Executive by the Election Committee in 1996 and was re-elected in 2002. He resigned in 2005 citing an arthritic leg.
Wong, Anthony 黃耀明	Canto-pop singer, vocalist of the 1980s boy band Tat Ming Pair, and civil rights activist. Like Denise Ho, Wong came out of the closet in 2012 and was one of the few local entertainers who openly supported the occupy movement.
Wong, Joshua 黃之鋒	Open University politics student and founder of Scholarism. Nicknamed G-phone, Wong rose to political stardom and international fame after thwarting C.Y. Leung's attempt to introduce the Patriotic Education Plan in 2012. He, Alex Chow and Lester Shum were the three most prominent student leaders of the occupy movement.
Wong Yeung-tat 黃洋達	Internet radio host, former member of People Power, and founder and leader of Civic Passion, known for his radical rhetoric and combative tactics against law enforcement, mainland visitors and even fellow pro-democracy activists.
Woo, Peter 吳光正	Property tycoon, chairman of Wheelock and Wharf Holdings, and one of the richest men in Hong Kong. Woo inherited a shipping empire from his billionaire father-in-law Pao Yue-kong.
Xi Jinping 習近平	Paramount Leader of the People's Republic of China since the 2012 leadership change, as General Secretary of the CCP, President of China, Chairman of the Central Military Commission, and the most senior member of the Central Politburo Standing Committee.

Zen, Joseph 陳日君	Chinese Cardinal of the Catholic Church and former Bishop of Hong Kong appointed by Pope John Paul II. Zen is an outspoken advocate of human rights and religious freedom in mainland China.
Zhang Xiaoming 張曉明	Director of the Liaison Office since 2012. Widely considered to be C.Y. Leung's partner-in-crime, Zhang intervenes in the city's governance behind the scenes and is known for his frequent gaffes. He once said to a pan-dem legislator that "the fact that you are still alive proves China's tolerance [toward dissent]."

IV. Major Political Parties in Hong Kong

The pro-Beijing camp

Party	Leadership*	Geographical seats at Legco*	Functional seats at Legco*	Background
Democratic Alliance for the Betterment and Progress of Hong Kong (DAB) 民建聯	Starry Lee 李慧琼 Tam Yiu-chung 譚耀宗	9	4 (including 1 super seat)	▪ Founded in 1992. ▪ Flagship party of Beijing loyalists with the most Legco seats and the deepest pockets. ▪ Known for using free meals and gifts to win votes from the elderly and low-income citizens.
Business and Professionals Alliance for Hong Kong (BPA) 經民聯	Lau Wong-fat 劉皇發 Andrew Leung 梁君彥	1	6	▪ Founded in 2012 after members split from the Liberal Party. ▪ Pro-business conservative party that advocates for the wealthy elite.
Federation of Trade Unions (FTU) 工聯會	Stanley Ng 吳秋北 Chan Yuen-han 陳婉嫻	3	3 (including 1 super seat)	▪ Founded in 1948. ▪ The city's largest labor group with nearly 400,000 members. ▪ Supposed advocates for the working class, but vote with the pro-establishment camp on important social policies.

* As of the time of the occupy movement.

Party	Representatives		Notes
Liberal Party 自由黨	Vincent Fang 方剛 James Tien 田北俊	1 4	▪ Founded in 1993. ▪ Pro-business conservative party that advocates for the wealthy elite. ▪ Strained relationship with C.Y. Leung after the party supported businessman Henry Tang during the 2012 Chief Executive election.
New People's Party (NPP) 新民黨	Regina Ip 葉劉淑儀 Michael Tien 田北辰	2 0	▪ Founded in 2011. ▪ Pro-Beijing, pro-business conservative party and a platform for Regina Ip to bid for Government House.
Others	N/A	1 9	▪ Include smaller pro-business conservative parties such as Economic Synergy (經濟動力) and Kowloon West New Dynamic (西九新動力). ▪ Also include independent members not affiliated with any particular political party who toe the party line with the pro-Beijing camp and often take direct orders from the Liaison Office.
		Total: 17 (out of 35)	Total: 26 (out of 35)

The pan-democracy camp

Party	Leadership*	Geographical seats at Legco*	Functional seats at Legco*	Background
Democratic Party 民主黨	Emily Lau 劉慧卿 Albert Ho 何俊仁	4	2 (both super seats)	▪ Founded in 1990 as the United Democrats in Hong Kong. ▪ Flagship opposition party with a moderate stance. ▪ Reputation irreparably tarnished after siding with the government on the 2010 Reform Bill.
Civic Party 公民黨	Alan Leong 梁家傑 Audrey Eu 余若薇	5	1	▪ Founded in 2006. ▪ Second largest opposition party with a moderate stance. ▪ Comprises mostly lawyers and professionals, and its liberal platform appeals to the middle class.
Labour Party 工黨	Lee Cheuk-yan 李卓人 Cyd Ho 何秀蘭	3	1	• Founded in 2011. • Center-left party that pushes for pro-labor policies and the creation of a social safety net.

* As of the time of the occupy movement.

Party	Leaders	Seats	Notes
People Power 人民力量	Erica Yuen 袁彌明 Albert Chan 陳偉業	2	• Founded in 2011 after Albert Chan and Raymond Wong (黃毓民) split from the LSD. • "Radical" wing of the opposition that filibusters government initiatives. • Went after the Democratic Party after the passing of the 2010 Reform Bill.
Association for Democracy and People's Livelihood (ADPL) 民協	Bruce Lee 廖成利 Frederick Fung 馮檢基	1 (super seat)	• Founded in 1986. • Center-left party that advocates for grassroots interests.
Neighbourhood and Worker's Service Centre (NWSC) 街工	Wu Wai-chung 胡偉忠 Leung Yiu-chung 梁耀忠	1	• Founded in 1985. • Center-left party that advocates for workers' interests.

League of Social Democrats (LSD) 社民連	Long Hair 長毛 Wong Ho-ming 黃浩銘	1	0	▪ Founded in 2006. ▪ "Radical" wing of the opposition that filibusters government initiatives and hurls objects at unpopular politicians. ▪ Architects of the De Facto Referendum in 2010.
Neo Democrats 新民主同盟	Gary Fan 范國威	1	0	• Founded in 2010 after members split from the Democratic Party. • Ally of the LSD and People Power on political issues.
Others	N/A	1	4	▪ Include smaller pro-democracy parties such as the Hong Kong Professional Teachers' Union (教協). ▪ Also include independents such as Raymond Wong who split from the LSD in 2008 and from People Power in 2013.
		Total: 18 (out of 35)	Total: 9 (out of 35)	

V. Glossary

Term	Meaning
50 Cent Party 五毛黨	Online trolls hired by the Chinese government and its operatives to harass journalists and opinion leaders critical of Beijing.
1967 Leftist Riots 六七暴動	A series of large-scale anti-government riots in 1967 involving pro-Communist protesters. The riots began as a minor workers' dispute that grew into citywide strikes, mass demonstrations, violent clashes with police, and multiple bomb threats and actual bombings. Demonstrators were funded by the Chinese government with the intention to subvert the British-appointed colonial government. The events lasted six months and left more than 50 dead (including five police officers and a well-known radio presenter) and hundreds injured.
2003 Mass Rally 零三年七一遊行	A mass demonstration involving an estimated 500,000 citizens on July 1st, 2003 in protest of then Chief Executive Tung Chee-hwa's inept response to the SARS outbreak, a decimated economy, and his poorly timed attempt to introduce an anti-subversion bill under Article 23 of the Basic Law. The rally resulted in the withdrawal of the controversial bill and the resignation of Security Secretary Regina Ip.
2005 Reform Bill 零五年政改方案	An electoral reform package introduced by then Chief Executive Donald Tsang in 2005 in response to mounting pressure from the pan-dems to achieve dual universal suffrage by 2007. The package attempted to democratize Hong Kong by, among other things, adding 10 new seats to the Legco. It fell far short of the pan-dems' expectations and was ultimately defeated in the Legco.

2007 Decision
零七年人大決定

A decision issued by the Standing Committee in 2007 in response to growing public demand to achieve dual universal suffrage by 2012. The decision stipulated a timetable for the implementation of Articles 45 and 68 of the Basic Law, pursuant to which the Chief Executive and Legco members would be elected by universal suffrage in 2017 and 2020, respectively.

2010 Reform Bill
一零年政改方案

A second electoral reform package introduced by then Chief Executive Donald Tsang in 2009 and modified in 2010. Based largely on the defeated 2005 Reform Bill, the 2010 package, among other things, would add 10 new seats to the Legco (including five super seats to the functional constituencies), and expand the size of the Election Committee from 800 to 1,200 members. The pan-dems rejected the package as regressive, causing five Legco members to trigger the De Facto Referendum in 2010. The 2010 Reform Bill was eventually passed after several Democratic Party and ADPL lawmakers met with representatives of the Liaison Office and subsequently changed their vote.

2015 Reform Bill
一五年政改方案

An electoral reform package introduced in 2015 by C.Y. Leung and the Electoral Reform Taskforce setting out the method for electing the Chief Executive in 2017. The package was based entirely on the highly restrictive 8/31 Framework issued by the Standing Committee. The bill failed to secure a super-majority vote in the Legco and was defeated by the pan-dems in June 2015.

6/10 White Paper
一國兩制白皮書

Formally titled "The Practice of the 'One Country, Two Systems' Policy in the Hong Kong Special Administrative Region," a document issued by the State Council of China on June 10th, 2014 to assert China's complete jurisdiction over Hong Kong. The 54-page document stated that the high degree of autonomy enjoyed by Hong Kong came from the Chinese government and was therefore subject to its unquestioned authority.

6/22 Referendum
六二二公投

An eight-day citywide referendum commissioned by OCLP asking members of the general public to choose from three alternate proposals for the method to elect the Chief Executive in 2017. Between June 22nd and 29th, 2014, 800,000 citizens reportedly participated in the referendum via the smart phone app PopVote or at physical voting booths set up at HKU and Polytechnic University.

8/31 Framework 八三一人大框架	Officially titled "Decision of the Standing Committee of the National People's Congress on Issues Relating to the Selection of the Chief Executive of the Hong Kong Special Administrative Region by Universal Suffrage," a document issued by the Standing Committee on August 31st, 2014 containing the guidelines for the 2017 Chief Executive election. The framework required, among other things, that the total number of candidates on the ballot be capped at two to three, that each candidacy be backed by at least half of the Nominating Committee, and that the size and composition of the Nominating Committee be based on the existing Election Committee. The framework, which significantly restricted the right to a free vote, triggered a series of protests that culminated in the Umbrella Movement.
9/13 Tamar Demonstration 九一三添馬示威	A student demonstration outside the Tamar Government Headquarters organized by Scholarism to oppose the 8/31 Framework. The demonstration began on September 13th, 2014 and later merged with the 9/22 Class Boycott and OCLP.
9/22 Class Boycott 九二二罷課	A campaign organized by the HKFS calling on students at all 24 higher education institutions to boycott classes for five days beginning on September 22nd, 2014 in protest of the 8/31 Framework. On September 26th, 2014, the student strike was extended and expanded by Scholarism to cover secondary schools across the city.
9/28 Crackdown 九二八驅散行動	A major police operation to disperse peaceful demonstrators in Admiralty with tear gas and riot gear in the evening of September 28th, 2014. The heavy-handed crackdown shocked the city and sparked the Umbrella Movement.
10/3 Mob Attacks 黑社會襲擊	A series of attacks on protesters at the Mongkok and Causeway Bay protest sites by unidentified counter-protesters on October 3rd, 2014. The assailants were believed to be connected to the Triads.
10/17 Mongkok Operation 光復旺角行動	A three-day operation by protesters on the weekend of October 17th, 2014 to reoccupy a section of Shantung Street in Mongkok that had been cleared by the police. The event left dozens injured and was one of the most violent police clashes in the occupy movement.

10/21 Talks 學生對話	Talks held on October 21st, 2014, between representatives of the HKFS and senior SAR government officials. The event was moderated by Lingnan University president Leonard Cheng and broadcast live on prime time television. The talks did not result in any resolutions, other than the government's promise to prepare a supplemental report to be submitted to the Hong Kong and Macau Affairs Office.
11/19 Wreck-and-run 闖入立法會行動	A failed attempt in the early hours of November 19th, 2014 by a small group of masked men to break into the Legco Building in protest of a copyright amendment bill that they feared would limit freedom of expression on the Internet. The men, some of them members of Civic Passion, smashed a pair of glass doors at the building's north entrance and urged protesters nearby to enter the legislature. Protesters refused to comply and the men later fled the scene when the police arrived. The incident worsened the infighting within the movement, as localist groups accused the student leadership and the site marshals of sabotaging their attempt to escalate the protests.
11/30 Tamar Siege 包圍政總行動	A failed attempt on the evening of November 30th, 2014 by the HKFS to escalate the occupy movement by laying siege to the Tamar Government Headquarters. 4,000 protesters congregated in Tamar Park for the operation but they were quickly overrun by an equal number of police officers responding with pepper spray, batons and water cannons. The overnight operation ended in the early hours of December 1st.
Apple Daily 《蘋果日報》	A tabloid-style newspaper founded in 1995 by Jimmy Lai and published by the Next Media group. It tends to side with the pan-dem camp and is one of only two Chinese language print newspapers in Hong Kong that remains critical of Beijing.
Article 23 二十三條	A provision in the Basic Law that requires the SAR government to introduce a national security law to prohibit, among other things, subversion against the Chinese government, treason, secession, theft of state secrets, and political activities in Hong Kong by foreign political organizations. The attempt by Tung Chee-hwa to pass an anti-subversion bill under Article 23 sparked the 2003 Mass Rally.

Article 45 四十五條	A provision in the Basic Law that stipulates that the Chief Executive be elected by universal suffrage. Article 45 does not provide a timetable for its implementation and leaves issues such as the nomination method to be determined by public consensus.
Article 68 六十八條	A provision in the Basic Law that stipulates that all members of the legislature be elected by universal suffrage. Article 68 does not provide a timetable for its implementation and leaves issues such as the continued existence of the functional constituencies to be determined by public consensus.
Asian Financial Crisis 亞洲金融風暴	A two-year financial crisis in Asia beginning in July 1997 that led to a series of stock market routs and devalued currencies in the region. The crisis started in Thailand after the collapse of the Thai baht and quickly spread to the rest of Southeast Asia, South Korea and Japan. In Hong Kong, the Hang Seng Index fell 23% within a week in October 2007. The Hong Kong Monetary Authority and then Finance Secretary Donald Tsang struggled to maintain the peg between the Hong Kong dollar and the U.S. dollar amidst currency speculations by international investors such as George Soros.
ATV 亞洲電視	Asia Television Limited, one of the two licensed free-to-air television broadcasters in Hong Kong at the time of the occupy movement. It was founded in 1957 as RTV, the first ever Chinese-language television station in the world. ATV had been in financial straits since the Handover, especially after its acquisition by mainland Chinese businessman Wang Zheng in 2010. In December 2014, a court appointed accounting firm Deloitte as ATV's manager to find a white knight to save the languishing broadcaster. Four months later, with no serious buyers on the horizon, the SAR government announced that it would not extend ATV's license when it expired in 2016.
Basic Law 基本法	Hong Kong's mini-constitution, a document heavily negotiated between China and Britain which became effective on July 1st, 1997.
blue ribbons 藍絲帶	A collective term for supporters of the police force – and the SAR and Chinese governments in general – during the occupy movement. Some of the blue ribbons were hired by the Liaison Office to manufacture dissent and counter the pro-democracy narrative.

border control unit 鐵馬組	Also known as the "local lords," an amorphous, self-organized team of protesters who guarded and secured the borders in Admiralty with steel barriers, trash cans and other objects. Tasked to keep intruders at bay and alert the Grand Stage of police operations, they had frequent run-ins with both law enforcement and site marshals who sometimes tampered with their barricades.
Cantonese 廣東話	The language spoken in Hong Kong, Macau, parts of Guangdong province, and among the overseas Chinese communities in Singapore and Malaysia. Cantonese has an estimated 60 million native speakers. In Hong Kong (and elsewhere in China), Cantonese is increasingly under threat as it is deemed by the Chinese government a regional dialect to be eventually phased out.
CCP 中國共產黨	The Chinese Communist Party, the sole governing party of the People's Republic of China. The CCP was founded in 1921 and defeated the KMT in 1949 in the Chinese Civil War. The CCP, the PLA, and the State Council of China form the three branches of power in the country.
CCTV 中央電視臺	China Central Television, a state-owned television broadcaster in mainland China and a mouthpiece for the CCP.
Central Politburo Standing Committee 政治局常委	Not to be confused with the Standing Committee of the National People's Congress (a 150-member body charged with the power to interpret and modify legislation), the Central Politburo Standing Committee is an ultra-exclusive seven-member committee that serves as the highest decision-making body of the CCP. Sitting members include President Xi Jinping and Premier Li Keqiang.
Chief Executive 行政長官	The head of the executive branch of the SAR government and the highest office in Hong Kong.
civil nomination 公民提名	A proposal to allow individual citizens to nominate Chief Executive candidates, thereby circumventing the pre-screening Nominating Committee stipulated by the 8/31 Framework. The proposal, first made by Joshua Wong in August 2013, was included in all three proposals in the 6/22 Referendum.

V. Glossary

corporate voting
公司票

Votes held not by individuals but by trade organizations and corporations. Some functional seats and many members of the Election Committee are elected by corporate voting.

CPPCC
全國政協

The Chinese People's Political Consultative Conference, a political advisory body in China consisting of delegates from political parties, social groups and individuals. Membership is conferred on the wealthy elite and celebrities in Hong Kong who are deemed loyal to the CCP. Access to the CCP network that comes with the membership makes it a highly coveted perk.

CSSTA
兩岸服務貿易協議

The Cross-Strait Service Trade Agreement, a pact between China and Taiwan to open up the service industry in both countries. The controversial agreement aims at creating cross-strait investment opportunities in dozens of service-related sectors, such as banking, healthcare, tourism, films and telecommunications. The KMT's attempt in March 2014 to pass CSSTA without proper vetting by legislators sparked the Sunflower Movement.

Dark Corner Beating
暗角打鑊

The beating of Civic Party member Ken Tsang in the small hours of October 15th, 2014, by a group of seven plainclothes police officers in a back alley off Lung Wo Road. A TVB cameraman captured the officers punching and kicking a handcuffed Tsang for close to five minutes. The seven assailants were convicted of assault in February 2017.

De Facto Referendum
變相公投

A campaign in 2010 initiated by the LSD to pressure Donald Tsang to revise the 2010 Reform Bill. Three LSD and two Civic Party lawmakers representing each of the five electoral districts in Hong Kong resigned at the same time to trigger a citywide by-election, which in turn provided a platform for citizens to take a stand on the 2010 Reform Bill. The idea was that if citizens voted the resigned lawmakers back into the Legco, it would be construed as a "yes" vote supporting a more progressive electoral reform package.

dual universal suffrage
雙普選

The twin goals to grant citizens a free vote to elect the Chief Executive and all members of the Legco.

Election Committee
選舉委員會

A 1,200-member committee vested with the power to select the Chief Executive under the current electoral procedures. The vast majority of the committee members are pro-Beijing loyalists. Every Chief Executive since the Handover has been chosen by the Election Committee.

Electoral Reform Taskforce
政改諮詢專責小組

Officially known as the "Task Force on Constitutional Development," a three-person committee headed by Chief Secretary Carrie Lam to oversee the public consultations for the 2015 Reform Bill.

Express Rail-link
廣深港高鐵

Officially known as the "Guangzhou-Shenzhen-Hong Kong Express Rail Link," a 26-kilometer high-speed rail that connects West Kowloon to Shenzhen. Funding for the HK$70 billion (US$9 billion) project was approved by the Legco in 2010 amidst vehement opposition from the pan-dems and civic groups.

fai ching
廢青

Literally a "useless youth," the Cantonese phrase refers to people in their 20s who are financially dependent on their parents and lack the motivation to apply themselves as a result of limited career prospects.

Five-party Platform
五方平台

A loose coalition of leadership during the occupy movement consisting of the Occupy Trio, the HKFS, Scholarism, the pan-dems, and a contingent of community leaders.

Four Great Tasks
四大任務

Believed to be Beijing's key political agenda for post-Handover Hong Kong to tighten control on civil society. The four tasks are passing an anti-subversion law, instituting patriotic education, reining in electoral reform, and taming the mass media.

functional constituencies
功能議席

One of the two "houses" of the Legco, taking up 35 of the 70 seats in the legislature. 30 of the 35 functional seats are selected by the lawmakers' respective industry sectors and special interest groups. The remaining five seats are democratically elected super seats.

geographical constituencies
地方議席

The other "house" of the Legco taking up the remaining 35 of the 70 seats in the legislature. All geographical seats are democratically elected.

gong'an
公安

Literally "public security," the Mandarin term for law enforcement in mainland China.

gong chu 港豬	Literally a "Hong Kong pig," the Cantonese phrase refers to people who choose a steady livelihood over civil liberties, or those who are thankful for economic handouts from Beijing despite having their freedoms gradually taken away.
gong hai 港孩	Literally a "Hong Kong child," the Cantonese phrase refers to local children born in the new millennium who have been raised by their domestic workers and spoiled by their middle class parents.
gouwu 鳩嗚	A form of flash mobs in which participants pretend to be shoppers and visit busy shopping areas in large numbers to overwhelm law enforcement as an act of defiance.
Government House 禮賓府	Built in 1855, the official residence of the Chief Executive located on Upper Albert Road in Midlevels.
Grand Stage 大台	The main command center in Admiralty for speeches and important messages during the occupy movement. The HKFS and Scholarism had de facto control of the Grand Stage, but their leadership was increasingly challenged by localist groups toward the end of the movement.
Handover 香港回歸	The transfer of sovereignty over Hong Kong from Britain to China on July 1st, 1997, when the city transitioned from a British colony to a special administrative region under Chinese rule.
Hang Seng Index 恒生指數	The main stock index in Hong Kong, similar to the Dow Jones Industrial Average in the United States and the FTSE100 in Britain. Critics call Hong Kong a "one-dimensional market," pointing to the fact that property developers and financial institutions account for over half of the index constituents by market value.
HKFS 學聯	The Hong Kong Federation of Students, an organization founded in 1958 by the student unions of the city's eight accredited universities. At the time of the occupy movement, the federation was led by secretary general Alex Chow and deputy secretary general Lester Shum. In March 2015, half of its members, including HKU, Polytechnic University, Baptist University and City University, voted to leave the federation as a result of its failings in the occupy movement.

HKTV Saga 香港電視風波	A political firestorm in 2013 after C.Y. Leung's cabinet rejected the application by Ricky Wong's HKTV for a free-to-air broadcasting license. Many believed that the decision had to do with Beijing's desire to control the local media, one of the Four Great Tasks handed to the Chief Executive.
Hong Kong and Macau Affairs Office 港澳辦	A Beijing-based administrative agency of the State Council of China responsible for coordinating political and economic ties between mainland China and the special administrative regions of Hong Kong and Macau.
ICAC 廉政公署	Independent Commission Against Corruption, an independent government division established in 1974 to prevent, combat and prosecute corruption within the SAR government. The Basic Law stipulates that the ICAC be directly accountable to the Chief Executive. Since the Handover, the commissioner of the ICAC has been appointed by the State Council of China.
Individual Visit Scheme 自由行	A scheme to relax travel restrictions on Chinese nationals visiting Hong Kong. It was implemented in 2003 after the SARS outbreak to revive the city's economy with mainland tourism dollars.
Joint Declaration 中英聯合聲明	Officially known as the "Joint Declaration of the Government of the United Kingdom and the Government of the People's Republic of China on the Question of Hong Kong," a Sino-British agreement signed in 1984 to memorialize the arrangement for the transfer of sovereignty over Hong Kong. The agreement contemplates, among other things, that the SAR enjoy a high degree of autonomy after the Handover.
July 1st rally 七一遊行	An annual event on July 1st – the Handover anniversary – for citizens to take to the streets to vent their anger over a range of social and economic issues. It begins at Victoria Park in Causeway Bay and ends at the Government Headquarters. Turnout at the rally is a barometer of public sentiment and (dis)satisfaction with government policies.

KMT 國民黨	*Kuomintang*, Taiwan's ruling party founded by Sun Yat-sen after the Xinhai Revolution of 1911. The KMT was defeated by the CCP in the Chinese Civil War in 1949, and was forced to relocate its government from mainland China to Taiwan.
leftard 左膠	Left-wing to the point of stupidity and self-delusion. The phrase is most used by radical splinter groups to criticize moderate pro-democracy activists who believe that shouting slogans, singing songs or occupying streets (without escalation) can bring about political change.
Legco 立法會	The Legislative Council, the legislative body of Hong Kong that enacts and amends laws, examines and approves government budgets and public spending, and raises questions about government operations. Of the 70 seats in the Legco, half are taken up by the functional constituencies and the other half by the geographical constituencies.
Liaison Office 中聯辦	The de facto Chinese embassy in Hong Kong tasked to coordinate Beijing's policies with the SAR government. Located in Sai Wan, the office was headed by Director Zhang Xiaoming at the time of the occupy movement.
Lion Rock spirit 獅子山精神	A can-do spirit and the belief that anyone who works hard enough can achieve the "Hong Kong Dream."
localists 本土派	Loosely organized radical coalitions in Hong Kong that are anti-immigration, anti-government and pro-independence. Some of them, such as Civic Passion, are splinter groups broken away from the pan-dem parties.
Macau 澳門	The other special administrative region under Chinese rule. The former Portuguese colony was handed back to China on December 20th, 1999. Best known for its gaming industry, Macau has a population of 643,000 (less than 10% of Hong Kong's).
Mainland China 中國大陸	Also referred to as the "mainland," the People's Republic of China excluding Taiwan and the two special administrative regions of Hong Kong and Macau.

Mandarin
普通話

Also known as *Putonghua*, the language spoken in mainland China and in Taiwan. Mandarin has more native speakers (nearly a billion) than any other language in the world.

Ming Pao
《明報》

A newspaper founded in 1959 by celebrated Chinese martial arts novelist Louis Cha. It is one of only two Chinese language print newspapers in Hong Kong that remains critical of Beijing.

National People's Congress
全國人大

The national legislature of the People's Republic of China with nearly 3,000 members. Under the Chinese Constitution, the NPC has the power to enact law, oversee government operations, and appoint major state officials.

Nominating Committee
提名委員會

A committee stipulated in Article 45 to elect the Chief Executive after the implementation of universal suffrage. The Basic Law is silent on the committee's size and composition, which were the main points of contention between Beijing and pro-democracy protesters before and during the occupy movement.

Occupy Trio
佔中三子

Co-founders of OCLP, namely Benny Tai, Chan Kin-man and Chu Yiu-ming.

OCLP
和平佔中

Occupy Central with Love and Peace, a civil disobedience campaign led by the Occupy Trio to take over parts of Hong Kong's financial district to pressure Beijing to deliver its promises under the 2007 Decision.

OCLP Legal Defense Team
佔中法律支援隊

The legal defense team represented by barrister Alvin Yeung, initially created to provide legal assistance to OCLP and later to participants of the occupy movement. The team consisted of nearly 50 lawyers at the peak of the protests.

OCLP Medical Team
佔中醫療隊

The medical team led by Dr. Au Yiu-kai, initially created to provide emergency medical services to OCLP and later to participants of the occupy movement. The team consisted of around 300 volunteers, including 30 doctors, over 100 registered nurses and many more medical students from HKU and CUHK.

one country, two systems 一國兩制	A constitutional framework created by then Paramount Leader Deng Xiaoping in the early 1980s allowing Hong Kong and Macau (and eventually Taiwan) to be reunited with the mainland as one country while retaining their distinct economic and political systems.
Pan-dems 泛民	The pan-democratic coalition, the main opposition force in the Legco consisting of pro-democracy political parties such as the moderate Democratic Party and Civic Party, and the more radical LSD and People Power.
parallel traders 水貨客	Day trippers from Shenzhen and other neighboring Chinese cities who cross the border using multiple-entry permits to stock up on daily necessities in Hong Kong and resell them at a higher price back home. They are a nuisance to residents in border towns such as Sheung Shui and Yuen Long, and one of the main sources of cross-border tensions.
Paramount Leader 最高領導人	The most prominent political leader in China. Although not a formal position, the Paramount Leader is often simultaneously General Secretary of the CCP, President of the People's Republic, and Chairman of the Central Military Commission. In the case of Deng Xiaoping, he was able to wield tremendous power without holding any official title long after stepping down from his formal roles.
Patriotic Education Plan 國民教育	Formally called the "Moral and National Education Curriculum," primary and secondary school coursework designed to inculcate among young citizens in Hong Kong a stronger Chinese identity and a sense of belonging to the motherland. C.Y. Leung's attempt to introduce the curriculum in 2012 was met with vehement opposition from the public. Mass demonstrations led by Joshua Wong eventually led to its withdrawal.
peanut eater 花生友	A passive bystander, in colloquial Cantonese. During the occupy movement, the phrase was used to describe idle protesters who stood by and watched while others braved pepper spray and police batons on the frontlines.
PLA 解放軍	The People's Liberation Army, China's 2.3-million strong armed forces and the largest in the world. The PLA, the CCP, and the State Council of China form the three branches of power in the country.

Princeling Faction 太子黨	One of the two major factions within the CCP. Princelings such as Bo Xilai and Xi Jinping are descendants of Communist China's founding fathers and they use their powerful family connections to acquire high-level political positions.
pro-Beijing camp 建制派	A coalition of political parties that are loyal to Beijing, such as the DAB, the BPA, the FTU and the Liberal Party.
qiang guo 強國	Literally a "superpower" in Mandarin, the phrase is used by netizens in Hong Kong to mock China's swagger on the world's stage as a nation of *nouveau riche*.
renminbi 人民幣	The official currency of mainland China. In the 10-year period between 2005 and 2014, the *renminbi* appreciated against the Hong Kong dollar by more than 30% as a result of the fast growing Chinese economy.
SAR 特別行政區	Special administrative region, a special status conferred on Hong Kong and Macau under the "one country, two systems" framework to allow the regions to retain their distinct economic and political systems.
SARS outbreak 沙士爆發	Severe acute respiratory syndrome was a highly contagious and life-threatening disease with a fatality rate of almost 10%. The SARS outbreak broke out in Asia in 2003 and killed 299 in Hong Kong within six months, including a half-dozen medical professionals. It also decimated many local industries, in particular, tourism and retail.
Scholarism 學民思潮	An activist group made up of secondary school students. Founded in 2011 by Joshua Wong, the group organized a series of mass demonstrations to oppose the Patriotic Education Plan in 2012 and successfully pressured the government to withdraw the curriculum. In March 2016, Wong disbanded the group to make way for a new political party called Demosistō.

SCMP 《南華早報》	The *South China Morning Post*, the leading English-language newspaper in Hong Kong. In recent years, the *SCMP* went through a number of high-profile staff reshufflings and personnel changes that raised some eyebrows. In December 2015, Jack Ma's Alibaba acquired the newspaper with the explicit purpose to "improve China's image" and to counter the "biased Western media."
se zai beng zung 蛇齋餅粽	Literally "snake soup banquet, vegetarian meal, mooncake and glutinous rice," the Cantonese acronym refers to the four popular handouts used by pro-Beijing political parties to buy votes from senior and low-income citizens. Like the Thanksgiving turkey and the Christmas ham, mooncake and glutinous rice wrapped in bamboo leaves are traditional holiday foods eaten during the Mid-autumn Festival every September and the Dragon Boat Festival every June, respectively.
separate vote count 分組點票	A two-step voting procedure applicable to bills proposed by individual Legco members but not to those proposed by the government. Any legislator-led bill must first be passed by the democratically elected geographical constituencies before being separately voted on by the functional constituencies who are mostly Beijing loyalists.
Shanghai-Hong Kong Stock Connect 滬港通	A cross-border equity investment platform that allows mainland investors to purchase stocks listed on the Hong Kong Stock Exchange, and Hong Kong investors to do the same with Shanghai-listed stocks. The scheme was announced by Li Keqiang on April 10th, 2014 and launched on November 17th, 2014.
small circle election 小圈子選舉	A phrase that refers to the selection of the Chief Executive by the 1,200-member Election Committee instead of by a popular vote.
stability maintenance projects 維穩工程	China's censorship and surveillance projects, such as the Great Firewall of China and the Golden Shield Project, operated by the Ministry of Public Security to block unfavorable information from foreign countries, intercept search engines, and monitor social media contents.

Standing Committee
全國人大常委會

The Standing Committee of the National People's Congress, a committee of about 150 members with the power to interpret and modify legislation. In China, constitutional and legal interpretation is considered a legislative activity rather than a judicial one, and the authority rests with the Standing Committee instead of the courts.

State Council of China
國務院

China's chief executive organ, synonymous with the Chinese government and the equivalent of the White House in the United States. The 35-member council is chaired by the Premier and includes the heads of major governmental departments and agencies. The State Council, the CCP, and the PLA form the three branches of power in China.

Sunflower Movement
太陽花學運

A student movement in Taiwan during which university students, led by Lin Fei-fan and Chen Wei-ting, occupied the legislature in Taipei in protest of the passing of CSSTA by the KMT without a clause-by-clause review. The movement began on March 18th, 2014 and ended on April 10th, 2014, and eventually led to the withdrawal of the controversial trade agreement.

super seats
超級區議會界別

Also known as the "district council constituencies," they are the five functional constituencies added to the Legco as a result of the 2010 Reform Bill. Only elected district councilors are eligible to run for these seats, which, unlike the other 30 functional constituencies, have a broad electoral base comprising 3.5 million registered voters.

Taiwan
台灣

Formerly called Formosa and officially the Republic of China, an island state founded in 1949 after the KMT was defeated by the CCP in the Chinese Civil War and was forced to relocate its government across the Taiwan Strait. The country has a population of 23 million (more than three times that of Hong Kong), and its capital and largest city is Taipei.

Tamar Government Headquarters
添馬政府總部

Officially known as the Central Government Offices, they are the headquarters of the SAR government. Together with the Legco Building and the Chief Executive's office, they make up the Tamar Government Complex on the Admiralty waterfront.

Tiananmen Square Massacre
六四屠城

Also known as the "June 4th Incident," the bloody crackdown of the Tiananmen Square Protests on June 4th, 1989. Hardline CCP leaders ordered the PLA in a pre-dawn operation to clear the occupied square with assault rifles and tanks, killing an estimated 3,000 civilians. The Chinese government condemned the protests as an anti-subversive riot and has prohibited discussion of the events ever since.

Tiananmen Square Protests
八九學運

A student-led pro-democracy movement on Tiananmen Square in the heart of Beijing that lasted seven weeks in the spring of 1989. The protests were triggered in April by the death of former General Secretary Hu Yaobang, a liberal reformer who was deposed by hardliners within the Communist leadership. About a million citizens, including many Beijing University students, gathered on Tiananmen Square to mourn Hu's death and demand political and economic reforms. The protests ended on June 4th, 1989 with the Tiananmen Square Massacre.

Triads
三合會

The collective term for organized crime groups in Hong Kong. The word was coined by the British before the Handover in reference to the triangular crest of one of the prominent gangs. Triad groups such as Wo Sing Wo and 14K operate the local drug, prostitution and gambling rings.

TVB
無線電視

Television Broadcasts Limited, one of the two licensed free-to-air television broadcasters in Hong Kong at the time of the occupy movement. It was founded in 1967 and its headquarters – TVB City – are the largest commercial television production center in Asia. The demise of its sole rival ATV has given TVB a near-monopoly in the free-to-air market.

UGL Scandal
UGL事件

A political scandal involving C.Y. Leung over his failure to declare a HK$50 million (US$6.4 million) payment by Australian engineering company UGL. The payment was made pursuant to a 2011 agreement in exchange for Leung's support of UGL's acquisition of DTZ Holdings (a property consulting company owned by Leung until 2011) and his advisory services for a period of two years (during which period Leung was elected the Chief Executive). Investigations into the scandal by the ICAC did not result in any charges against Leung.

West Kowloon Development
西九文化區

A development project to create a world class arts and culture district in West Kowloon. The project was the brainchild of Tung Chee-hwa, and has been repeatedly delayed as a result of budget concerns and frequent changes in management. In 2012, C.Y. Leung was embroiled in a conflict of interest scandal for failing to declare that his company DTZ Holdings was a consultant to one of the contestants while he acted as a panel judge in a concept planning competition for the development project.

---

wo lay fay fay
和理非非

Literally "peace, rationality, non-violence and no profanity," the Cantonese acronym refers to the four tenets of political moderation practiced by the pandems. During the occupy movement, the phrase was used by the localists and escalation-prone protesters to mock the leadership's ineffectiveness.

---

yellow ribbons
黃絲帶

A collective term for supporters of the Umbrella Movement. They were sympathetic to the protesters' pro-democracy demands despite the disruptions they caused.

Youth League Faction
團派

One of the two major factions within the CCP. Leaguers such as former Paramount Leader Hu Jintao and Li Keqiang came from ordinary family backgrounds. They joined the Communist Youth League at a young age and worked their way up the CCP hierarchy.

Also by Jason Y. Ng and available from Blacksmith Books:

HONG KONG State of Mind

ISBN 978-988-19003-1-9
2010, US$13.95 / £9.99 / HK$118

Hong Kong is a mixed bag of a city. It is where Mercedes outnumber taxi cabs, partygoers countdown to Christmas every December 24th, and larger-than-life billboards of fortune tellers and cram school tutors compete with breathtaking skylines.

HONG KONG State of Mind is a collection of essays by a popular blogger who zeroes in on the city's idiosyncrasies with deadpan precision. At once an outsider looking in and an insider looking out, Jason Y. Ng has created something for everyone: a travel journal for the passing visitor, a user's manual for the wide-eyed expat, and an open diary for the native Hong Konger looking for moments of reflection.

No City For Slow Men

ISBN 978-988-16138-7-5
2013, US$14.95 / £10.99 / HK$128

No City for Slow Men examines some of the pressing social, cultural and existential issues facing Hong Kong. It takes the reader on a *tour de force* from the gravity-defying property market to the plunging depths of old age poverty, from the storied streets of Sheung Wan to the beckoning island of Cheung Chau, from the culture-shocked Western expat to the misunderstood mainland Chinese and the disenfranchised foreign domestic worker.

The result is a treatise on Hong Kong life that is thought-provoking, touching and immensely entertaining.

Hong Kong 20/20

ISBN 978-988-77927-6-5
2017, US$18.95 / £14.99 / HK$148

Two decades after Hong Kong reverted to Chinese rule, the real impact of the sovereignty change is just starting to register: the city's near-total economic integration with the mainland, a massive influx of Chinese visitors, simmering cross-border tensions and a rapid erosion of freedoms. To mark the 20th anniversary of the Handover, PEN Hong Kong invited some of the city's most prominent literary and creative minds to reflect on its post-colonial development, in a definitive compendium of essays, poems, fiction and artwork.

Co-edited by Jason Y. Ng, Tammy Ho, Mishi Saran, Sarah Schafer and Nicholas Wong, *Hong Kong 20/20* features Ng's story "Castaway," an allegorical tale about a man who survives a shipwreck and must fight for his life with everything he's got – not unlike the dire straits Hong Kong is in.

With forewords by Timothy Garton Ash and Kevin Lau Chun-to.

Hong Kong Noir

ISBN 978-988-77928-7-1
2018, HK$125

Akashic continues its ground-breaking series of original noir anthologies, launched in 2004 with *Brooklyn Noir*. Each story is set in a distinct neighbourhood or location within the city of the book.

What will Hong Kong look like in five years, ten years, or thirty years when the "one country, two systems" promise expires? It's impossible to foresee. Hong Kong's future may be beyond our control, but some things aren't. We can continue to write about our beloved city and work our hardest to preserve it in words.

Hong Kong Noir features brand-new stories by Jason Y. Ng, Xu Xi, Marshall Moore, Brittani Sonnenberg, Tiffany Hawk, James Tam, Feng Chi-shun and Shannon Young, among other leading authors who write about the city.